SO-EKZ-899

M044 A3 1971

3 0050 00032 2130

CAL STATE HAYWARD LIBRARY

THIS BOOK IS DUE ON THE LAST DATE STAMPED BELOW

Failure to return books on the date due will
result in assessment of overdue fees.

DUE   NOV 03 '90

RET'D OCT 2 2 '90

90-71

RADICAL ADVENTURER

RADICAL ADVENTURER

The Diaries of Robert Morris
1772–1774

Edited with an introduction by J. E. Ross

ADAMS&DART, BATH

CT
788
M6 44
A3
1971

© 1971 J. E. Ross
First published in 1971 by
Adams & Dart, 40 Gay Street, Bath, Somerset
SBN 239 00076 5
Printed in Great Britain by
Alden & Mowbray Ltd

CALIFORNIA STATE UNIVERSITY, HAYWARD
LIBRARY

Contents

List of Illustrations

Acknowledgements

In seeking recorded details of the life of Robert Morris before and after his disastrous elopement with his ward in 1772, I have been greatly helped by librarians at the University College of Swansea; the Reference Department of the General Library, Swansea; the Royal Institution of South Wales, Swansea; the British Museum; the Public Record Office; Guildhall, London; Lambeth Palace; Lincoln's Inn; Dulwich College and the County Record Office, Chichester. Without ready replies from Official Departments and individual correspondents the search might have yielded very little.

For tracing and supplying illustrations I am indebted to the Frick Collection, New York (plate no. 2); the National Portrait Gallery (plate no. 1); the British Museum (plates nos. 8, 9, 13, 14); Dulwich Picture Gallery (plates nos. 3, 4); the Public Record Office (plate no. 12); the Honourable Society of Lincoln's Inn (plates nos. 10, 11, 15); and again, to the University College of Swansea; Mr W. C. Rogers and Mr Peter Johns.

My chief debt, however, is to Mary Janes who followed the trail with me for three years and to her family who maintained a convincing curiosity to the end.

J. E. Ross

'I do love bustle, variety and disturbance to my very soul'

Diary, 12 May 1774

'It is the cause of liberty I wish to promote, and I care not by whose hand it triumphs'

Letter to John Wilkes, 27 May 1771

Introduction

THE Morris family was attracted from Shropshire to the Neath and Swansea valleys in the first years of the eighteenth century by the promise of industrial development firmly based on plentiful coal supplies near a good port on the Bristol Channel.

By 1724, when the 'Llangavelach' Copper Works, just over the Swansea boundary, were threatened with bankruptcy, Robert Morris, father of the diarist, was already involved in the metal industry and, as an expert, was called in to value the company assets. He saw great possibilities for development; and, after some difficulty, succeeded in forming a partnership based on London capital, to take over the works, later becoming a shareholder himself.

In the next forty years he made a considerable fortune; and, when he died in April 1768 at his London home in Mortimer Street, Cavendish Square, he was able to leave his wife and six surviving children well provided for.

He married[1] on 9 September 1725, at St John's Church, a mile or so from the works, Margaret Jenkins, an heiress of Machynlleth, descended through Owain Gwynedd 'from one of the fifteen tribes of North Wales, arms sable between three flowers de luce—a chevron argent'.[2]

They acquired a dwelling-house in the town and two small estates, Tredegar Fawr and Penderi, in the rising hinterland of the Tawe Valley. Twelve children, baptized at St Mary's Church, were born of the marriage: six of them succumbed either to the frequent epidemics of smallpox or to childhood illnesses like 'breaching of the teeth'. Four girls, Bridget (b. 1730), Margaret (b. 1731), Mary (b. 1736) and Jane (b. 1739) lived to welcome the last two boys, Robert (b. 1743) and John (b. 1745).

By 1745 Morris and Lockwood's large new works at Fforest, higher up the Tawe valley, were in full swing and everything appeared propitious

I

for Robert, the long-awaited heir. (Two other boys had died in infancy.) He had four sisters to dote on him and a brother, very near in age, to play with.

His education seems to have run smoothly to a creditable end. His diary entry for 20 May 1774 (page 179) mentions his early school in the north of England.

I put up at the Bull's Head: Old house, which I perfectly remember ye situation of, when formerly returning from Heath School in Yorkshire. Happy times those! Not happy in being at school but happy in returning from it.[3]

The lists at Charterhouse (1759–65) record two boys, Morris and Morris junior, of Bathurst House. Robert was one and John, who later sent his own sons there, was the other. The fact that the name of the Reverend Dr Salter, preacher, and later Master of Charterhouse, appears in Robert's list of acquaintances in London in 1772 suggests that he was reasonably content; nor does his own reference to the school in the entry for 17 May 1774 (page 175) suggest otherwise.

Then he [Green] askt about ye Charterhouse, which I chose to acknowledge; then he purposely recollected me in every other respect than my name; in which to the last I deceived him; for I told him it was Chapman.

At the age of 16, in 1760, Robert matriculated at Oriel College, Oxford. He graduated in 1764. The Admission Registers of Lincoln's Inn, vol. 1 (1420–1799) state that Robert was admitted on 13 January 1763* when he was described as being of Oriel College. A further entry in the Black Books of Lincoln's Inn runs:

At a Council held there on the 6th Day of May in the seventh reign [sic] of our Sovereign Lord King George III and in the year of our Lord 1767
Present: Arthur Jones Owen Salub^y Brereton Richard Spooner Lewis Jones Theodore Johnson
Ordered that Mr Robert Morris one of the Fellows of this Society having been regularly admitted to the Degree of Master of Arts in the University of Cambridge[4] and being thereby of full standing in this Society according to the order of June 1762 and having kept twelve Terms Comons and conformed himself to the rules of this Society be called to the Bar on paying all Arrears and Duties and that he be published at the next Exercise in the Hall.[5]

Abst Coms.	4. 5. 6
Vacation do.	6. 0. 0
Preacher	3. 1. 6
Pensions	1. 2. 8

* On 3 June 1763 Alexander Wedderburn Esq. KC, was 'admitted into a whole chamber, 3 stories high, No. 20 Kitchen Garden Court'. He became 'Sollicitor General'. Treasurer 1772, Master of Library 1773 at Lincoln's Inn.

Call	5. 0. 0
Library	5. 0. 0

Bill Book No. 5

Calls were made in only two terms of the year, Easter and Michaelmas terms: the call took place in open Council in term time: 3 or more Masters of the Bench meeting in the Council Chamber or Buttery were made a sufficient Council for calling any gentleman: the quorum was summoned by the Quattuor in Hall on the application of any gentleman desiring to be called to the Bar. The masters were attended by the Chief Butler with the Books of Admissions, and by the second Butler with the book of exercises. Each Master was entitled to a service of Sweetmeats value 5/- and a bottle of wine from each gentleman.[6]

Robert lived at 21 Kitchen Garden Court, near Hugh Hamersley (No. 22) and Thomas Lloyd (No. 25), two fellows of the Society who were to become closely involved in his tumultuous life. He applied for and was granted the use of the cellars at a Council held on 11 December 1767 and in November 1768, after the death of his father and his success in the Baltimore case, he 'prayed leave to new fashion in the Venetian stile the windows of his Chamber at No. 21,* in Kitchen Garden Court and Field Gate Row and to make a bow window looking into Kitchen Garden'. This was granted on 13 December as was a later request on 13 February 1769 to 'Continue the wall of the cook's storeroom to such a heighth as to make a closet over the same to his chambers'.[7]

He 'joined the Great Sessions, later known as the South Wales Circuit'[8] and first came to public notice in 1768 when he helped in the successful defence of Frederick Calvert, 6th Lord Baltimore (1731–71) 'a fast young man who did not live to be an old one. He was a man of shallow intellect and overweening self conceit' according to an entry in volume 38 of the *Gentleman's Magazine*; while Winckelman wrote of him,

with an income of £30,000 he knows not how to enjoy it. He became so intolerable that at length I frankly told him of my opinion. . . one of those worn-out beings, a hipped Englishman who had lost all moral and physical taste.

Lord Baltimore had married Diana, seventh daughter of the Duke of Bridgewater, who died on 18 August 1758. By then he was the father of two children; Juliet, aged five, and Henry Harford, aged one, the son of Hester Relhan or Rhelan, an Irish woman known as Mrs Harford. By the time of his trial for rape, ten years later, Frances Mary Harford, born on 28 November 1759 at the New Bond Street house of her grandmother, Dorcas Relhan, had been followed by three more illegitimate children; Sophia and Elizabeth Hales, children of Elizabeth Dawson, spinster; and

* Council Meeting records reveal constant internal and external building adjustment. The bow window is now in No. 20.

3

Charlotte, an infant, born in Hamburgh to Charlotte Hope of Munster. 'A man universally known to be one of the most licentious of his times, cordially hated by the people and not respected by the nobility', he appeared at Kingston Sessions on 26 April 1768, accused by Sarah Woodcock, the trial lasting from 7 a.m. on Saturday till 4 a.m. on Sunday.

The report by Joseph Gurney[9] published in *Modern State Trials* gives a verbatim account of the proceedings. Sarah described how a customer called several times at the milliner's shop where she worked, bought several trifles, and invited her to the play. She refused; in any case, as a Dissenter, she disapproved of such pleasures as plays and cards.

On 14 December a Mrs Hervey, tried with Mrs Griffenburgh as an accessory, called and ordered some ruffles, asking for them to be delivered. Sarah went to Curtain Row, Holloway, where she was inveigled into a grand coach 'on pretence of having a lift to see a new customer'. She was shown into a room while Dr Griffenburgh, a member of the Baltimore household, who had himself been imprisoned for rape, went to call the new client. A man in a nightgown (Lord Baltimore) came in but Sarah then had no idea who he was, though she recognized him as the man who had approached her about going to the play.

They had tea, supper and a game of tee-totum while she waited for her lady customer, who failed to arrive. She was now growing agitated but was refused permission to leave and it grew too late for a coach home. She was, she averred, imprisoned under the vigilant eyes of Mrs Hervey, an obvious procuress.

Later she was forcibly taken to Lord Baltimore's country seat, Woodcote, Epsom, where, after much cloak and dagger work, 'she was ruin'd'. On Christmas Day Lord Baltimore, who had sent £200 to her father, introduced her to his children, Juliet and Fanny, and to their governess, Mme Saunier, saying she had been recommended by her father as a companion to them.

When asked how she spent the weeks of her bondage Sarah invariably answered, 'I cried'. She also admitted by stages, under pressure from Lord Baltimore, to being 36, though in the charge she was described as 26. Lord Baltimore's counsel, guided by Hugh Hamersley and Robert Morris, called many witnesses in the employ of the accused; the house steward, Broughton; the cook; the linen maid; the gardener; the coachman and boatman who testified to her cheerfulness and pleasure in the excursions undertaken and to her opportunities to escape, especially when the party, including Fanny, returned to Lord Baltimore's house in Southampton Row.

Meanwhile Sarah Woodcock's fiancé and family had 'taken up' Mrs Hervey, who was safe in prison, and had gathered an enraged group of friends outside Lord Baltimore's house. Later Sarah appeared before Lord Mansfield, the supreme magistrate in criminal matters in the kingdom, and was asked to choose whether she would go to her father or stay with Lord Baltimore. She chose her father but made no complaint against her violator which it was essential to do if her case were to succeed. She pleaded fear at the trial in April as the cause of her silence before Lord Mansfield.

Her story became sufficiently discredited to acquit the noble lord who said in his defence,

'Libertine as I have been represented I am sure I have sufficiently atoned for every indiscretion by having suffered the disgrace of being exposed at the bar as a criminal in the County which my father had the honour to represent in Parliament.'

He was most severely censured for this atrocious act of seduction and the conviction of his guilt was universal.[10]

England had no room for him. He left for the Continent with Mrs Hales (according to Robert) and the Griffenburghs, staying at various towns in the north and finally settling in Naples.

His title had come to him from George Calvert, a great favourite of James I, who granted him a large estate in Ireland and created him Lord Baltimore of Baltimore in Ireland in 1624. He had invested a large sum of money trying to colonize Newfoundland; but, defeated by the climate, he applied for a charter to a new colony and was granted Maryland, though he died before the seals passed. George's descendants inherited the province which eventually came to Frederick Calvert, who was not sufficiently interested to visit the source of his great wealth but bequeathed it in his will, made just before his trial, to his illegitimate son, Henry Harford. His executors were Robert Eden, his brother-in-law; Hugh Hamersley; Robert Morris and Peter Prevost, 'Sollicitor and Attorney', a much older man from Epsom.

Baltimore's trial over, Robert now became immersed in family affairs. His father died; and from his London home the body was borne back to St John's Church, Swansea, where he had been married and 'where I buried four of my dear deceased children'.

On 6 June his will was proved.

I give and bequeath to my son, Robert Morris, now of Lincoln's Inn Esquire the reversion of all my lands and tenements before mentioned after the decease of his mother [Note. A house in Swansea, Tredegar Fawr, Masmillan and Kae Cadwgan,

Penllan Owen and Gwair Tire in Montgomeryshire.] and from the time of my
decease I give him my estate called Pengravenny in the parish of Llanrhidian in the
County of Glamorgan, my estate called Pwlar Oir in the parish of Llanguvelach
and my house in the strand [Swansea] wherein dwells Thomas Lott. Likewise three
of my shares in the capital stock of the Copper Trade and Collerys in which I am
co-partner with John Lockwood Esquire and others and I also give to my said son
the sum of five hundred pounds.[11]

A considerable increase in income for a twenty-five-year-old lawyer!

Politics in 1768 offered all the 'bustle, variety and disturbance' that
Robert could desire. He threw himself wholeheartedly into the storm
which was steadily brewing over freedom of election to Parliament and
liberty to inform the public of what was being decided there.

John Wilkes, the outlawed member of Parliament, had returned from
France in February; and, having won the Middlesex election for the first
time a month later, was committed to prison on 18 June for publishing
No. 45 of the *North Briton* and the *Essay on Woman*.

Mounting enthusiasm of the people for Wilkes as a champion of liberty,
both at home and in America, the outrage felt over 'the massacre of St
George's Fields' and Wilkes's provocation of the government by accusing
them of planning it, 'made clear the emergence of a political movement
not confined to the City of London only but general to the whole
metropolis'.[12]

Nowhere was the situation more eagerly discussed than at the London
Tavern where Robert and his circle gathered regularly. On 20 February
1769 the group met 'to untangle the finances'[13] of the public hero, also an
extravagant libertine and former member of Sir Francis Dashwood's
degenerate circle at Medmenham.

An extract from the books of the society formed at this meeting states:

1769, Feb. 20, Serjeant Glynn in the chair.
Resolved, That the gentlemen present at this meeting will contribute, as far as lies
in their power, to the independence and support of Mr. Wilkes, and that the
Rev. Mr Horne be desired to draw up a paper expressive of these intentions; who
in pursuance of this desire instantly drew up the following article, which received
the subscription of all gentleman present.
'Whereas John Wilkes, Esq., has suffered greatly in his private fortune from the
severe and repeated prosecutions he has undergone in behalf of the public, and as
it seems reasonable to us, that the man who suffers for the public good should be
supported by the public. . . the public is called upon to rescue Mr Wilkes from his
present encumbrances and to render him easy and independent.'[14]

£3,023 was subscribed immediately: an association called the Supporters of the Bill of Rights was formed, and on 25 February Robert
Morris was elected its first secretary.

The members included men either already or soon to be prominent in City politics: Sawbridge; his father-in-law and business partner Sir William Stephenson; his cousin Richard; Frederick Bull, a leader of dissenting interests; Sir Watkin Lewes; one or two barristers; and a number of attorneys in the City, among them George Bellas, 'of famous memory', deputy alderman, and of ripe experience in opposition politics. Sawbridge and James Townsend, leading freeholders of Middlesex, provided a link with another of the metropolitan constituencies as did also the Wilkite member for the county, Serjeant John Glynn. Sir Joseph Mawbey, a wealthy Vauxhall distiller, furnished contacts with Southwark and the urban populations of East Surrey. From Westminster came Parson John Horne, the restless political adventurer to whom the formation of the society was largely due, and two or three country gentlemen whose support he attracted, notably the Huntingdonshire baronet, Sir Robert Bernard.

Some had wealth and assured position, but others were young, aspiring, and not very successful members of the less socially regarded professional classes, discontented for one reason or another with the existing social and political order.[15]

Parson John Horne and many others objected to devoting so much publicly raised money to the debts of Wilkes; and on 27 February Horne inserted an advertisement in the papers which stated that 'many gentlemen divested of every personal consideration and unconnected with any party formed a society whose sole aim was to defend the liberty of the subject. They would support Wilkes's cause so far as it was a public cause.'[16]

Wilkes maintained 'that he was plainly the primary though not the sole object' as could be seen 'by such explicit declarations at the first meeting'.[17]

On March 7th a committee was appointed to inquire into several demands upon Mr Wilkes; and 300 l was immediately sent to Mr Wilkes for his present use. At the ninth meeting, on June 6th an account of Mr Wilkes's debts was delivered in, which amounted to 17,000 l, seven of which have been already compromised. A circular letter was at the same time read and approved by the Chairman. This letter has since been sent to the gentlemen of the minority who are to promote it, and is also to be sent to all the city and borough towns in England, with Mr Wilkes's case written by himself.[18]

The society then adjourned to 10 October; and on the 17th, Wilkes's birthday, members presented him 'with a silver cup on which were several emblematical figures expressive of his sufferings in support of liberty'.[19]

Meanwhile, from prison, Wilkes stood for Middlesex a third time only to have his election again declared null and void. An intense war of words followed in the press on this exclusion from Parliament of a duly elected candidate which culminated, on 19 December, in the publication of Junius's letter to the King in the *Advertiser* of Mr Woodfall.

Robert's enthusiasm blazed both in the City and in Wales when he was 'on the Circuit'. He rallied his friends, among them the Hanburys of Pontypool; wrote frequently to the press and carried out his secretarial duties with a flourish. In December 1769 the Assembly of South Carolina sent a very practical token of its sympathy for the aims of the society.

Gentlemen, [they wrote to Messrs Hankey & Co] the Assembly of this province having yesterday, in a very full house, voted ten thousand five hundred pounds this currency, to be remitted to Great Britain for the support of the interest and constitutional rights and liberties of the people of Great Britain and America, and applied to us to carry their resolution into execution,

We, being certain that it is their intention to present that sum to the Supporters of the Bill of Rights, to assist them in carrying on the great and good intention, do enclose the following bills of exchange, which you will please to pay to the order of the Society . . . We shall be much obliged to you, gentlemen, to signify immediately to Mr Robert Morris, Secretary to the Supporters of the Bill of Rights, the remittance that we now make, that the Society may be informed thereof; and also to favour us with a line, under cover, to Pieter Manigault, esquire, acknowledging receipt of the enclosed bills.[20]

Messrs Hankey & Co. wrote to Robert who immediately passed the good news on to Wilkes.

Lincoln's Inn N21, Feb. 6, 1770

I have this day received a Letter from the Speaker and other Gentlemen of the hon[l] house of Assembly in South Carolina informing me of their having remitted the Sum of £1,500 sterling to be paid to the order of the Supporters of the Bill of Rights 'to be applied by them in defense of all subjects of the British Empire & particularly for supporting such of our subjects, who by asserting the just rights of the people have or shall become obnoxious to Administration & suffer from the hand of power' . . .

The remittance is in consequence of the Circular Letter sent to Mr Gadsen (Mr Speaker) above named.[21]

Robert now had the task of replying in suitable terms, thanking the Assembly for its generosity. 'Parson' Horne was highly critical of his letter and complained to Wilkes, who sprang to the defence of his friend, refuting at the same time Horne's accusation that Wilkes hated America. He quoted two letters sent to Boston while he was in prison.

Are these, Sir, the letters of a man who hates Americans, who is the declared foe of their liberties? The folly of this attack is unparalleled, except in your former letters.

I proceed to the business of the letter to the honourable the Commons house of assembly of South-Carolina, in answer to their letter and noble subscription of 1,500 l. You say, 'One of the members of the society [of the Bill of Rights] a gentleman of the clearest public principles and of much merit, drew up very hastily a letter of thanks on the occasion, which he shewed to Mr Wilkes for his opinion. Mr Wilkes commended it extravagantly, and earnestly pressed the committee to adopt the letter; and he took some extraordinary measures that it might be adopted by the society.'

Mr Morris, the secretary at the time, drew up an answer, which he shewed to me, first in the rough draft, and afterward finished. It was diffuse, but sensible and spirited. I approved it but did not commend it warmly to any of my friends, for it contained many compliments to me personally. On this account I know that you disliked it. You complained that Mr Morris was a mad man, that the letter was execrable and would bring the society disgrace. I said that perhaps the letter might be thought here rather too diffuse and copious, but Mr Morris had considered it was proper to give the g/men of S. Carolina a full exposition of the sentiments of the society: that in Am. [America] our brethren were more studious of expressing themselves with force and clearness than with conciseness and classical energy: that the copious style was theirs: that their own productions abounded more in reasoning than elegance of diction: that they often preferred to our close style a diffuse mode of writing, to avoid any possibility of any doubt of their meaning: that in this style Mr Morris excelled: that I should even regret their rivalling Europe in the meretricious arts of eloquence, fine writing and polite literature, for they would probably make such acquisitions at the expence of strength of thought and manliness of sentiment, in which they excelled the Europeans: that we ourselves were greatly deficient: that most of the modern refinements of Europe were the luxurious effects of a debauched vitiated, enervated taste, wh. had lost sight of antient and true elegance of simplicity: that v. few among Am^s [Americans] had in fact succeeded in either the sister arts of poetry or painting: that spirit, not taste, was their characters: that I knew no fault in Mr Morris's letter, except comps [compliments] to myself: that language was, after all, merely the dress of our thoughts; and that it was peevish and ill-bred to find fault with Mr Morris, only because periods of strong sense were not tuned to the nice ear of Mr Horne. I was never with the Committee. The transaction happened during my imprisonment. At the London Tavern I am told that you were furious and unmannerly about the secretary's letter. Mr Morris in a good-natured manner, withdrew his intended answer to the gent^n of S. Carolina. You produced another letter wh. after many important alterations made by Serjeant Glynn & other gentlemen was at length adopted. I have given the whole of this business. Will you prevail on your new friend Mr Morris, to favour the public with his intended answer; and will you give us your own uncastrated letter as it was first proposed to the Bill of Rights. The public will then be able to determine on the merits of each performance.[22]

Like many other admirers of Wilkes, Robert tried to lighten the closing days of his imprisonment. He wrote on 16 April, while on the South Wales Circuit,

I hope you have by this time found the three pots of potted Lamprey from Glos'ter. I was much piqued that I had it not in my power to pay you one more visit or two, before I left town; & shall be more so, in not attending you upon your enlargement, which I hope there is at this time no obstacle to, for it's taking place on the 18th. As I have long interested myself to remove all such difficulties, you will do me singular satisfaction & favour, if you wou'd take the trouble of

9

informing me by a line directed to Cowbridge in Glamorganshire, how the matters
stand in this respect; I mean whether the way is actually paved for a farewell to
your present situation, that I may not in vain take the steps I intend to do, for the
due celebration of the time, both at Swansea, & wherever else I shall be upon the
Circuit.[23]

A week after his release Wilkes went to the Mansion House to be
sworn in as Alderman of the City of London. On 8 May he was elected
to the Bill of Rights Society and on 22 May dined at the London Tavern
to thank the members for their support. He continued to attend their
meetings regularly until 1774, when he became Lord Mayor and demands
on his time became very heavy.

On 30 June (John Almon having already been tried and fined) Henry
Woodfall was charged with printing Junius's letter to the King. Robert
submitted an affidavit in which he declared that, in his opinion, the letter
was not a libel.

This called forth the animadversions of Mr Justice Asten, who observed from
the bench, 'that he was astonished there should be a single man in the kingdom,
who did not consider it as calculated to vilify a most gracious and virtuous king, to
alienate the minds of the people from their sovereign, and to excite insurrection
and rebellion and as to the affidavit of that man', he added, 'who had, though but
in a parenthesis, put into it, that he did not think the letter signed Junius to be
a libel', he should for his part, pay very little attention to any affidavit he should
make.
Mr Morris replied by means of a pamphlet, in which, after animadverting on
the indelicate conduct of a judge so anxious to vindicate the characters of great
men; he expressed his astonishment that, while condemning a libeller, he should
in the same breath, subject himself to a similar imputation.'[24]

The Bill of Rights Society itself was also in trouble. 'In July many
talked of quitting', and on 4 September Robert resigned as secretary.

For my own part I will confess that the cause of Mr Wilkes, as an injured and
persecuted individual, has been the first and hitherto the only motive of my appearing in public. I have the satisfaction to say, that I leave the cause in a better
situation than I found it: though not the vanity to think, that much of our success
(which indeed ought to have been greater) has been owing to my endeavors: I am
resolved, however not to act any longer in the office of secretary. I shou'd not have
undertaken it at first, but in expectation that it wou'd soon have fallen to the lot of
others in turn. I have repeatedly desired to resign and as consistently received no
other answer than your compliments to my conduct. I must now therefore resign
without leave, because I cannot continue in my office with the same alacrity I have
done, being tired of my share of the burden, and having something else to do. As
for odium which may have fallen on my name from the conspicuous part I have
appeared in, I shall esteem that my greatest reward, being satisfied it will only come
from a quarter, whose enmity will be my greatest honour. When you proceed to

the election of another secretary I hope your choice will fall on one more worthy than

      Gentlemen etc. etc.

        Robert Morris[25]

He did not, however, cut himself off from the society; nor was he less solicitous of Wilkes. In October he invited him to South Wales.

                    Octr 9, 70.

I conceive by this time most of great City business wch seem'd to detain you in town, is concluded, and, what is more, happily so. You have therefore nothing to do now, but to take a ramble with your friend in this part of Wales. I know many *good* houses where you w^d have as *good* a welcome, but it is the Country & open air, that I imagine w^d suit your taste the best. If Mountains, Rivers, Seas can charm, here, you may have your fill; in short we have all sorts of prospects I think, and all sorts of animals to command, but women, for whom I shall say nothing. I don't know indeed, what conquests you may be able to make, for you are certainly a great favorite with the Ladies. There is one, a very elegant creature & former acquaintance of yours' Mrs Gomm, who dies to see you; & you will have this advantage besides, that she has retired into the Country having parted from her husband. I write this from Hanbury's* at Pontipool, & am now going with a large Glamorganshire party to the Races at Monmouth; from thence I return to Cowbridge† in Glamorganshire, whither if you form an early resolution, & write to me by the return of the Post, I shd be most happy to meet an appointment from you to come & conduct you from Bath, Bristol or the Passage‡ upon whatever schemes & to whatever part of the Country you please. At least let me have the pleasure of learning some of your intentions by as early a letter, as you can write, and I remain,

        with much esteem,

           Y^r sincere friend

            Robert Morris

Direct me at J. Edmondes, Esqr at Cowbridge in Glamorganshire.[26]

Wilkes declined the invitation:

                  Swansea, Oct. 27

Your letter reached me yesterday at this place. I had given over expecting you, and now find it was really impossible, since the enchanting Mrs G. cou'd not even bring you down. If I find a moment to whisper your soft things into her ear, I will: and yet I can promise you no hopes, as I shall have no good opportunity to talk to her, & am not yet sufficiently upon a footing of intimacy. Were you down yourself, I don't think it w^d be for you a difficult matter to succeed. What a prize shd I bring you, were she to accompany me to London, that she might throw yourself [herself] into your arms! Cou'd you trust your friend upon such an occasion as that? Yes, you might. I was myself struck with her at first. Yet I found out afterwards, that she pleased more by Art, than by nature; and my love was cured.

* John Hanbury, MP, 1744–84.

† Refugee American Loyalists stayed at Cowbridge during the War of Revolution.

‡ The ferry.

I am satisfied She has more in her of the affected, than the tender; and that whatever rapture you might taste in her arms, she wou'd not do for the female friend, in whose bosom you might repose your cares. That you may meet with such a one, I heartily wish. There is no happiness without them; at least, when our thoughts are turn'd that way. We live by the hopes of such an acquisition, which is rarely, if ever obtained. There may be the widow'd Bachelor, as well as the widow'd husband, & widow'd wife. I am now in the former state, having no connexion with females: and I sometimes think myself the happier for it.

I leave this Country for your busy scene in London upon Wednesday next, which, by the dalliance I shall have upon the road, will bring me to Lincoln's Inn by the first day of term. That is a place I have not seen you in yet; and Yet I hope, we shall sometime pass an agreable hour there. I entirely join wth you in the affair of Press-warrants. You shall have all my assistance in it. It rests upon no better footing than General Warrants. All the usage in the world w^d not have made them legal, as the Judges declared; and I don't see, why the same might not be said of Press-warrants.

I take my leave of you only for a short while.

        I am, Dear Sir,
            yrs most sincerely,
               Robert Morris.[27]

Wilkes dined with Robert 'tete-a-tete at No. 21 Lincoln's Inn'[28] on 19 November; and on the 27th 'the Bill of Rights Society met at the London Tavern and accepted Robert Morris's resignation with a vote of thanks'.[29]

Robert busied himself with Mr Justice Aston, writing to Wilkes,

I daresay you will excuse my not waiting upon you today at Fulham, when you know that my detention will give more time to trim that Bully Asten whom I do not intend to spare. By staying here, I shall have the letter out in the middle of next week – and Monday morning it will be ready for your perusal, when I shd be glad to see you in your way to the City – that you may throw in where you see occasion a little of seasoning. I shall esteem such a call very kind in you. Believe me it is great mortification that I cannot attend upon you.

Lincoln's Inn   Dec. 1, '70[30]

Bully Asten was 'Sir Richard Aston, a Judge of the Court of King's Bench and Chief Justice of the Common Pleas, who had accused Robert Morris of wilful perjury in an affidavit, and to whom Morris addressed a letter [on 11 December] 'Containing a Reply to his scandalous Abuse and some Thoughts on modern Doctrine of Libels'.[31]

In the following year, 1771, Robert's political activity reached its peak. Wilkes and Horne and their factions were still bickering. On 15 January 'a paper having appeared in the *Gazetteer*, supposed to have been written by a friend of Mr Wilkes, charging Mr Horne, among other things, with subscribing to the Bill of Rights but never paying a shilling, Mr Horne replied "he never did subscribe to the Bill of Rights but had paid 5 guineas into the hands of Mr B. and numerous little sums besides" '.[32]

But Wilkes was quite sure of his supporters. On 1 February he recorded,

Dined at the Devil's Tavern Temple Bar with the Retribution Club,* present Messrs Charles, Martyn, Adair, Robert Jones, Trevanion Wm Ellis, Bissel, Reynolds, Ch. Pearce, Morris.

Society disputes could not stem the great tide of feeling which finally overwhelmed the efforts of Parliament to restrict the freedom of the press.

On 5 February Colonel Onslow drew the attention of the House to misrepresentation in reports of their proceedings in certain newspapers. Reporting was forbidden by standing orders of 26 February 1728 but the rule was not strictly enforced and Wilkes encouraged printers to defy it. Taking warning, some editors desisted but the *Gazetteer* and *Middlesex Journal* (7 Feb.) became more provocative, even insulting:

It was reported, that a scheme was at last hit upon by the ministry to prevent the public from being informed of their iniquity; accordingly on Tuesday last little cocking George Onslow . . .

On 8 February the printers were ordered to attend for punishment on the 11th. Thompson of the *Gazetteer* appeared but Wheble of the *Middlesex Journal* ignored the summons. Orders were issued several times and on 26 February, Parliament having given the benefit of doubt over the summons to attend, the arrest of Wheble for contempt was moved but both Thompson and Wheble disappeared. Colonel Onslow moved that an address be sent to the king asking 'that he will be graciously pleased to issue his royal proclamation for apprehending the said John Wheble and R. Thompson with a promise of reward for same'. This appeared in the *London Gazette* on 9 March and a reward of £50 was offered.

Although it was known that opposition was being organized in the City, Colonel Onslow persisted on 12 March in his attack on the printers: 'It was nonsense to have these rules and not put them into execution.' After an all-night sitting and numerous divisions, six more printers were ordered to attend on 14 March.

---

* Next to Temple Bar (now Child's Place). Rules were devised in imitation of Roman entertainments.

> Let none but guests or clubbers hither come.
> Let dunces, fools and sordid men keep home.
> Let learned, civil merry men be invited
> And modest too; nor be choice liquor slighted.[33]

At the same time Robert Morris was addressing the Supporters of the Bill of Rights at the London Tavern.

Mr Chairman,

The proclamation issued for apprehending the printers, is on all hands, I think, allowed to be illegal. I do not believe that there is in the whole kingdom a lawyer's clerk, who does not know it to be equally repugnant to the spirit and letter of the law and the constitution. The law, though not so well known is as clear against commitments by the House of Commons. They have nothing to support their pretensions but their own vote, wh. certainly is not binding on any but themselves; an act of the three branches of the legislature being the only authority that is, besides the common law, acknowledged by England as valid. Matters being thus circumstanced, I am sorry to find that such magistrats of London, as belong to this Society, do not afford protection to the printers & rescue them from lawless violence. My concern for this neglect, this fear, or this tergiversation, is the greater, that, if the officers of the House of Commons, or any other person but a minister of this city properly authorised, takes these obnoxious men into custody the rights of the city are violated, it being legally impossible for King, Lords & Commons, to seize any citizen of London without the consent of its own magistrates. Were they even to make an act for that purpose it could not have any force; because the act made in favour of the city in the reign of William and Mary, ought to be considered as a constitution and as irreversible as Magna Carta; for indeed it is the Magna Carta of the City. For all these reasons, it gives me pain to see the printers deserted; and I wish Mr Alderman Townsend were present, that I might complain to him, face to face, of his having forfeited his word by refusing to be the man who would release them if they were apprehended in consequence of this illegal proclamation. Indeed I have already talked to him on the subject & asked why he did not perform his promise? His answer was, that he did not find he should be supported by any great man, & otherwise it would be folly.[34]

The next day he sent a hasty letter to Wilkes.

I have been all this day upon the wing about the business of the printers, and hitherto unable to call upon you, agreeable to my inclination. I w^d not have the affair sleep for the universe. The ministry take care it shall not on this side; we must therefore be staunch on ours. You know what they proceeded to yesterday. Some six newly ordered to attend, I believe make their appearance at the house. These are Bladon (Gen. Ev^g) Wright (Whiteh.) and possibly Evans (Lond. Pack.). There will be business for all of us; & each must have his share. Different Games must be played. But if we can, we must take into our assistance some more Aldermen, & I hope also we shall have the Sherriffs. Messengers may be sent to Newgate; & printers lodged there be let out. I saw Wheble & Thompson this day. The direct opposites of each other in patience; & the hasty one is the former. I gave your message to the latter. He thanks you, as he has much reason, for your alacrity to serve him; though I know it is also to serve the public. You have too great a regard for that consideration, ever to alter in your conduct from paltry jealousies. Therefore I gave it as my opinion, that the Printers shou'd wait, 'till Monday to see if the other Aldermen wou'd bear a part. If they do not by that time, we shall have waited long enough. And I hope, & do not doubt, that you will be equally ready to act with that firmness & coo unaltered resolution, of which you have always been the master. In the conduct of this affair I hope I have your concurrence, & shall endeavour to see you to-morrow. In the meantime,

I am most sincerely yours,

Robert Morris.

Lincoln's Inn N21
March 13, '71[35]

On 14 March four of the printers obeyed the summons, were reprimanded and discharged. Woodfall was in the hands of Black Rod; and Miller did not appear. He was ordered to be taken into custody.

On 15 March Wheble wrote a public letter to the Speaker in which he declared 'he would yield no obedience but to the laws of the land'. He had found a piece of paper on which he had asked Counsel's opinion 'about the summons of February 21, delivered to a servant and not to himself'.

Case for Mr Morris's Opinion

I have attentively perused the above written case.

1. To the first Q., I am clearly and decisively of Opinion, that Mr Wheble is not compellable by Law to attend the House of Commons in pursuance of the written order above.
2. The first Q. being answered in the Negative the second requires no consideration; but if the attendance was requirable, pursuant to the above Order, it would not be difficult to shew what penalties the refusing party would be liable to upon resort to the legal Courts of Justice, which have cognizance of such offences.
3. If the Summons be invalid, the subsequent Warrant by the Speaker must be invalid also; for the defects of the Summons were not cured by the appearance of Mr Wheble. A form of a warrant no more makes a legal authority (for so much the Word imports) than a Constable's Staff makes a Peace Officer. If the Warrant were legal, a Messenger of the House is not a proper person for executing it but only the Serjeant at Arms and the Deputy Serjeant. But these are trifles with respect to the Question; for the Answer is most plain and positive, that the Speaker of the House of Commons is no more a Magistrate appointed to issue Warrants of Apprehension, than the House itself is a Court of Justice appointed to punish.
4. This Question admits of no hesitation of Dispute. The pretended Proclamation of the King is clearly illegal. Proclamations have no intrinsic Force in this Country; nor have they any at all but by special Act of Parliament.
   Upon the whole I advise Mr Wheble to pay no Attention or Obedience either to the above-mentioned Summons Warrant of Application, or Proclamation. All are equally unjust and illegal. Mr Wheble will be protected by Magna Charta and by numerous Statutes which confirm our valuable code of Liberties. The Proclamation, moreover seems to me to levy a Cruel War upon 2 individuals without colour of Law: and I do give it as my Opinion, that Mr Wheble may well institute an Action against the Counsellors, Promoters, Aiders, Abettors and publishers thereof.

Robert Morris

March 14.   Lincoln's Inn

On 15 March, following a scheme of Wilkes's faction, advised by Robert Morris, Wheble was arrested by Edward Carpenter, one of his own employees, and appeared before the presiding magistrate at Guildhall. This was none other than Wilkes, who discharged Wheble and bound him over to prosecute Carpenter for assault at the next quarter sessions.[36] Carpenter, who was given a certificate so that he could collect the £50, 'did not accuse Wheble of any crime: he had apprehended him merely in consequence of His Majesty's Proclamation'.[37]

The great clash began with the arrest of John Miller, also on 15 March.

Mr Miller was also taken into custody by a messenger of the House of Commons; and on his refusing to go with him, the messenger took him by the arm; upon which a constable was sent for, and Mr Miller gave him charge of the messenger Whittam for assaulting him in his own house; whereupon he was carried to the Mansion House and at ½ past 6 o'clock came on a hearing before his Lordship [Crosby] and Mr Alderman Wilkes and Oliver.

In the meantime the Sergeant at Arms being informed of the transaction, came to demand the bodies of the messenger and of Mr Miller; upon which the Lord Mayor asked the messenger if he had applied to a magistrate to back the warrant, or to any peace officer of the city to assist him: he replied in the negative. His Lordship then said, that as long as he was in that high office, he looked upon himself as a guardian of the liberties of his fellow citizens; that no power had a right to seize a citizen of London, without an authority from him or some other magistrate; and that he was of opinion the seizing of Miller and the warrant were both illegal: he therefore declared Miller at Liberty and proceeded to examine witnesses to prove the assault on him by the messenger; which being done, his Lordship asked the latter whether he w^d give bail? if not, he shd be committed to prison; he at first refused, but the commitment being made out, and signed by the above 3 magistrates, the Sgt. at Arms said, that he had bail ready for him; and 2 sureties were bound in 20 l each and the messenger in 40 l for his appearance at the next session at Guildhall. The Lord Mayor told the Sgt at Arms that he was surprized he shd trifle with him, and not give bail at first; he replied, that he had done no more than his duty. About 7 o'c in the evening, R. Thompson, printer of the Gazette was also apprehended at his own door in Newgate St. and carried before Mr Alderman Oliver at the Mansion House as being the person described in His Majesty's proclamation: but not being accused of having committed any crime, he was discharged and set at liberty. The man who had apprehended him then desired a certificate of his having acted in pursuance of the proclamation in order to obtain the reward of 50 l which was immediately granted.[38]

Robert Morris acted as counsel for John Miller, and made repeated interventions on legal points to add to the discomfiture of the Commons' officials.[39]

In the morning following [16 March] the following handbill was dispersed about this city.

'To the liverymen, freemen, and citizens of London. Although our Lord Mayor had been confined to his room for 15 days with a severe fit of gout and is still much indisposed, he is determined to be this day in his seat at the House of Commons to support your rights and privileges, even tho' he shd be obliged to be carried in a litter. He leaves the Mansion House at 10 o'clock.

And in the afternoon two, following
The citizens of London, and all the friends of Freedom in the metropolis, are expected to bring the Lord Mayor back again in triumph, and attend him to the Mansion House.

The freemen of London are requested to attend at the House of Commons in order to conduct the Lord Mayor back to his own Mansion.[40]

The King himself declared that

the authority of the House of Commons is totally annihilated if it is not in an exemplary manner supported, by instantly committing the Lord Mayor and Alderman Oliver to the Tower.

On 20 March a motion was passed at the House of Commons

that the Lord Mayor of the City of London be at Liberty to be heard upon Friday morning next, by his Counsel, upon all such points as do not controvert the Privileges of the House.[41]

As Alderman Brass Crosby was ill, his appearance was postponed to 25 March.

The Lord Mayor attending accordingly in his place, acquainted the House, that he had received the Resolution of this House of Friday last, for allowing him Liberty to be heard by his Counsel, upon all such points as do not controvert the Privileges of the House; but that finding the Counsel were, by that Resolution, restrained from speaking to many points material to his Defence; and that the Counsel he could depend on and whom he wished to employ were on the Circuit; he therefore would not give the House the Trouble of hearing Counsel on this occasion.[42]

Two days later both he and Alderman Oliver were sent to the Tower and on 29 March, a letter ascribed to Junius and addressed to the prisoners and Mr Wilkes, praised Robert's arguments on the illegality of the printers' arrests.

I have two observations to make upon the late attempt of enforcing the order of the House of Commons by the Royal proclamation.

First, that the calling in the aid of the King upon that occasion was weakening the authority and dignity of the House, & tends to make the execution of the orders of that house dependent on the pleasure of the King; & in the next place such an interposition on the part of the King carries this appearance with it to the public, that it is not the independence or the just liberties & privileges of the Commons of England that are anxiously sought to be preserved, but the gratification of the spleen & resentment (to say no worse of it) of the administration. I shall conclude this letter by saying, & thinking till I am better informed, that the late proclamation was an unwarrantable exertion of power, tending to mislead all judges & justices throughout England, & to put them upon imprisoning an English subject contrary to law, & the rules of evidence wh. make part of the law of this kingdom; & therefore I, for one, applaud the conduct of Mr Wilkes in this instance. In another letter I shall deliver my sentiments as to the proceedings of your Lordship, Mr Alderman Oliver, and Mr Alderman Wilkes, when the messenger of the House of Commons was brought before you. I have forborne to take this business up on the same grounds as Mr Morris has done, as it would only be a repetition of what he has very judiciously before transmitted to the public. It is sufficient for me to say that I think he has sufficiently demonstrated the illegality of the order of the House of Commons: I only meant to give add^n strength to his observations.[43]

Exactly where Robert acted is not clear but his letter to Wilkes of 11 December 1772 recalls his appearance against the Speaker of the House, and the Records of the Court of Aldermen register the City's appreciation of his work.

This day [23 April 1771] the Right Honourable the Lord Mayor having presented unto this Court Robert Morris Esquire to be made free of this City as the first of three due to his Lordship's Prerogative it is ordered that Robert Morris Esquire be admitted into the Company of Drapers paying unto Mr Chamberlain for this City's use the sum of Forty-six shillings and eightpence.
Trecothick Locum Tenens; Crosby Mayor.[44]

In spite of its success however, the Bill of Rights Society was still in turmoil.

This day [said the *Annual Register* on 9 April], was a very full meeting of the Society of the Bill of Rights in pursuance of the special summons upon important business. The meeting opened with a confirmation of the gratification before agreed upon the printers; and a vote of thanks was then resolved upon to the Lord Mayor for his upright and intrepid conduct in defending the undoubted liberties of the subject against the illegal and arbitrary proceedings of the present House of Commons. During the progress of the debate upon the first motion, a very violent altercation passed, as usual, between Mr Wilkes and Mr Horne. Mr Wilkes in particular declared that Mr Horne's conduct both to him and the public had neither been consistent with the truth of a clergyman, or the faith and honour of a gentleman. Mr Horne said, that the Society was becoming nothing more than a scene of personal quarrel; the public interests were absorbed in the petty faction of one individual; that regularity, decency, order, and concord, were banished together; he therefore moved 'That the Society should be dissolved'. It was in vain objected that a motion of such consequence should not be put so suddenly, whatever cause to it the present disturbance might afford; that, in fact the ferment in which the society then was, shewed an improper temper of discussing so serious a question; and that, at least, the sense of the society should first be taken, whether they would rescind the restrictive resolution against opening any new subscriptions whatsoever, but for the private purposes of Mr Wilkes, till the whole list of his debts was discharged; as the charge against the society for existing only in the capacity of Mr Wilkes's committee might then be obviated. Both parties, equally sure of a victory, or desirous of meeting their defeat, were eager to put the question. The motion to defer the consideration of a dissolution was only supported by five members among them Dr Lee, Mr Morris, Mr Grieve &c. The main question was then put when there appeared for dissolution 24: against it 26. Mr Alderman Townsend was in the chair, and the whole number present was 53, being the fullest meeting which had ever been held in the society. Lord Mountmorres, and another gentleman, retired before the division. For dissolving the society there appeared Mr Alderman Sawbridge, Sir Francis Bernard, Sir Francis Delaval, Mr Bellas, Mr Tooke, Mr Horne, Mr T. Oliver, Mr Twogood &c. Against it, Mr R. Jones, Mr Ellis, Mr Bull, Mr Baldy, Mr Adair, Dr Wilson, Mr Wilkes, Mr Churchill &c; the gentlemen divided against putting the question. Those who were for dissolution having failed in their motion, then immediately proceeded to strike their names out of the society's book, which was first done by Mr Alderman Townsend, who also struck out at the same time, the name of Sir Cecil Wray and Mr Charles Turner, who had authorized him for that purpose. After this, they withdrew into another room, and there signed a resolution to form a new society to exist only upon the public ground, Mr Morris, Mr Grieve, Dr Lee, Mr Sayer, and others declared they would follow them in their secession, unless the remaining members of the society came to a resolution to rescind the vote of restriction against opening new subscriptions, as public exigencies should require, whether gentlemen were willing to contribute farther to the discharge of Mr Wilkes's debts or not.[45]

Wilkes offered to settle for a large lump sum instead of £1,000 a year but his popularity did not extend so far. He continued to dine regularly with the Society, even taking the chair for Serjeant Glynn on one occasion.

There were several pleas on behalf of the imprisoned magistrates, who were finally released at the close of the prematurely ended session of Parliament. Fifty-three carriages escorted them triumphally to the Mansion House, and, on 13 May, the case against Whittam was stopped.

The printers now that the impotency of the House was discovered laughed at an authority which had been so much dreaded before it was wantonly brought to a test that exposed its weakness.

This discovery being made, the effect naturally followed; and in the succeeding session, the votes of the house, a thing before unknown, and contrary to its orders, were printed in the public newspapers, without notice or enquiry; and thus the point in contest was apparently given up by the house.[46]

This victory failed to heal the breach in the membership of the Society. Horne now had no room for Wilkes and did not hesitate to show it. Robert maintained that Horne never had approved of Wilkes. The latter thereupon produced a letter written by Horne from Montpelier in 1766, couched in most flattering terms:

To John Wilkes, Esq. Paris.

Dear Sir,

I well recollect our mutual engagement at parting, and most willingly proceed to fulfil my part of the agreement.

You are now entering into a correspondence with a parson, and I am greatly apprehensive lest that title should disgust; but give me leave to assure you, I am not ordained a hypocrite. It is true I have suffered the infectious hand of a bishop to be waved over me; whose imposition, like the sop given to Judas, is only a signal for the devil to enter.

I allow, that usually at that touch—'fugiunt pudor verumque, fidesque. In quorum subeunt locum fraudes, dolique, insidiaeque &c, &c.' but I hope I have escaped the contagion; and, if I have not, if you should at any time discover the BLACK spot under the tongue, pray kindly assist me to conquer the prejudices of education and profession. . . .

I passed a week with Sterne, at Lyons, and am to meet him again, at Sienna, in the summer. Forgive my question, and do not answer it, if it is impertinent. Is there any cause of coldness between you and Sterne? He speaks very handsomely of you, when it is absolutely necessary to speak at all; but not with that *warmth and enthusiasm*, that I expect from every one that knows you. . . .

I have this moment seen a letter from England, that tells me that Fitzherbert has sent you a power to draw on him to the amount of 1000 £, a year:

> Eutrapelus, cuicumque nocere volebat
> Vestimenta dabat pretiosa.

I am afraid this is Eutrapelian generosity; and that, by furnishing you with the means of pleasure, they intend to consign you over to dissipation, and the grand points of national liberty and your glory to oblivion. I am sure they will be mistaken; nothing little or common is for the future to be pardoned you.

The public have done you the justice to form extravagant notions of you; and though they would be sorry to see you neglect any opportunity of serving your private interest; yet they hope never to have cause to reproach you as Brutus did Cicero. 'That it was not so much a *master* that he feared, as Anthony for that master.'

You perceive how freely I deliver my sentiments; but all this is uttered in the openness of my heart, and ought not to offend you, as it proceeds from a man who has always both felt for your sufferings, and spoken highly of your conduct in the public cause. In the meantime,

I am, dear sir,
Your most obedient and very
humble servant,
John Horne.

Wilkes was now accused by Horne of publishing a private letter wantonly but claimed he brought it forward only to refute Robert Morris's statement. A wordy argument between Robert and Wilkes ensued:

To Mr John Wilkes.

Sir,

I am unwilling to interfere in the dispute between you and Mr Horne, who have both deserved well of the public, and are so fully qualified to fight your own battles; but as I perceive a mistake in your last letter, where you mention my name, which it is in my power to correct, and as it is a position agreed, that people have a right to truth, I cannot by my silence admit you to have given an exact representation of your conduct respecting Mr Horne's letter from Montpellier.

The sentiment you would have the world adopt is, that the first production of that letter was in consequence of what I said, and to corroborate your answer; therefore not a wanton or designed publication of a private and confidential letter. I am persuaded that no conversation passed between us, which can justify such a construction upon your conduct. I first heard of the letter, not from yourself, but from persons to whom you had previously shewn it; and it was first produced to me at a meeting at the Devil Tavern, called the Retribution Club, where I believe I was at that time the only stranger to it's contents, amidst a dozen other gentlemen in the room, and before which time you had never spoken to me of such a letter. Some of the company asked me, 'Whether I had not seen the letter which Mr Wilkes had of Mr Horne's?' and as soon as the letter was mentioned, you produced it. I confess that I frequently took occasion, and probably did so at that meeting, to declare that Mr Horne had made some such assertion as you mention; because his former connection or intercourse with you, which he had then quitted, created the only difficulty in my mind respecting Mr Horne's conduct, in other respects equally honourable to himself and serviceable to you. But your action is now coupled with my declaration, in a manner to which they have no relation.

Having rendered this justice to Mr Horne, I shall be equally ready to do the same justice to you; whenever I find him trespassing upon truth, either through wilfulness or mistake, in any matters which come immediately within my knowledge. As to the parties who are now contesting, I have no reason to wish success on one side more than on the other; and I certainly shall not decide upon a dispute till it is ended. As yet, I may say with Lucan,

.... Quis justius induit arma
Scire nefas; magno se iudice quisque tuetur.

It is the cause of liberty I wish to promote, and I care not by whose hand it triumphs. Of that cause alone I desire to be esteemed a partizan, and not of any individual. I have the honour to be,

With regard, SIR,
Your most obedient humble Servant,
Robert Morris.

Lincoln's Inn
May 27[47]

To Robert Morris, Esq.

Prince's-Court,
Wednesday, May 29.

SIR,

The fact is that you, Sir, had frequently said so to several of your friends, 'Mr Horne told me he had always the same opinion of Mr Wilkes,' and once to myself before the meeting at the Devil Tavern. My answer had been to you, 'Not always the same. When I see you next, I will convince you of it.' I knew you were to dine at the meeting at the Devil Tavern. I brought the letter with me for your perusal.

You came late. Several gentlemen before your arrival mentioned your declaration about what Mr Horne had said. I then produced the letter, which was read before you came by the other gentlemen, and by yourself afterwards. You confirmed to us what had been said by Mr Horne. I desire you to ask any of the dozen gentlemen present, whether I have not exactly stated the fact.

The letter from Montpellier is dated 3 Jan. 1766. Will you please, Sir, to name any one gentleman who read it prior to the late dispute between Mr Horne and myself, and likewise to your own declaration that 'Mr Horne told you he had always the same opinion of Mr Wilkes.'

I am, SIR,
Your very humble Servant,
John Wilkes.[48]

However equivocal Robert's attitude was towards Horne, that of the London mob admitted of no doubt. On 1 July

in the evening, the effigy of Mr Horne, in a canonical habit, with a pen in one hand, and in the other a salt-box, intended to represent the treasury box of the bill of rights, after being carried through the principal streets in the city, was consumed in a bonfire which the populace made for that purpose before the Mansion House.[49]

From this struggle between the City and Parliament stemmed the Freedom of the Press in England and Robert Morris, through his knowledge of the Law, played a very active part in the fight for it.

Now that Lord Shelburne and his party had broken off to form the Constitutional Society pledged to support Liberty but not Wilkes, those who were left produced a political programme which Junius was quick to attack.

I cannot but resent the injury done the common cause by the assembly at the London Tavern, nor can I conceal from you my own particular disappointment. They had it in their power, [he wrote to Wilkes] to perform a real, effectual service to the nation; and we expected from them a proof, not only of their zeal, but of their judgment. I object, in the first place, to the bulk and much more to the style of your resolutions of the 23rd of July though some part of the preamble is as pointed as I could wish. You talk of yourselves with too much authority and importance. By assuming this false pomp and air of consequence, you either give general disgust, or what is infinitely more dangerous, you expose yourself to be laughed at. The English are a fastidious people and will not submit to be talked to in a high tone, by a set of private gentlemen of whom they know nothing but that they call themselves Supporters of the Bill of Rights. There are questions, which, in good policy, you should never provoke the people in general to ask themselves. At the same time, I am far from meaning to undervalue the institution of the Society. On the contrary I think the plan was admissable; that it has already been of signal service to the public, & may be of much greater; and I do most earnestly wish that you would consider of and promote a plan for forming constitutional clubs all through the kingdom. A measure of this kind would alarm the government more, and be of more essential service to the cause, than anything that can be done relative to new-modelling the House of Commons.[50]

Frances Mary Harford
(1759–1832). *George Romney*.
Aged 25. 'white dress, cut
low with light brown
trimmings, a pearl necklace
and lace head-dress, light
brown hair, brown eyes and
beautiful complexion'.

Frederick Calvert, sixth
Lord Baltimore (1731–1771).
Artist unknown.
He succeeded to the title in
1751; married Lady Diana
Egerton in 1753, who died in
1758; and bequeathed his
estate in Maryland to Henry
Harford and £30,000 to
Frances Mary Harford, his
illegitimate children.

Margaret Morris (1731–1813).
After Joshua Reynolds.
Aged 26. 'in a blue dress with
rows of pearls, left hand
holding a bunch of flowers
to her breast, dark hair
trimmed with feathers'. She
married Desenfans in spite of
opposition.

Noel Joseph Desenfans
(1745–1807).
David Owen (1769–1825).
He left France *c.* 1769;
worked as a tutor and sold
lace. After his marriage he
became a dealer in pictures.
In 1799 he published a plan
for the advancement of
British Arts and the
establishment of a National
Gallery; and he was the
author of its first descriptive
catalogue in 1802.

Clasemont 1782. *P.F. Bourgeois (1756–1811)*.
Built *c.* 1772 by John Morris (1745–1819). It was removed to Sketty by his son
in 1820 because of industrial pollution. Bourgeois was the protégé of Desenfans.
Their combined collection was left to Dulwich College in 1813.

Landore with 'Morris Castle' 1792. *J.C. Ibbetson.*
This was the centre of the Morris and Lockwood copper and mining interests.
The 'Castle', built by John Morris, housed 40 families of colliers, a tailor and a
shoemaker. It was occupied until 1850.

Singleton Abbey. *P.F. Robinson*
This incorporates Marino, built by Jernigan *c.* 1784 for Jane Morris (1739–1810) and Edward King (1750–1819). It was leased to the Vivian family in 1817 and extended several times.

Corporation Meeting,
2 November 1787. The
quarrel was caused by
Gabriel Powell's attempt to
mortgage Corporation
estates to oppose 'new
paving the town and
improving the harbour'.
Powell won and Morris, in
the black hat, left in disgust
without signing the minutes.

The Steward, 1787.
Gabriel Powell (1710–1789)
was Steward to the Duke
of Beaufort, and by 1740
became Portreeve. His
nickname was the 'King of
Swansea'. He opposed the
petition for a paving bill in
Parliament.

21

TO
HALE·COURT

21

The Great Hall. *Photograph by Peter Johns.*
'On Wednesday last the affair of Mr Morris and his ward was taken into consideration by the Lords Chancellor at Lincoln's Inn Hall.' *London Evening Post 8 August 1772*

Lincoln's Inn. *Photograph by Peter Johns.*
The Admissions volume I, 1420–1799, include the names of many from Wales.

Harford his Wife, and further to the said
Article or Exhibits he knows not to Answer.

3° & 4th — To the third and fourth pretended additional
positions or Articles to the said pretended
Libel and to the paper Writing or Exhibit
marked N° 24 in the said fourth additional
Article pleaded and Exhibited this Respondent
answereth and admits the same to be true.

5th & 6th — To the fifth and sixth pretended additional
positions or Articles to the said pretended
Libel and to the paper Writing or Exhibit
marked N° 25 in the said sixth Article pleaded
this Respondent answereth and admits the
same to be true.

7th — To the seventh pretended additional position
or Article to the said pretended Libel this
Respondent answereth and confesses and
believes what he hath confessed and
believed, and denies and disbelieves what
he hath denied and disbelieved:/—

26th October 1782.   Robert Morris.

Repeated and Acknowledged
before Dr Andrew Coltee Ducarel
one of the Judges in the within
mentd Cause, in his Chambers in
Doctors Commons London Present
(Here time for Jushington conformity to and
Registered)   Nath Bishop Notary Publick one of the
Deputy Registrars,

Lady Henrietta Musgrave, *c.* 1774. *Joshua Reynolds (engraved by R. Smith).*
Fourth daughter of Sir Philip Musgrave of Eden Hall and Kempton Park. She
married John Morris in 1774 and was called 'The prettiest woman in Town'.
She died in 1812 and was buried at St John's Church, Swansea.

Answers of Robert Morris (see pp. 38–9). Written by Morris himself, the answers
occupy 27 pages and give an excellent picture of his facility. He finally withdrew
most of them.

Ranelagh House and Gardens, 1750. *Artist unknown.*
'It may be said that as a public place of amusement it is not equalled in Europe for beauty, elegance and grandeur.'

Window in the Venetian Style, Lincoln's Inn. *Photograph by Peter Johns.*
28 November 1768: 'Robert Morris prays leave to new fashion the windows of his chamber at 21 Kitchen Garden Court to make a bow window looking into Kitchen Garden.' (It is now numbered 20.)

Swansea Castle and the River Tawe. *Artist unknown.*
Morris and Lockwood sailed their own ships to Cornwall for ore and to London with products. 'How beautiful was the seashore covered with low roses, yellow snapdragons and thousands of other plants.' W.S. Landor.

Six weeks later, on 4 September 1771, Lord Baltimore died of a fever in Naples and the whole course of Robert's life was deflected. The body was brought eventually to lie at the Exeter Exchange in the Strand before burial at Epsom; but although three years had passed since the trial at Kingston, feeling against him was still so high that the mob plundered the room as soon as the corpse was borne away.

According to a letter to his daughter Wilkes received a call from Robert at Bath on 1 January 1772; and on 13 January Lord Baltimore's will was certified in Naples and carried on the 17th 'by two men domestiques of long service' to London to be delivered to Hugh Hamersley in Serjeant's Inn, Fleet St., or Peter Prevost in Serle St. and 'not to be read but in the presence of Hugh Hamersley, Peter Prevost and Robert Morris and Henry Harford or in the presence of any three'.

The two main beneficiaries were Henry Harford and Frances Mary Harford.

I do bequeath my said province of Maryland and all other premises thereto belonging last mentioned to and unto the use of a certain youth called or known by the name of Henry Harford, the son of Hester Rhelan of the kingdom of Ireland born in Bond St. and now of the age of nine years or more* and to the heirs male of his body lawfully begotten and to the default of such issue to the heirs male begotten on the body of a certain female Frances Mary Harford daughter of the said Hester Rhelan and born in Bond St. aforesaid and now of the age of eight years or more and to the heirs of the said Frances Mary Harford and if there shall be failure of issue of the said Frances Mary Harford then to the use of the Honourable Mrs Eden my youngest sister.[51]

If Henry died before the age of twenty-one the estate was to go to Frances Mary, who was left £30,000. To Hester Rhelan, now of Rathbone Place, he left an annuity of £200; £1,000 to Elizabeth Dawson (Mrs Hales) and £4,000 to her two children, Elizabeth and Sophia; £2,000 to Charlotte Hope, an infant, but nothing to her mother who, Lord Baltimore declared, had treated him badly. To his executors he left £1,500 each and an annuity of £100. He had remembered his obligation for the acquittal at Kingston Assizes.

I make it my earnest request to my Executors that they will superintend and take upon them the care of the persons and fortunes of the said Henry and Frances Harford and they will to their utmost support the dispositions made in this will.

Both children had now to be placed in schools fitting their new station in life. Henry, nearly fifteen, was taken from the care of the Reverend Dr Loxton at Richmond and sent to Eton where he stayed until 1775.

* In 1768.

Frances Mary, now twelve, on the recommendation of Robert, was taken from her governess and daily masters and

was placed to receive an education suitable to her fortune at a Boarding School kept by Mrs Martha La Touche at Little Chelsea.

Robert Morris in company with Henry Harford inquired what were the terms of admission into the school and asked the said Henry Harford how he liked the same as a school for his sister.[52]

Fanny was 'brought at the end of March by her mother Hester Relhan and fetched for the Easter Holidays on April 16th. She returned on May 1st'. Robert visited the school, but usually alone 'unknown to the other executors and without arousing any suspicion that he was visiting her with any view or account other than merely as a guardian'. He wrote her little notes:

Mr Morris presents his compliments to Miss Harford & sends the Papers he promised which have an account of the Masquerade, is sadly fearful he shall not be able to do himself the Honor of waiting upon Miss Harford today but will endeavour to form a Party for Ranelagh on Monday. Left Harry very well on Saturday & as pleased as is supposed to be at School.[53]

Fanny, although she had lived in a part of the house well separated from the quarters of her licentious father at Woodcote, Epsom, was already showing a sophisticated taste for the amusements of the town.

Robert took her with her mother to the Pantheon,*

the much-talked-of receptacle of fashionable pleasure in Oxford Street, which had opened [in January 1772] to a crowded company of between 1,500 and 2,000 people. Imagination cannot well surpass the elegance and magnificence of the apartments, the boldness of the paintings or the disposition of the lights, which are reflected from the gilt vases, suspended by gilt chains. Beside a number of splendid ornaments that decorate the rotunda or great room, there are a number of statues, in niches below the dome, representing most of the heathen gods and goddesses, supposed to be in the antient Pantheon of Rome. To these are added three more of porphyry, the first two representing the present King and Queen and the last Britannia. The whole building is composed of a suite of 14 rooms all of wh. are adapted to particular uses; and each affording a striking instance of the splendour and profusion of modern times.

In point of company, the company were an olio of all sorts: peers, peeresses, honourables and right honourables, jewbrokers, demireps, lottery insurers, and quack doctors.[54]

Also at the Pantheon on the day of Fanny's visit were Susanna, wife of Richard Vaughan of Golden Grove, Carmarthenshire, an old friend of

* Near Gt. Marlborough St. and Poland St. Destroyed by fire on 14 January 1792 at a loss of £60,000.

Robert, and his youngest sister, Jane, who was staying with the Vaughans. Robert asked if he might present Miss Harford and Fanny 'was led across the room from her mother's side' to meet them. Later he begged Mrs Vaughan to invite Fanny to dinner and on to Ranelagh for the entertainments, a treat she eagerly desired.

Mr Morris has the honour to present his Comps. [compliments] to Miss Harford & has the pleasure of mentioning that Mrs Vaughan will form a party on Friday next. Will wait upon Miss H. at the dancing time tomorrow & if it should be in his power will drink tea at Chelsea this afternoon about 7. Is in hopes to bring Mrs Vaughan tomorrow with other ladies. Hopes the Buckles will meet with Miss H's approbation.

Tuesday, May 12, 1772[55]

He had not, however, reckoned with Mrs Martha La Touche's sense of propriety. She declared she did not know Mrs Vaughan and had never heard of her. Fanny could not be permitted to go. Robert called at Chelsea and declared his friend to be 'a lady of Fortune, Figure and Character'. Mrs La Touche nevertheless insisted on a written invitation from Mrs Vaughan herself and a promise that Fanny would be safely returned to the school. Jane Morris wrote the letter for her.

Mrs Vaughan presents her Comps. to Mrs La Touche and desires she will permit Miss H. to dine with her and go to Ranelagh in ye Evening.

Berners St. Wensday night.[56]

Mrs La Touche was satisfied and sent a note 'via a liveryman' to Mrs Vaughan (who never received it) giving Fanny permission to accept her invitation.

On 15 May about 2 o'c. in the afternoon Robert Morris went to Mrs L.'s in a coach, having the appearance of a gentleman (but borrowed*) attended by a footman & coachman cloathed in the same livery.'[57] [Robert said] 'that Mrs Vaughan w^d have come herself but she was not well'. [But Mrs Vaughan] 'was not privy to or in any manner acquainted with Robert Morris's intention of making use of her name other than to dine'.

In the forenoon of Fryday 15 May 1772 Mrs Vaughan and Jane Morris, spinster went in Mrs V's coach to the Exhibition of pictures & on their return to Mrs V's in Berners St. about 4 o'c they were much surprized to find R.M. & F.M.H. were not come & at 5 p.m. before they sat down to dinner Mrs V. received a note from R.M. 'Mr Morris presents his compliments to Mrs V. & is sorry to disappoint her but Miss Harford & himself are obliged to set out directly for Eton.'[58]

But Christopher Talbot's coach did not go so far. Just out of sight stood

* From Christopher Mansel Talbot, 2nd son of Rev. Thomas Talbot of Collingbourne; entered Oriel College on 9 October 1768 and Lincoln's Inn on 4 December 1771, described as the 2nd son of Rev. T. Talbot, late of Margam, clerk, deceased. He died at Penrice Castle.

a post chaise and four which 29-year-old Robert and 12½-year-old Fanny hurriedly boarded.

Unaccompanied by any other servant or other person whatever & without any other clothes than what she had upon her person he did carry her to Dover. He hired a small open boat to Calais in Picardy and arrived in Boulogne and stayed the night. F.M.H. expressed herself uneasy and wished to go home again. Whereupon R.M. used all kinds of words & expressions he could to pacify her but finding she persisted in her desire of returning he pretended to grow desperate and swore he w^d kill himself if she left him whereat F.M.H. greatly terrified consented to stay with him.[59]

In her eagerness to escape from school where she spent only four weeks, broken by the Easter holiday, Fanny must have been an accomplice. As soon as their flight was discovered Robert's fellow executors entered 'a plea for Henry and Frances Mary Harford to have the care and protection as to their persons & estates during their minorities'.

Robert's diaries, beginning baldly, 'At six in the afternoon F. & I left London in a chaise and four' tell the story of the next two years. The documents of the ten-year-long libel and appeal fill in details which delineate a character scarcely credible when considered against Robert's professional training, acknowledged skill and upbringing.

He gives the barest details of their first marriage at Ypres on 21 May. Witnesses, however, stated

having failed at Furnes they finally set out for Ypres, arriving between 9 and 10 in the morning and after a little stay there sent their servant [they had hired two, Louis Podevin and Françoise Raisin] to Pieter Antoine Douze, inn-keeper of Hôtel de la Chatelaine, desiring to know if there was at that place any minister of the Reformed Church to marry them. He took them to the Reverend Joannes Carolinus van Byler. R.M. said they were French subjects; he was a bachelor of twenty-two and F.M. a spinster of sixteen but she did not appear so old. She had no father, mother or Guardians and both signed a document to that effect. They left immediately for Lille.[60]

Robert then wrote to Peter Prevost

acquainting him that Miss Harford and he had that day united together in a marriage & in a Postscript to the said Letter he wrote that he would not have been so ungenerous as to propose a marriage with Miss H. without a proper settlement of her Fortune which he had transmitted to her brother who was at Eaton School acquainting him with the marriage.[61]

He knew that two Englishmen were in pursuit; and on 24 May Robert Spottiswoode and John Jolly, sent by Hamersley and Prevost, 'applied to the Commandant at Lisle to arrest both'.

The next day Robert complained to Wilkes and Serjeant Glynn.

Sirs,

As one of your constituents, & one who with some satisfaction gave a voice to your election, as he now reflects upon your conduct, I make my appeal to you from an unjust confinement in the french king's dominions by Mr de la Merveille Commandant of this town, who, after arresting me by four Grenadiers, now confines me within the walls of it, under the pretence of a young lady (who accompanied me from England) being reclaimed by some two Englishmen, who assume a greater right to her company than myself, which is a matter that concerns him not. The dominating spirit of his office, & the infectious air of slavery which pervades this country are the only causes of his conduct. Your interposition I doubt not will be as spiritedly exerted in my behalf, as my own actions have hitherto been spirited in your support. As you have never been wanting to the care of Public Liberty, so I doubt not you will be attentive to that of an individual, however remote from his home; leaving the name and character of an Englishman everywhere to be respected, especially amongst our vanquished enemies.[62]

Robert's rage, and fear of the formidable champion of liberty, John Wilkes, produced the desired effect. The guard was taken off and Robert and Fanny were free to leave, but his money had run out. In a fortnight he has spent £200, including sixty guineas for wardrobeless Fanny and seventy-six at a Paris watchmaker's. He sent Louis Podevin off post-haste to London for funds and, as soon as he was back, they all set out on the road for Paris but 'turned towards Holland by Tournay and travelled all night'.

The next day Prevost 'proceeded for Lisle accompanied with Mrs Hester Harford, the mother of Frances Mary Harford, and Mrs Relhan, sister of Mrs Harford with letters from the French Ambassador in London'. But their quarry was well away. Prevost hurried as far as Amersfoort but gave up the chase and returned to his neglected practice.

By 1 June the party was at Dordt where their feeling of security was badly shaken at dinner by news from Fanchon (Françoise) that Robert Spottiswoode and Hay Ferrier were enquiring about them on board the ship in which they had sailed from Eccluse for Rotterdam. Leaving everything, they crossed the river twice and finished the journey by coach. 'Five days and six nights incessantly travelling and living on coffee and toast brought them to Hamburgh.' Robert was again down to his last few guineas.

On 12 June Spottiswoode and Ferrier caught up with them and 'applied to the Senate to have Frances Mary Harford delivered up'. On the 17th an order was made to place a guard on her but Robert, once more warned by the hotel-keeper's son, snatched her from beneath their noses and, hiding her in the bottom of the coach, rode to Wandsbeck. Here he applied to

Baron Schimmelmann (the richest subject in Germany and Lord Wandsbeck, a town three miles from Hamburgh). Wandsbeck has the privilege of protecting all persons from being arrested. Now to arrest any refugee within the territory the previous assent of the 3 Chanceries of Denmark, Bareuth and of the Grand Duke of Holstein must be obtained. If any one of these Chanceries does not assent eodem tempore then no warrant can be granted to arrest such refugee and before the united assent of the 3 Chanceries can be accomplished the fees of office attending such applications amount to £100,000 sterling. By this device Baron Schimmelmann has established the privileges of his territory and Mr Morris with his lady enjoy the rights of liberty.[63]

On 23 June Robert wrote again to the Members for Middlesex, John Wilkes and Mr Serjeant Glynn.

The liberty of myne and my wife's person is again attacked at Hamburgh. I beg, as one of your constituents in Parliament your interposition in our behalves. My solicitor Mr Lloyd of Grays Inn can furnish you with an authenticated Copy of my marriage certificate.[64]

The letter was immediately sent on to the Earl of Rochford, one of the Principal Secretaries of State; but Robert's old friend, Tom Lloyd, believing Robert guilty of the worst of all crimes, a betrayal of trust, parted from him for good.

Mr Lloyd presents his Compliments to Mr Wilkes, is sorry he was prevented being at Guildhall this morning. Mr Lloyd has received a Letter from Mr Morris dated the 23rd instant but does not understand from it that he or his wife is under any confinement. Mr Lloyd so much disapproves of Mr Morris's conduct that he does not wish to be thought to be in any manner connected with him.[65]

Robert now began to keep close to Wandsbeck for fear of arrest. Pressure from London was increasing and as yet no seal had been set upon the marriage. Fanchon was Fanny's bedfellow. Early in July, as Fanny lay ill, he declared in his diary that he 'found the force of my true affection for her'.

On 9 July the Lord Chancellor made an order that 'Robert Morris should attend personally and produce Frances Mary Harford on August 5'. By the 20th Ferrier and Spottiswoode were back again. They called on Robert twice but failed to serve the Lord Chancellor's writ.

Eventually, after much subterfuge on the part of Ferrier and Spottiswoode and a great deal more by Robert, the writs were served. Robert thrust them out of the house and afterwards burnt them. Once more he applied to Wilkes, writing from Hamburg on 21 July:

As a persecuted constituent of yours & one who has shown himself your friend, I have written to you, but received no answer to my letters. I beg to know whether you have received any lines from me, & what you have done in that respect.[66]

Two days later he recorded the consummation of the marriage in code at the head of a detailed list he was to keep while Fanny stayed with him.

Fanchon and Louis Podevin were interrogated for two days about the circumstances of the Ypres marriage at Baron Schimmelmann's Court of Judication; Robert was taking no chances over recognition of its validity. He also had bought three houses at Wandsbeck on 19 July.

At the Lord Chancellor's Court on 5 August, the day after his thirtieth birthday, Robert was restrained from acting in the trusts of Lord Baltimore's will and interfering in the care of Frances Mary Harford and, since he had defied the court, was to be committed to the Fleet Prison and restrained from matrimony.

For a time pressure from London seems to have eased, though Robert complained to Baron Schimmelmann about the intermediary who served the writs and wrote again to Wilkes on 18 September:

I think my former connexion with you, & the conduct which I observed in every dispute relative to yourself at the least intitled me to a civil answer. But you have chosen only to inform me, that my letters have been received by letting it be inserted in the Newspaper.[67]

On 27 October, to raise money 'he executed a Bargain & sale to J.M.' [his brother John] (p. 59) and early in November decided that another marriage ceremony in Denmark could only further cement his tie with Fanny. He drew up a petition to the King, making only a brief reference to it in the diary entry for 3 November 1773.

The petitioner Robert Morris of Wandsbeck humbly prays his Majesty to be married at home with Frances Mary Harford.

May it please your Majesty to permit me submissively to represent to you that I have for some time resided in Wandsbeck & become an inhabitant having purchased a house there & being resolved to be united in marriage by the hands of a Priest with Frances Mary Harford and wish the same to be solemnized & to avoid the usual formalities I therefore humbly petition your Majesty praying to be dispensed therefrom & grant me your gracious concession. That I may without the usual preceding leave & notice from the Chancel at any time & place where I please be married by the hands of the Priest with Frances Mary Harford.
I devotedly remain, etc.[68]

Robert left Wandsbeck for Hamburg and, on 13 November, there presented the petition. Permission was granted by King Christian on 5 December at a 'cost of 3 Rix dollars and 9 Sch. current cash' and the Commission reached Wandsbeck from Copenhagen on 19 December.

We Christian 7 by the Grace of God, King of Norway Wenden & Gothen, Duke of Schleswick Holstein, Starmen & Ditmarchen &c do hereby make it known that upon the petition presented we have graciously permitted & granted &c by these presents in like manner we do permit & grant that the subscribed Robert Morris of the Lordship of Wandsbeck may with his betrothed bride Frances Mary Harford by the Hands of a Priest be married & given to each other without the usual anteceding public licence & notice from the Chancel at any day or place they shall think proper provided there be no lawful Impediment to prevent the same & so that the Church Schools & their officers be in no ways wronged from the just dues & fees.

Granted under our Royal Seal. 5.12.1772[69]

During this fortnight in Hamburgh he met Edward King who had been 'appointed to the post of second Assistant Rider on February 17, 1770. George III had a stud at Celle (Zell) in Hanover where Edward King was doubtless employed'. Although he was a good deal younger than Robert – he was born in 1750 – he was to become the friend on whom Robert most relied.

In December news came from John Wilkes.

Mr Wilkes has had the honour of writing four letters to Mr Morris in France and Hamburg, but as he has not heard of any of them being received, now makes a last effort, and if this paper reaches him, begs Mr Morris to do Mr Wilkes the justice of believing the real and warm sense he entertains of many past favours.
Princes Court &c   December 11.1772[70]

Robert was most gracious and lengthy in his reply.

The few lines which you did me the favour of writing upon the 11th Inst. are the only ones of your hand that have reached me, since I have been abroad. I do not know to what to attribute the miscarriage of your former favours; but they none of them cou'd have laid me under greater obligation than your last. By the step I have taken in relation to matrimony my private & public reputation I know has greatly suffered: which I did not at first foresee; but if I had, I confess to you I shou'd not have altered my inclination or resolution. I have a sensible regard for the good opinion of my former acquaintance & of the Public; but in the matter of a private nature, concerning my own happiness, I cannot after all help thinking myself the better judge. I expected to have it said by Cavillers & Enemies, that I had taken advantage of the share which had been given me in the trust of a young Lady's person & fortune, & when she was of too young an age to determine for herself upon such a subject. Those who knew me intimately I conceived wou'd acquit me of such penuriousness, and who knew the Lady I was satisfied wou'd acquit her of such infantine weakness. The trust which I accepted did not exempt me from marrying, therefore marriage was no breach of it. After all, taking this matter in a contrary light, are there to be no temptations for me in a woman, & is she to be less charming for being young? The Lady, young as she is represented, is allowed to have been of an age, by Law capable of marrying. If she ought not to have married at that age, the Law is in fault, which gives her the capacity of doing so, not I. This is what I might have said to my friends upon the occasion. Yet what had my friends to do with it? They are not Censors, set up to make a nice disquisition into my conduct, though some of them seem to have thought them-selves such. Was I obliged to tell them, whether I loved my wife, & how much she loved me in return? But if we loved each other all is justified.

Of the private ill-usage I have received I wou'd not complain to you, but for your acquaintance with some of the particular persons at whose doors I lay it. I will instance to you one, in Mr Watkin Lewes. But ——! To you I need not say more. The blank will be a secret to none but himself. The public ill-treatment I have received I place to two quarters, his Majesty's Secretary of State, and that tool of every fool in office, the Lord Chancellor.* The Secretary of State has at least countenanced my oppression, by not enjoining, after my repeated applica-tions & complaints, his Majesty's minister here & the Ambassador in France, to obtain redress for me from these parties, in these respective countries, who, by pretences of office & in reality from other motives, had authorized the arrest & interruption of English subjects pursuing legally their own affairs abroad, and that for a matter transacted in the dominions, where oppressive orders were issued.

In these situations I scorned all applications to great men in power or interest, with whom I might have had recommendation. I knew none, whom I rather chose to apply to than yourself & Mr Serjeant Glynn, not from any hopes of your power to serve me, but from the connexion that subsisted between us, which gave in my opinion a propriety to the application both on my side and yours, you being my legal representative in parliament. I had a greater reason to expect relief from you, in particular, from the Chancellor's silly order against me, 'that I shou'd stand committed to the Fleet prison for not attending his Court in person, & pro-ducing there a young Lady described in her maiden name, who was then my wife'; a matter studied to be concealed by my opponents, & which I had not an oppor-tunity of proving by witnesses before him, incompetent as he is to the question, though I acquainted him with it by letter. This order too was made whilst I was abroad, unheard, and the Chancellor not having assumed to take cognizance† of the affair, till both myself & my wife were out of the kingdom & consequently out of his jurisdiction. Neither was there a pretence of informing me of his supreme order 'till within a fortnight of his sentence of outlawry; I being then too at the distance of Hamburgh. Yet all comes very properly within the notion of a contempt; a term not less dangerous to the people of England, than General warrants and Seisure of Papers from which you have so gloriously relieved your countrymen, and in the room of which this has started up. I am satisfied that you will not be less active to relieve them from this new-fashioned instrument of Tyranny, because it happens to be exerted in the case of another. I ought to inform you, that I have lately made an application to Mr Townsend, the Lord Mayor, offering the Chancel-lor to return to London, if he will protect me in the same manner against the Chancellor, as you & the other magistrates did some other citizens, in whose behalf I appeared then as Counsel, against the Speaker of the house of Commons, upon their pretence of privilege, which is the same word with them, as Contempt is within the Courts of Law. Whether my conduct is approved, excused or con-demned in what has passed relative to my marriage, I ought not to be delivered over to an arbitrary power, contrary to the genius of the English Laws. I demand a trial by a jury before I am condemned; and till then, whoever inflicts a

* Lord Apsley, later Lord Bathurst.
† As Robert left so suddenly this argument is quite untenable.

punishment upon me, I shall esteem him to be in a state of war with me, & myself intitled to use him as I wou'd an enemy or an assassin. If you esteem my case worthy of your interposition, extend it to me not for the sake of friendship but for the sake of justice. I will not have you talk to me of obligations for past favours; I know of none, that have not been amply requited to me by your public conduct. My feeble efforts in your support, I esteemed & still think no more than the duty of an honest man.

Private jealousies I trust will not affect your public sentiments; and that you will be as ready to unite with the present Lord Mayor, for whom you knew my friendship, as you were with any former one upon patriotic grounds. Yet in your own history I have been witness how much private jealousies do really alter the sentiments of men; a fault which I place not intirely to one side or the other, but to the general frailty of human nature. I own for myself, that from your neglect, as I apprehended, of my application to you, I had almost been tempted to exclaim against you, even as a public man; in the same stile, as some in the City have done, who were formerly your friends, & have become your detractors, too much upon the principles of private quarrels.

If there is any matter communicated in this letter, which, upon my account or any other, you may think proper to give to the Public, you are welcome to do so, with your answer: which I hope I shall soon have the honor of receiving: and am, Sir,

Your most obed^t humb^l servant
Robert Morris.

John Wilkes Esqr Prince's Court, Storey's Gate,
Westminster, England.[71]

Ever since the elopement Robert had been romping through his inheritance but it seems he still had an estate worth bequeathing, for in November he spent a few days making fair copies of his new will. By 25 December, his plans were complete and he held a small dinner party for those who were to accompany him and Fanny to their second marriage at Ahrensburgh.

On January 3 [Sunday] 1773 Robert Morris produced the Royal Licence to Henning Johann Eicke, pastor of the parish of Ahrensburgh and left it with him and about 1 o'clock a marriage was solemnized in a room at an inn at Ahrensburgh by Eicke according to the rites of the Lutheran Church in the presence of John Parish George Thomsen, George Parish, Jacob Wolffe and others.[72]

'Thou, Robert Morris' [read Eicke] 'here acknowledges before their worships and all bystanders that thou hast taken and dost take to thy lawful wife here present whom thou does promise never to forsake and that thou shalt cleave to her the days of thine and her life, love her and faithfully take care of and maintain her to live and keep house with her in all reasonable honesty and honour and hold faith and belief with her in all things as becomes an honourable man and as he ought to treat his wife. Dost thou promise this?'

The bridegroom was required to answer 'yes'.[73]

Fanny acknowledged that she had taken Robert to her lawful husband whom she promised

never to abandon, to cleave to him the days of his life, obey him, serve and help him in all right reasonable things, live and keep house with him in all reasonableness, honesty and honour and hold faith and belief in him upon all things as becomes a faithful and honourable wife and as she ought to treat her husband.[74]

Then she gave him her right hand, the company wished them joy, and they all sat down to dinner.

On the following day Eicke issued a certificate which the four friends witnessed at Hamburgh on 11 January.

Robert now considered himself beyond the reach of Prevost, to whom he wrote that

to avoid any further occasion of dispute he had been that day again married by an authority that cou'd not be disputed, the King of Denmark's Special Licence in the King's own dominions and that he offered a certificate.

Nevertheless, early in February, the pair went to Hamburgh and

at the request of Robert Morris and Frances Mary Harford the marriage was certified* and entered and registered in the Protocol or Registry of the Court of Judicature and judicial testimony granted.

There are no signs that Fanny was a reluctant bride on the second occasion.

As the year advanced the little group of master, mistress and servants began to break up. Fanny made her will in Robert's favour. A new companion, Miss Hodgson, edged Françoise Raisin (Fanchon) from her rôle as confidante and bedfellow and began to sow seeds of resentment against Robert in the mind of her mistress, talking of successful marriages Fanny might have made with her fortune.

The diaries tell the story of growing separation and, by the end of 1773, Robert acknowledged defeat. Fanny refused yet another marriage ceremony now she was 14 and rejected him as a husband.

Overwhelmed, he wrote to Prevost from Geneva, 'I shall be anxious to bring the two marriages already passed between us to a decision.' He then prepared to leave for Paris where he arranged that Fanny, who had written to her brother about her decision, might be collected.

She arrived at her mother's house in Rathbone Place on Saturday, 8 January 1774 and a fortnight later the Lord High Chancellor ordered 'Mr Pechell to enquire into the marriage and in the meantime Frances

* See the entry for 7 February 1773 in F's Sayings &c. 'Now I can bring ye certificate entry'.

Mary Harford should reside with and under the care of Hester Harford'. The long legal process to annul the marriages had begun.

Robert, in danger of arrest for debt, went into hiding in Paris until money came from his brother John; and, since he could not with safety return to England, he set out by sea on a tour of the low countries with Edward King. But this distraction had to end and when King left Rotterdam for England, Robert suddenly sailed for Harwich. Three days later in London he was 'blest yth ye sight of my most dear and affectionate Brother John Morris' (page 169)[75] who was about to marry Lady Henrietta Musgrave and wanted no impediment through scandal.

From safety in the rooms of a fellow barrister, Henry Howarth* of Mitre Court, Inner Temple, he prepared his answer to the charges against him; but to his letter 'saying he was ready to be forthcoming in the Court of Chancery' the answer was a warrant for arrest. 'Being disrespected he became less inclined to appear at all.'

His escape north to board a ship back to Hamburgh is well described in volume 2 of his diary but whether he sailed or not is unknown since the account suddenly ends on 5 July 1774.

September found him back in Swansea.

Robert Morris (our dear and ever honoured Father) preserved copies of all business letters so, after returning from an unfortunate two-years, ill-bestowed absence abroad, Robert, the eldest surviving son, took up the suggestion of his younger brother John to make extracts of the 'material parts' concerning the conduct of the conducted enterprises of his father, as a means of giving pleasure and instruction.

If in what I shall here execute I may prove of any assistance to my Brother, who has so well deserved to succeed my father in the management of these concerns, it will be a peculiar happiness to me at this juncture. Though I left him oppressed with a load of business and most important engagements I never failed experiencing from him an attention to my interest equal or superior to his own.[76]

The next year, 1775, saw the battle of wits between Robert and the Law truly joined. Fanny 'being in her minority and therefore by law incapable of standing in judgment or of commencing or prosecuting any suit otherwise than by a guardian' acted through Hugh Hamersley, Peter Prevost and Henry Stevens.[77]

On 18 May they applied to the Bishop of St David's to grant Fanny

'letters of request that she may apply for such citation of nullity in the Arches Court of Canterbury . . . which will be of advantage to both parties not only from the better assistance they can have of advocates and Proctors than in the Consistory

---

* Entered Lincoln's Inn 23 November 1764: listed as 'gentleman, son of Rev. Hy Probert?H. of Meslough, co. Radnor, clerk'. Called to Bar Trinity 1769. Died 11 May 1783.

Court of St David's but as the same will also be more ready and expeditious a way for the hearing and finally determining the said cause'.

The next day Fanny appeared in court at Lincoln's Inn before the Chancellor and the decree was granted. Robert was summoned to appear 'six days after he received the citation in the dining room adjoining the Common Hall of Doctors' Commons in the Parish of St Benedict near Paul's Wharf'.

But on 26 May 'the decree under seal had been executed but not returned'[78] and the court was forced to continue the certificate through June and July, finally extending it to the first session of Michaelmas term. Meantime 'the decree was personally served on Robert Morris at Swansea in the County of Glamorgan under seal and leaving same with him, a true copy by Rees Davies of Swansea, sworn before Iltid Thomas, a master Extraordinary in Chancery'.[79]

On 3 November

on which day Stevens junior returned the said decree and then proclamation being thrice publicly made for Robert Morris, the party cited and he in no wise appearing Stevens Jr accused his contumacy and prayed and the Judge at his petition pronounced him in contempt and in Pain of his contumacy and at the petition of Stevens continued the certificate until the next court day.

Again Robert did not appear on 13 November: he was called three times and declared in contempt. Further continuations followed until 20 January 1776 when 'Lushington exhibited under Seal of Robert Morris a proxy (signed on 9 December) and made himself a party and prayed a libel be given on his party to be dismissed with costs'.[80]

'Now know all men by these presents that I the aforesaid Robert Morris for divers good causes and considerations me thereunto especially moving have constituted and appointed by these presents, do nominate and appoint Messieurs Stephen Lushington and James Heseltine, public and Procurators General of the Arches Court of Canterbury . . . to be my true and lawful proctors for me and in my name to appear before the Right Worshipful Sir George Hay, Knight, Doctor of Laws Official principal of the Arches Court of Canterbury.'[81]

Meanwhile Fanny's advocates were busy seeking evidence abroad from Witte Tullingh of the legality of the marriage at Ypres according to the laws of Holland; as a garrison town its position with regard to Law was in doubt, which Robert duly made use of. For Holland, the absence of banns called personally before witnesses was crucial, a special grant being necessary for strangers. Then, Fanny had been carried away by her guardian who was 'highly punishable on the body as the case requires, even Death'.[82]

35

In no circumstances could Robert benefit from her estate, even if consent were later obtained.

All through 1776, for lack of vital documents, which had to be sought abroad, translated and certified, the libel dragged on. Then, on 2 December the Judge, Sir George Hay, 'rejected the said libel and Exhibits annexed and dismissed Robert Morris from the suit and further observance of judgement therein'.[82]

Robert had won the first round. The marriage at Ypres was pronounced valid and Fanny's complicity to some degree established, 'she being of proper age, being free and the marriage voluntary'. But the matter was not to be left there. In January 1777 Fanny 'acting by Prevost Prevost asked for leave to appeal which was granted in May'; and in June the High Court of Delegates requested

Sir George Hay Knight, Doctor of law official Principal of the Arches Court of Canterbury, his Surrogate or Register that they fully plainly and entirely and faithfully transmit on the first session of the Michaelmas term next ensuing all documents which do in any way relate to or concern the said cause in the Common Hall of Doctors Commons.[83]

The opinion of Witte Tullingh on the Ypres marriage had failed to settle the issue. Prevost now turned to the carefully planned and documented marriage at Ahrensburgh. In 1774 papers from Hamburgh had declared that Robert's elopement had been concealed and that he had falsely called himself an inhabitant or Liegman of Wandsbeck, betrothed to Miss Harford, but that her youth was no bar to marriage since, under Roman Law, girls of twelve could marry.

Through constant postponements and objections from Robert's counsel the case hung fire for several years, though Robert, both in London and in Swansea managed to provide sensation in other spheres of life. On 29 June 1779 an article appeared in the Morning Post in which the writer cast aspersions on the loyalty of the Dulany Family. The author, the Reverend Bennet Allen,

published a variety of American characters and among them that of Dulany, who in return called the anonymous writer in the same paper a scoundrel and a coward. Allen avowed himself the author in 1782, when after verbal and written communications thro' their friends the terms of a meeting were arranged in Hyde Park. Dulany was attended on the ground by Mr Delancy and his antagonist by Mr Robert Morris. Dulany and the two seconds I conclude 'American Loyalists' who had taken refuge in England. The duel was fought with pistols at eight yards about ten o'clock in the evening. The Reverend duellist before firing put on his spectacles. His shot was fatal. Dulany fell but rose, ran a few feet and fell again. He was conveyed to his lodgings and expired two or three days afterwards.

Allen at the fall of his adversary absconded, but finally surrendered himself on July 22nd. He and his second Morris were indicted for murder and tried at the sessions house at the Old Bailey. . . . There was evidence that while Allen was the original aggressor he invited the conflict and had applied the most insulting epithets to the ill-fated Maryland loyalist. It also appeared that his second, Morris, repeatedly urged a postponement of the duel until a proper hour the next day.

Mr Justice Butler stated 'as to the law there is not, nor ever was, any doubt that where two persons meet together deliberately to fight a duel and one of them is killed the other is guilty of murder and his second likewise'. The jury after twenty minutes' deliberation returned a verdict – Allen guilty of manslaughter, Morris not guilty. The recorder then pronounced sentence that the convicted party should pay a fine of one shilling and be imprisoned for six months in Newgate.[84]

[Robert was also the reputed author of] a pamphlet published in London in 1782 in which an attack was made on an American, General Arnold, who had fought with distinction against the British and later joined them. It was asserted that General Arnold had been transported from England for horse stealing, though in fact he was born in Connecticut. Captain James Battersby of the 29th Regiment of Foot challenged Morris to a duel but luckily a reconciliation took place.[85]

In the meanwhile on 21 February 1781

before the Archbishop of York, the Earl of Hillsborough, the Earl of Galloway, Viscount Hampden, the Bishop of Rochester, the Lord Bishop of Peterborough, the Reverend Ed. Willes, justice of His Majesty's Court of King's Bench, Sir James Eyre, Knight, Sir Beaumont Hotham, Knight, two of the barons of the Court of Exchequer, His Worshipful Peter Calvert, Sir James Marriott, Knight, and William Macham, doctors of Law, Judges among other delegates in the Common Hall of Serjeant's Inn, Chancery Lane, between the hours of 6 and 11 in the evening, present Nathaniel Bishop and Maurice Swabey, Notarys public, deputy registrars, the libel of Harford against Morris re-opened.

Their lordships assigned the cause for further informations and sentence on the next day at six o'clock.

They did so too on the next three days. Then in March it was declared that

the Judge below had done wrong in rejecting the Libel and Exhibits and additional articles and Exhibits . . . and Dr Calvert Official Principal of the Arches Court of Canterbury was monished to bring and leave the original articles before the first session of Michaelmas term to the Judge Delegates.[86]

Time after time the certificate for decree for answers was continued at the request of one side or the other. Lushington, for Robert, was 'assigned to give an answer to the libel under pain of suspension'. He rejected the charge; and in the following year Prevost brought to the court a succession of witnesses to bolster his case – Fanny's mother, Hester Relhan, spinster; Elizabeth, her aunt; Martha La Touche, her teacher;

Robert Spottiswoode who had pursued Robert across the low countries; and his childhood friend, Susanna Vaughan, of Golden Grove.

In June 1782 Stevens

put forward a Schedule of Excommunication in pain of Robert Morris the party principal thrice called and not appearing but the judge at the petition of Altham for Lushington directed Excommunications not to go under Seal till after the next Court.

However, it was 26 October before Robert 'brought in his said answers in writing subscribed with his name, which subscription he acknowledged to be of his own handwriting and the said answers true'. They took up thirty beautifully written pages.

On 15 November

Heseltine for Lushington alleged his Client's answers to be in private [and they were] repeated and acknowledged before Dr Andrew Coltee Ducarel, one of the judges in the within mentioned cause in his Chambers in Doctors Commons. Present Heseltine for Lushington consenting to one Judge only.

In his answers Robert admitted the parentage of Fanny and her inheritance of £30,000 and the £100,000 she would inherit if her brother died before the age of 21, but he denied he was a trustee as Lord Baltimore had no authority in law to make trustees. He agreed Fanny was placed at the Chelsea School but denied recommending it and writing notes except the two shown, and denied he had any design of getting possession of the person of Fanny.

He admitted writing to Mrs Vaughan, wife of Richard Vaughan, 'a woman of respectable character desiring her to send a regular invitation and that the letter shown was in the handwriting of Jane Morris, now the wife of Edward King,* and written at Mrs Vaughan's request'. He admitted 'the facts of the elopement but that such journey was so undertaken with the entire free will and approbation of the said Frances Mary Harford and she was desirous of going abroad'. He denied that any Arts or pretences whatsoever were made use of by him.

He admitted the journey to Calais but denied Fanny ever wished she were home and admitted he treated her with tenderest care and affection. He denied he ever pretended to grow desperate or threatened to kill himself in order to prevail on her to stay with him. He admitted applying to Joannes Carolinus Van Byler, the Dutch Chaplain to the Garrison at Ypres – a minister of the Reformed Church – to solemnize a marriage but

---

* Jane married Edward King on 13 July 1777. His post at Celle was taken by a William Parnham in July 1776.

he 'denied he said either was a French subject or that he was only 22 and she 16 but, being under 30, said he was upwards of 21 and she of marriageable years but under 16'.

He admitted he told Byler that Fanny had no father or legal guardian whatever and that they were married according to the rites and ceremonies of the English Church in the presence of Pieter Antoine Douze, Louis Podiver and others, since 'Frances Mary Harford made a scruple to being married according to any Roman Catholic form'. He denied that Robert Eden, Hugh Hamersley and Peter Prevost or Hester Relhan had any legal right or authority to consent or dissent from the marriage. He denied that any consent, banns or a dispensation was necessary and that the decrees of the Council of Trent held in the Austrian Low Countries.

He denied that he carried Fanny away clandestinely; 'he had heard that certain persons were sent in pursuit and that a centinel was placed at the Hotel but why he did not know'. (See Diary: vol. 1, 24–25 May 1772.)

He had travelled to Hamburgh for pleasure and did not escape to Wandsbeck in consequence of any notice received. (See Diary: vol. 1, 20 June 1772.) He denied that the Lord Chancellor's order to attend on 5 August was delivered personally at Wandsbeck. He admitted obtaining a concession but denied it was done 'fraudulently or surreptitiously but for the mutual satisfaction of him and his wife'.

He acknowledged all official documents on the Ahrensburgh marriage and considered the licence sufficient authority. He denied that local regulations could affect the validity of the marriages of British subjects: the marriage was at their mutual request when Fanny was of marriageable age by the laws of Great Britain.

Through December 1782 and January 1783 the appellant's advisers brought in a succession of witnesses: Hester Relhan again; Peter Prevost; John Hopkins; Hugh Hamersley and Sir Robert Eden, Lord Baltimore's brother-in-law from Maryland.

Lushington, once more under pain of suspension, denied various articles produced while Robert's solicitor and brother John made energetic efforts to find him and urge him to attend the Court.

On 11 July 1783 the judges 'having heard informations on the part of the appellant and pain of Robert Morris the Respondent and Lushington being thrice called and not appearing assigned the cause for sentence before the whole commission at Serjeant's Inn'.

At last, on 11 May 1784 'appeared personally Robert Morris and without reasking his proctor' withdrew most of his answers and admitted the facts of the marriage. He rested his case on its legality. On 21 May, before the full Court of King's Bench 'at a quarter before 7 o-clock in the evening came on the final hearing of Mr Morris's cause to establish his matrimonial contract with Miss Harford'.

At ten o'clock the final judgment was given.

The marriage at Ahrensburgh was founded on fraud and illegality: both pretended marriages were void: Miss Harford falsely in the libel called Morris was at full liberty to marry again and Mr Morris was condemned in full costs.[87]

Fanny was now nearing 25. Romney's* portrait for which she had been sitting from February 1780 until 14 November 1783 shows her 'three quarters face looking to left, white dress, cut low, with light brown trimmings, a pearl necklace and lace headdress, light brown hair, brown eyes and beautiful complexion'.[88]

'She had £36,000 three per cent consolidated Bank annuities in the bank of England' and young twenty-one-year old Frederick William Wyndham as a prospective husband. He had £10,000, expectations of a similar sum and the 3rd Lord Egremont to pay off his debts of £1,000.

Peter Prevost was drawing up a marriage settlement which was to be concluded

so soon as Henry Harford, late of the Parish of St. James's, Esquire and who is now resident in the province of Maryland shall arrive in England to assign, transfer and make over all and singular the said trust monies and premises and the estate funds and securities so that the said Henry Harford shall and may from henceforth be a trustee with George, Earl of Egremont and Peter Prevost.[89]

Another annuity of £200 was settled on Hester Harford until her death.

Exactly two months after the verdict in her favour, the *Gentleman's Magazine* announced, 'On July 21, by special licence the honourable William Wyndham, brother of the Earl of Egremont, to Miss Harford, of Russel Place, late Mrs Morris'. Not quite the title that Robert swore she coveted but a fair chance of one, especially as the 3rd Earl had only a quiverful of illegitimate children who could not inherit it. The noble lord did, however, marry the faithful mother of his six children in 1801.

In August Edward King 'took a lease of Tir y Powell parcel of the manor of East and West Millwood'[90] in the presence of Robert Morris. Here he demolished the farm house and built Marino,† an octagonal mansion, in the beautiful sloping site running to the centre of Swansea Bay.

On 10 September Peter Prevost, now a widower, married Mrs Harford, Fanny's mother, and left Serle Street to live in Russell Place. When

---

* Romney stayed at Clasemont with John Morris.
† Now part of Abbey Buildings, University College, Swansea.

he died he left her considerable effects and money which she could add to the £200 annuity from Lord Baltimore and to the additional £200 settled on her as part of Fanny's marriage settlement.[91]

Eleven months passed with constant postponements before the full costs of the litigation were assessed. In April Fanny, now pregnant, appeared in court for the last time and on 10 May Stevens produced the Bill of Expences

which the judges taxed at the sum of £1,348.13.7 besides the expense of the monition. There was a sum of £617.0.8 for expeditions in Ypres and £136.5.7 for searches in Hamburgh, payable in fifteen days after service.[92]

Luckily for Robert Counsel appeared as friends. Then, according to the Register Book of Marriages solemnized by Licence in the Parish of St Andrew's Holborn

Robert Morris of the Parish of Saint Andrew Holborn and Sarah Prichard of the same Parish Spinster, were married in this Church by Licence on the Twentyeighth Day of June in the Year one thousand seven hundred and eighty five; by me Arthur Owen Minister. This marriage was solemnized between us
Robert Morris
Sarah Prichard
In the presence of us Anne Lucas
Mich[l] Southcote.[93]

Sarah, whose family lived at Bach y Gwreiddyn, very near Tredegar Fawr, signed in a small neat hand.

On 30 August Fanny's first child, George Francis, was born. He was not to succeed to the title until 1837, fifteen years after his mother's death in Florence. When he died in 1845 the title became extinct. It has recently been revived.

Fanny had three other children, the last born in Florence where her husband held an official post as envoy to the Grand Duke of Tuscany. The eldest married at 20 but left her husband and went to live in Paris: she got no mention in her mother's will, the greater part of her personal estate going to the youngest daughter, Laura, wife of the Reverend Boultbee, 'who was to pay 100 sequins for a stone or an Urn wherever I am buried'.[94]

In 1786, sponsored by John Morris of Clasemont and his son John, of Brynn, Sketty, Edward King was appointed Deputy Comptroller of the Customs in the Port of Swansea,[95] and in July 1810 he was promoted to Collector, a position he held until 1815 at a salary of £500.

A month later his wife, Jane, died 'in advanced age' according to the Cambrian. She was 71. He retired to Bath, having sold the lease of Marino to the Vivian family, and died there in August 1819.

Henry Harford found his inheritance tangled in the American War of Independence and finally applied for compensation from the British Government for his loss. He asked for £477,850: he was awarded £70,000 but was still well able to support his first wife, Louisa Pigou and their four children, Frederick Paul, Louisa Ann, Frances and Frederica. He married secondly Esther Rycroft, daughter of Nelson Rycroft, Baronet, by whom he had two sons and two daughters, George, Esther, Emily and Charles. His country home was Down Place, Water Oakley, Windsor, and his town house was in New Cavendish Street.

In 1786 Robert's mother died at the home of his sister, Margaret, in Charlotte Street, leaving him all her real estate in North Wales and £50. He already had the reversion of her other property.

Margaret had by 1778 married Noel Desenfans who established himself very successfully with her dowry as a picture dealer; his collection eventually formed part of the Dulwich Gallery Collection, London.

Robert busied himself with his small estates in Swansea and Gower and joined in minor moves to develop the town. He was involved in efforts to improve the river embankment and in November 1787 acted as peacemaker in the fracas at a Corporation meeting over paving the streets. A cartoon perpetuates the scene.

A man holding a document has had his wig snatched off. His assailant (Powell*) is being restrained, but a very thin man wearing bands, his arm linked in Powell's, kicks him. Others look on . . . A form has been overturned . . . Robert Morris, Esqr., bursts into the room, restores the wig and puts an end to the Affray.[96]

The year 1788 brought further tragedy. After just over four years of marriage his wife, Sarah, became ill and by December 1789 – the year which saw the completion of his alterations to Tredgar Fawr – she was dead. Under her marriage settlement she had left him her estate for life.

In June 1790 Robert sought permission to proceed to Bengal to practise as a Barrister in the Supreme Court of Judicature. This was granted at a Court of Directors and a message dispatched on 15 December stating 'We have permitted Mr Robert Morris to proceed to your Presidency'.[97]

In April 1791 he made his will and devised

all my estate in the town and Franchise of Swansea to my nephew Robert Morris and his heirs for ever, free from all encumbrances and in case of any existing I direct that all my other real Estate shall be sold and my personal property in the first place applied to clear the same. I devise that all my other landed property should descend in the course of law . . . and I devise to my nephew to include St. John's Field and house newly built thereon which I have agreed to purchase.

* Gabriel Powell's eldest son, also Gabriel, entered Lincoln's Inn on 12 June 1770.

He left a hundred guineas to his sister, Margaret Desenfans, 'free of all controul of her husband' and ten guineas to Noel Desenfans as a token of remembrance: £50 to his sister Mary (who never married) and a hundred guineas to Jane, 'free of all controul'; ten guineas to Edward King and 'he forgave him all his debt which is above Three hundred'.[98] He left ten guineas to all his brother's children and £50 to Mr George Bowser. John Morris was to be sole executor.

He sailed on the *Airly Castle*, and while on board added a codicil, witnessed by cadets and by Thomas Hudson, the Captain's servant, on 14 May 1791.

In his memoirs William Hickey gives a racy and somewhat inaccurate account of Robert's affair with Fanny. He also describes in some detail Robert's arrival at the Bengal Courts:

Another circumstance that operated against Mr Morris was his not having brought out a single letter of recommendation to either of the Judges, nor to any one individual belonging to the Court, though he had a number to some of the principal gentlemen of the Settlement, both civil and military. A few days after his arrival which happened to be in term time, he addressed a letter to each of the four Judges, wherein he informed them of the date of his being called to the Bar of the Court of King's Bench at Westminster, and that his object in coming to Bengal was to practise as an advocate in the Supreme Court. Sir William Dunkin thereupon related to his brethren what he knew of Mr Morris's former conduct, which, he added, in his opinion rendered him unworthy of a place at their Bar, or of being allowed to mix in the society of gentlemen. The other Judges' sentiments being the same, an answer was written by the Protonotary and sent to Mr Morris, telling him that the power of admitting Advocates at the Bar of the Supreme Court rested entirely with the judges, and as they thought the number already sufficiently large to execute the business that occurred and to save something annually to do which was what brought professional men so far from home, they did not consider it either prudent or just to increase them. Sir William Dunkin objected to this softening off and proposed sending the rejection in direst terms without evasion, by assigning the actual reason for their refusing his demand, but the other Judges conceived such a proceeding might be unnecessarily wounding the feelings of a man who perhaps had seen his errors and resolved upon a complete reformation.

Upon receipt of the answer through the principal officer of the Court, Mr Morris again addressed the Judges, and told them that he never meant to ask, nor did he expect or wish for the smallest favour at their hands, either jointly or individually; that he required nothing but his inalienable right which, as a true-born Englishman, he would insist upon to his latest breath; that out of the respect that he felt for them as Justices of one of his Majesty's Courts he had communicated his intention, a compliment he did not conceive himself bound to pay them, for as a Barrister of the highest Court in England he contended he had a right to plead in any inferior Court he might choose to enter: that he should therefore attend in the Supreme Court of Calcutta the following morning, and trusted their Lordships would shew that they possessed common sense and common good manners, by receiving him like gentlemen, and not attempting to prevent his pursuing the profession he had been brought up to.

No notice whatever being taken of this second address, Morris made his appearance the next day equipped in gown, band, and wig, and upon the Judges taking their seats upon the Bench he rose, and in an eloquent speech renewed his claim of being permitted to plead as an Advocate. To which the Chief Justice replied in nearly the same terms as the written answer had been given. Mr Morris thereupon, in forcible and pointed terms, accused them of partiality and injustice, observing that as they had thought proper thus publicly and openly to traduce the character of a professional man, he hoped they would not refuse to assign their reasons for so doing. The Chief Justice, after consulting with his brethren, said he did not consider himself bound to give any other reason than he had already done for exercising a discretionary power which the legislature had vested in them. Morris thereupon interrupted the Judge violently exclaiming, 'Then I will make you individually and personally responsible for your illegal and wanton tyranny.' Mr Justice Hyde, offended at his conduct, said, 'You had better be more circumspect and guarded in your expressions, otherwise I certainly shall propose that you be delivered into the custody of the Sherriff. As to publicly declaring the motives that actuate me upon the present occasion, I shall not indulge you, nor will I, while I have a seat upon this Bench, submit to be dictated to by any pirating coxcomb whomsoever.'

Sir William Jones agreed in opinion with the two Judges who had preceded him (Morris the whole time being busily engaged writing down what each Judge said). Sir William Dunkin, as the junior Judge, next addressed him to the following effect, 'Mr Robert Morris, you have in very unbecoming and indecorous language called upon the Judges of this Court to assign their specific reasons for refusing to allow of your practicing as an Advocate, and notwithstanding the other Judges have declined to comply with your desire, I have no hesitation in publishing to the whole world what my sentiments are upon the occasion. I object to your being admitted an Advocate of this Court from the notoriety and infamy of your character, and from the vile, abandoned and disgraceful* life you have led for many years past.' Morris appeared to be utterly confounded; after shewing the utmost agitation, he suddenly rose from his seat and left the Court without uttering another syllable.

Shortly after this Morris went up the country, making himself conspicuous by his violent conduct wherever he remained twelve hours. Among other whims he made it a practice to visit the gaols of every town he stopped at, enquiring into the particulars of each prisoner's case, and then assuring them that nine out of every ten were illegally confined and would be justified in using forcible means to obtain their liberty. In a letter he wrote from Patna to an acquaintance in Calcutta, he says that in prison there he had found a native nearly related to one of the oldest and best families of Hindostan who many years before had murdered and, as was supposed, robbed an English gentleman who was travelling with considerable property in money and jewels about him. There being great reason to suspect the above person, who had the title of Rajah, was a party concerned, a warrant was

---

* Dunkin had seen Robert caught playing with loaded dice.

issued for his apprehension, of which, however, he got notice and absconded. After living in secret for some time, he went to Lucknow, where the Governor-General, Mr Hastings, then happened to be, to whom he got introduced, and through the medium of the Vizier, procured the said Governor-General's free pardon for the above-mentioned murder and robbery, but for which pardon he paid a large sum of money (as Morris plainly insinuated) to Mr Hastings. Morris further stated that such pardon was written in the Persian language, and had Mr Hasting's seal affixed to it, and there could be not the least doubt of its authenticity: that the Rajah had shewn him this pardon, but would not suffer it to be taken out of his sight, though he made no scruple of letting him (Morris) make a copy thereof, and he actually had taken a true and faithful transcript. He adds, 'What a precious morceau this pardon would be for the Right Honourable Edmund Burke to produce to the House'. Happily for society this dangerous and troublesome man was carried off by an attack of liver about eight months after he left Calcutta.[99]

It is certain that Robert took some steps to inform the Court of Directors of his reception by the Bengal Judges as the Bengal Public Letter of 25 January 1792, para. 51, shows: 'You will receive in this Dispatch an address from Mr Robert Morris, who arrived here in your ship the Airly Castle.'[100]

Public Dispatch to Bengal 25 June, 1793 Para. 25, replied: 'The Memorial of Mr Robert Morris referred to in this paragraph (51) is under the consideration of the Company's Law Officers.'[101]

Their conclusions are at the moment unknown: so are details of Robert's activities in India until his death five months later. Of his end there are two records: the burial certificate,[102] and in his brother John's* notebook, among jottings on his business and family, this poignant entry:

My poor brother was buried at Fattigur† in the East Indies, November 29, 1793. Attach yourselves to those most nearly allied to you for the ties of blood are most to be relied upon.[103]

So ended a life full of early promise and success and a tie between two brothers which stood against all misfortune.

---

* John was knighted in 1806 for his success in raising volunteers in the County of Glamorgan on the recommendation of Lord Bute. He and his father appear to have been men of outstanding ability and great integrity.
† Probably Fatehgharh, now in the Uttar Pradesh. The Rev. J. Clark officiated and Thomas Blanchard, Senior Chaplain to the presidency of Fort William, signed the certificate. Robert was described as a Barrister-at-law, aged 51 years.

Notes to the Introduction

1. Parish Register: St Mary's Church, Swansea. (One of two interpolated entries about the Morris family.)
2. Morris, John: Notebook, MS, U.C.S. Library.
3. Morris, Robert: Diary, vol. 2, 20 May 1774, MSS, U.C.S. Library.
4. Venn, J. A.: *Alumni Cantabrigensis*, part II, vol. IV.
5. *Records of the Society of the Lincoln's Inn*: vol. XIII, p. 500.
6. Ibid., Black Book III, Preface. Lincoln's Inn.
7. Ibid., Book XIV, p. 19, 25.
8. Jones, E. A.: *Two Welsh Correspondents of John Wilkes*, p. 141, note 1.
9. Gurney, Joseph: *Modern State Trials*, Guildhall Library, London.
10. *Gentleman's Magazine*: vol. 38, pp. 140–80.
11. Morris, Robert: Will, Secker 248, Somerset House.
12. Christie, R.: *Wilkes, Wyville and Reform*, p. 33. (By permission of Macmillan & Co.)
13. *Annual Register*: 1769, p. 75.
14. Ibid.
15. Christie, p. 34.
16. Fitzgerald, P.: *Life of John Wilkes*, vol. II, p. 77.
17. Wilkes, John: *Controversial Letters*, p. 170, Williams, 1771.
18. Almon, John: *Correspondence of John Wilkes*, vol. IV, p. 8.
19. *Gentleman's Magazine*: vol. 39, p. 509.
20. Almon: vol. V, p. 42.
21. Morris, Robert: Add. MSS, 30871, f. 7, B.M. Library.
22. Wilkes: *Controversial Letters*, p. 167.
23. Morris: Add. MSS, 30871, f. 25.
24. Stephens, Alexander: *Life of John Horne Tooke*, vol. II, p. 287.
25. Morris, Robert: Letter of Resignation, *Town and Country Magazine*, 4 September 1770, p. 500.
26. Morris: Add. MSS, 30871, f. 40.
27. Ibid., f. 42.
28. Wilkes, John: Diary, MS., B.M. Library.
29. *Public Advertiser*: 6 December 1770.
30. Morris: Add. MSS, 30871, f. 48.
31. Jones: *Two Welsh Correspondents of J. Wilkes*, p. 143.
32. *Annual Register*: 1771, p. 68.
33. Thornbury: *Old and New London*, pp. 39–43.

34. Morris, Robert: Speech at the Meeting of the Bill of Rights, *Annual Register*: 1771.
35. Morris: Add. MSS, 30871, f. 69.
36. *Annual Register*: 1771, p. 281.
37. Ibid., 1771, p. 184.
38. Rota Book: Guildhall Library, London.
39. Thomas, P. D. G.: *Bulletin of Historical Research*, vol. 33, p. 91, 1960.
40. *Annual Register*: 1771, p. 82.
41. *House of Commons Journal*, 20 March 1771.
42. Ibid., 25 March 1771, p. 283.
43. Junius: *Letters*, no. 93, ed. Wade, John, vol. II, p. 355.
44. Court of Aldermen Records, 1770–71, p. 157, Guildhall Library, London.
45. *Annual Register*, 9 April 1771.
46. Ibid., 1772, p. 81.
47. Wilkes: *Controversial Letters*, pp. 107–9.
48. Ibid., p. 110.
49. *Annual Register*: 1 July 1771.
50. Junius, *Letters*, vol. III, p. 276.
51. Baltimore, Lord Frederick: Will, Somerset House.
52. Cause Papers: Del 2/40, P.R.O.
53. Ibid., Exhibit 2.
54. *Annual Register*: 1772, p. 69.
55. Cause Papers, Del 2/40, Exhibit 3, P.R.O.
56. Ibid., Exhibit 4.
57. Ibid., Article 10.
58. Ibid., Article 11.
59. Ibid., Article 12.
60. Ibid., Article 13.
61. Ibid., Exhibit 5.
62. Morris: Add. MSS, 30871, f. 131.
63. *London Evening Post*: 26 June 1772.
64. Morris: Add. MSS, 30871, f. 135.
65. Ibid., f. 137.
66. Ibid., f. 142.
67. Ibid., f. 144.
68. Muniments Book: 1781–1815, Doc. 21, Lambeth Palace Library.
69. Ibid.
70. Jones: *Two Welsh Correspondents of J. Wilkes*, p. 147.
71. Morris: Add. MSS, 30871, f. 166.

72. Cause Papers: Del 2/40, Article 28.
73. Ibid., Estates General Service at the Hague.
74. Ibid., Article 29.
75. Morris: Diary, vol. 2, 29 April 1774.
76. Morris: History of the Copper Concern, MSS, U.C.S. Library
77. Process of the High Court of Delegates: Del 1/621, P.R.O.
78. Ibid.
79. Cause Papers: 16 September 1775.
80. Cause Papers: Del 2/40.
81. Especial Proxy: G142/7, Lambeth Palace Library.
82. Ibid.
83. Process of the High Court of Delegates: Del 1/621, P.R.O.
84. *European Magazine*: 1782, p. 353.
85. Sergeant, Winthrop: *Life of Major John André*
86. G 151/18. Lambeth Palace Library.
87. *Annual Register*: 1784–85, pp. 19, 21.
88. Romney: *Catalogue Raisonné*, Ward & Roberts.
89. Marriage Settlement: Petworth House Archives.
90. Rogers, W. C.: The Swansea and Glamorgan Calendar, MSS, Swansea Public Library.
91. Prevost, Peter: Will, Macham 3, Somerset House.
92. Process of the High Court of Delegation: Del 1/621.
93. Marriage Register of St Andrew's Holborn, Guildhall Library, London.
94. Wyndham, Hon. Frances Mary: Will, P.H.A.
95. Swansea Oaths of Admission, 1774–1857.
96. Engraving 7222: B.M. Library.
97. India Office Records: E/4/636/49.
98. Morris, Robert: Will, Exeter 753, Somerset House.
99. Hickey, William: *Memoirs, 1791–1792*.
100. India Office Records: E/4/50/820.
101. Ibid., E/4/640/114.
102. Ibid., N/1/4/153.
103. Morris, John: Notebook, MS, U.C.S. Library.

Note See Egerton MSS 226, p. 151, B.M.; House of Commons Journals, 1772, B.M. re Morris and Miller.

The original diaries are in the library of the University College of Swansea (Morris MSS 1, 2).

The Diaries

15 May 1772 – 20 February 1774

15 May, Friday At six in the afternoon F. [Fanny] & I left London in a Chaise & Four.

16 May Arrived at Dover 3½ of morning. At 6 Departed in a small boat 4 oars & men. At 11 Arrived in Calais Harbour – without either of us having been sick. Hired Louis Podevin 6 livres a day and Franchoise [Françoise] Raiesin [Raisin]. At 5 set out from Dessein's Hôtel D'Angleterre for Boulogne – where we lay.

17 May Went back to Marquise within 2 posts of Calais – turned off to Ayre & lay at St Omer.

18 May Came to Pafoin's Hotel de Bourbon at Lille.

19 May Started at 8 in ye Evening to be married to ye dear F. – went all night to Dunkirk – got there in ye mon^g. [morning]

20 May Went to Furnes. Plagued by a cursed Scotchman in ye Dutch service on garrison Here called Capt. Iornes. Pretended he cou'd ajust about our m. [marriage] Pickt my pocket of 5 guineas – wanted us to be contented with some fellows reading the service to us in a room. The protestant minister declined marrying us without the Commandant's permission, who wou'd not give leave to any without papers of Consent & certificate of an abode in France. Lay down in our clothes on. Hotel de la Chatelenye at Donzez.

21 May At 5 set out for Ypres. Signed Mar^e [Marriage] articles. Happily married that evening 9 o'clock to my sweet little angel, in the Dutch Protestant Church – Parson Byller [Byler] – gave him 25 G^s [guineas] gave Douze 10 G^s Parson ask'd me whether I w^d be constant – and I promised it, before God & man. All night sat up writing Letters to England. F. Lay as before on an bed, clothes on, Fanchon over room in another D°. I writing.

22 May Came back to Lisle by 11 o'clock – setting out at 5. Louis at 4 set out for London.

23 May   At Lille.

24 May, Sunday   Pope shou'd have the letter from Donze [Donzez] informing him of 2 Englishmen coming after us to Ypres, & w^d be at Lille that night. Went to the Play – at Return found they were come – Robt. Spottiswoode & John Jolly – 2 Blackguards – called them at once Bombailiffs or Hackney writers – was obliged to go with Major Peffe to the Commandant, Mr de la Merveille – from whence my dear little wife w^d certainly have been sent to a Convent, where a rescue was ordered, but that I show'd my Certificate &c. Brot [brought] there with the Grenadiers. Commandant ordered a guard at our door, till they heard from England.

25 May   Guard taken off in ye afternoon on my writing to M^r le Commandant, that I sh^d apply to the English Ambassador at Paris & to Mr Wilkes & Mr Serjeant Glynn my repres. [representatives] in Parl^t in England. Mr Commandant first offered me liberty to go away privately at a back door wch I refused. He also ordered first no Post Horses to be given us.

26 May   Liberty of Post Horses & to go away.

27 May   At Lille I much tired of it – cou'd not go away till Louis returned with money from London.

28 May   Louis about 5 in ye morning came from England with Frederic – brot money & the things I sent him for – Had actually spent £200 which I brought from England – Louis reced [received] on my account from Gosling besides £200 more – Of this he brought me to Lille about £180 (I had given him 25 gns at Ypres) I paid all Bills at Lille – that at the inn 30 gs in 10 days – milliners about 60 gs – gave Draught besides to Caillet Watchmaker for 76 gs at Paris. Set out from Lille – cou'd get no more than 3 Post horses & 1 Bidet. Went on Post the road to Paris then turned towards Holland by Tournay. Travelled all night.

29 May   This Evening by Gent Bruges to Eccluse.

30 May   Took shipping for Rotterdam. Lay aboard.

31 May   Still aboard ship. Sunday.

1 June, Monday   Was at dinner at Dordt in Holland within 2 or 3 hours of Rotterdam, ye vessel being at Andier, when Fanchon [Françoise] came to inform us that the same English Rascals who came to Lille, were come to the Vessel in search of us saying they had Letters to arrest us – I thought best to go off immediately, not so much from fear of arrest, or any forcible transport to England, as from ye trouble, that any appeal to the Magistrates w^d create us, & from other disagreable circumstances wch might possibly arise from interviews with persons I did not chuse to see, having my doubts whether Prevost himself, Mrs Harford of Rathbone

Place, or some other besides the first Rascals being there. But if there were any timidity in it, ignorance is always an excuse for fear. We came this evening, by crossing twice the River in a Coach to Rotterdam, leaving Louis, & everything behind, except what we had about us.

2 June At Rotterdam, I found I c^d muster in all about £60. I had first thought of going to Bures & some other place called Villengen, I believe – 2 free towns in Holland, as more exempt from ministerial interruption thinking the animosity in England had been prevailed upon to interfere. But Hamburgh being mentioned, & that too called a free town – It being also at a good distance off, though I did not think it as far as it was by half, having no map, & my little wife having seen & still liking the Place – I resolved immediately to go there – wch I did without any stopping in ye way. I had pressed one Favier, a Gold Lace weaver, into my service, as a Dutch interpreter – He came in the Vessel with his wife as Passengers & happening to be with us in the English Coffee house at Dordt, I took him by the shoulder & hurried him on with us, no time for speaking to his wife, & it happened too, that he had left his coat in the Ship.

3 June Went by Utrecht to Di'aventer this Evening – Sandy Barren heathy country all through Gueldres, belonging to Prince of Orange – most disagreeable, I ever saw. Several young Plantation Birch grow well. Sent Favier back – 5 gns – & promised to pay his expences 10 more.

4 June to Rhune

5 June Dispenau

6 June Vishellestin

7 June Harbourg (Sunday morning)

Hanover what we saw of it a cursed sandy country – now & then a pretty wood, into wh. we always used to get out and play – travelled in ye vile waggons of ye country wh. we mended by buying at Osnabruck some wax-cloth & Hoops that served for a tilt – a good deal of Show, & we made a shift to sleep – especially ye Dear Fanny – I c^d not persuade her to go to Bed on the Road, though whenever I saw her tired I much prest it – Now and then we got heated, with a vile coach for one Post. The Posts in this road are generally from 5 or 6 hours long – went with 4 horses – did not seem to be slow – when the road lost any of its sandiness. Cou'd get hardly anything to eat. A little minced veal now & then – no other flesh to be found but Veal – often no bacon – never found any cheese – mostly lived on Coffee & ye Toast & Butter wch Frederic made. The Dear Fanny touched nothing else. 5 days and 6 nights incessantly travelling to reach Hamburgh from Rotterdam. By water from Harburg in an hour to Hamburgh being on Sunday June 7, 72. Took up our quarters at Mr

Prinschausen – Humfer Strasse, Ymffid Junter, Maiden's Walk – by the side of the large piece of waters. I found my good friend Mr Willes here – who had been attending ye Queen of Denmark, & just left her at Stade tother side of water in Hanover Country. We were most happy to meet each other. He wondered what fate had brought me there – thought of Treasons & Duels – & at last (from having seen ye young lady) running away with a girl – but never dreamt of a wife. I left his curiosity to work upon him for some time, & did not satisfy him in the first interview. I wanted his assistance about money – my own being pretty near exhausted. It cost about £50 to come from Rotterdam. Willes's cash was gone, except a few guineas. He went with me the next day however to Mr Hanbury's & offered to endorse any of my Bills. Hanbury seemed suspicious – did not refuse – said he w^{d} advance cash both to Mr Willes & me, if the British Minister, Mr Woodford w^{d} send a note, that he knew Mr Willes had been upon the King's service. Went to Woodford. Left our names. Did not chuse to be at home to us.

8–11 June Spent these days at Hamburgh in company with Willis, & his English Companions – who were Ramiez[?] (whom I had met before) Ld George Fitzgerald (Duke of Leicester's 2d son) a Lieutenant – Captain Collins (Marines) Lieutenant M'Cormac – surgeon M. [Man] of War – who dined with us one day. Went with Willis to Mr Parish wine Merch^{t} on ye Quay i.e. Foresettel, to buy some wine, where he had also bot [bought] some – told him my situation – He immediately offered to advance some money from Willis's endorsing – (he had taken Willis's Bill before upon the Board of Green Cloth for some stores he wanted.) He gave me the next day £50 for my draught & in all advanced me £125 on my draught so endorsed Besides paying several small bills for me – Lending me in cash £10 & being of ye greatest utility to me – accompanied with the utmost kindness and therefore I am greatly obliged to him, & hope I shall live to be able to requite it. Dr Ross was an English gent^{n} I became acquainted with – & whom I sent for as a Physician & surgeon, the first day I came to Hamburg. He did me also great service, by his assiduous attention, & advice to us – & also procuring us the Professor's house at Wansbeck – to which we afterwards made so good a retreat.

10 June Willis &c went to join their vessels off Stadt.

12 June I went with my dear little girl in a large Boat. Tilt cars & sails & Band of 5 Musicians – down the water to hear on board the King's Ships – Obliged to land on ye Hanover side – before we could get there on account of tide – walked a long way – dark[er] – carrying my dear Fanny fell into a Ditch – sprained her foot – wh. sprain lasted bad a fortnight longer. Did not get on board the Commodore's ship till 10 at night – very politely and kindly received by ye Commodore. Found Sir Rob' Keith there. Lay in ye cabin. Lady with Fanchon at the Upper end. Curtain between them and the Commodore & me.

13 June Came back to Hamburg. Landed about half way on ye Danish shore – in 2 waggons to Altona – thence in a coach – Altona about an English mile off.

14–19 June Past these days in ye usual Rotine [routine] at Hamburg – buying things – airings – & going to the Play – & inquired after a country house. Bill at Prinshausen's was brought in at the End of ye Week without asking for it – wh. I found usual Practice – £20 in one week – Lodging in the house very dear.

20 June, Thursday Enter'd into an absolute agreement in writing with Mr Professor Nolten to take his house at Wandsbeck till March 1st 1772 [1773] for 1,000 marks – £66.13.4 Banco – £83.6.8 But N.B. These were Marks. After this, when at Dinner at Prinshausen's with Mr Parish, & Mr Crester, the Guittar-master – Mr Prins^{ns} youngest son called me out of the Room, & told me, 2 soldiers were sent by the Praetor to be a guard upon my wife – described by them under her maiden name – Liberty to go everywhere, except out of Hamburg – Said that his father had informed them we were not at house – advised us to go to Wandsbeck as a diff' [different] territory – But sooner after this told us the men wd not go away with his father's answer, but one was at the fore door, the other backwards – I ordered the coach, my dear little girl went down into Prinshausen's room – I lept into the Coach to go to Mr Woodford – saw nobody at the door – went back – took my wife by the hand, put her into the Coach & Frederic behind – told to drive to the English Minister's. Nobody in ye house knew otherwise. Soon altered the direction – & to drive to Wansbeck. Frederic told us, a man was following us – Bid the Coachman drive as fast as he could (though in Burgher's clothes, as a compl' [compliment] to a Burgher's House) The Guard, who had watched our going out – & only waited to come to the gate to stop us, ran on out of Breath – his hat in his hand we outstripped him – Frederic saw him speak to the Guard at the first gate – we were too much before – my little dear w^d lie at ye bottom of ye coach under the feet – till out of ye Gates – Got safe to Wansbeck – lay that night at the Inn.

19 June Called upon Mr Woodford the English Minister – assured by him he had no hand in what had past. Lay at the Professor's house – he still there.

20 June, Saturday Assured by Mr Mateson (the banker) & Mr Hanbury

C

the Court-master of ye English Mercht[s] [Merchants] that they had given me security for assistance to the English Assassins – as reported. N.B. Hanbury lied. Hanbury and Evatt gave security.

21 June Assured of protection by the Baron Schimmelmann upon whom I personally waited – saw his eldest son – talks English – great civilities from them both. Called upon ye Praetor – no news from him.

21 June, Sunday At Wansbeck. Had the house given up to us intirely by ye Professor.

22 June–2 July These days we past in our usual course – mostly at home accordingly – days, now out of house & [in] garden – much amusement in ye Garden – Writing Master – Harpsichord – I learnt Guittar of Crester – Fanny not. F. one day ill – Then found the force of my true affection for her – Left off going to Hamburg – doubt as to my safety there – went last time I believe Wensday June 24. N.B. In a month after went there several times. also went to Berlin.

3–5 July Dined at the Baron Schimmelmann's Castle at Aurensburg – 2 G. [German] miles off – a very agreeable family – well recv[d] [received] with my dear F.

6–12 July At Wansbeck – Fun with old Gossling the Writing Master – hardly toucht the Guitar more. Dancing Master – Helen i.e. Maria Magdalena Cornellison. Cook Christina Elisabeth York. Housemaid – Anna Margaretta Schorn. John Frederic Selze. Louis Podevin. Françoise Raiesin (The servant names)

13–19 July I bought 3 houses at Wansbeck. Still at Wansbeck In the old stile. A horse.

20 July Farrier [Ferrier] & Spottiswoode called twice; presented a third time by my letter. Had treacherous designs in pretended offers of friendship.

21 July Brown an English Coffeehouse or Tavern-keeper at Hamburg Introduction from having known D.B. [Duke of Baltimore] before &c – calls and offers a Packet from F. & S. – directed him to take it to——? . & say he had left it here – so said he w[d] – left a letter from F. & S. for me at Parish's – called again in ye evening – askt for a note from me to assure F. & S. that I had rec[d] the letter – gave it him – went to the door – put a packet close to me wh. fell down – I refusing it [he] said, 'I am very sorry for it but I must deliver this – these are ye originals. I w[d] not have done it for £100, but was commanded by Mr Woodford' – Run off – spun to his House – I pushed the paper out of house & it was afterw. [afterwards] burnt.

Lloyd (Tom) of Grays Inn – an honest lad of good dispositions – no fool, but no strong sense. Easily led away by others took into his head & heard others say so, that my marriage was a Breach of Trust. A Breach of Trust he had always heard call'd infamous. Was himself by his profession of a Solicitor much in the way of Trusts – Had learnt therefore as by rote or a rule of practice to hold breaches of them in great detestation – Thought there was no distinction between one Breach & another & that no circumstances cou'd excuse. It was all infamous. He might have said Forgery is infamous – therefore he held me as bad as a forgerer and treated me as if I had been so. (After the greatest friendship & many intercourses of business which had passed between us for a long while, having been at school together, by his letter of June 23rd '72 – he writes me, that I had been guilty of a breach of trust, therefore I was infamous – was utterly inexcusable & desired no longer to appear in ye character of my friend or Solicitor. Poor Tom – I pity thy honest Prejudices. So Poor Tom – adieu.

N.B. However I shall call him to account for this affront.

23 July This Day F.f.b.m.w.h.l.f.*

24–25 July, Saturday Louis & Fanchon exam^d [examined] in Baron Schimmelmann's Count of Judication rel^n [relation] to our marriage – evidence recorded.

27 July Louis Podevin paid & went to Calais – at his own desire. Fred. & he cried at Parting – & to solace themselves got drunk. Louis exprest great regard & affection for me – w^d lose his life to serve me.

F. ag. gr. m. poss. of h.f.p. & n. y. up a h.v. shd.th. l. of it, w. m. a.v.t.

28–30 July F.f.ag.

4 August Birthday. [He was 29.]

5–6 August At Wansbeck – sent memorials to the Senate & to Mr Woodford – Also to Baron Schimmelmann about Brown.

7 August Set out for Berlin

8–9 August Arrived at Berlin – White Pidgeon Inn near Post-house.

10 August, Monday at Berlin. Plagued with diarrhoea – Took some Pills made of Rhubarb, Ginger & Laudanum. Mostly obliged to stay at home – low spirits fear and doubt – at play at night – French – long Theatres quite dark – candles drawn up, when play begins that nothing might be lit but the stage, & so that show to more advantage.

11 August Went about the town &c – still ill – next to Death. At night – German Play – Nobody in the Boxes all the ladies in the house were in ye pit & amphitheatre.

12–13 August At Berlin

* Marriage consummated.

14 August Went to Potsdam. A fine town. Saw the King of Prussia a horseback, passed close by me looked at me very hard – made me a bow. Very old look, seemed penetrating & sensible. Saw the Prince Royal – seem'd about 40 – heavy – made me three bows. Prussian soldiers fine men – exercise well – like the English. Potsdam a fine town – number of new buildings. King encourages building there & at Berlin very much.

15 August A fine work carrying on at Berlin on a swampy bottom – Draining & Stables for ye King – soldiers most at work receive 10 pence a day or 5 Grossens. A curious way of raising the water, about 6 foot – by a slope & a number of small loose upright boards like the flappers of a water mill linked together, drawn up & down the Slope. Saw the repository of Berlin China – very fine but very dear – Saw Plates for the Empress of Russia at 5 Guineas a Plate.

16 August, Sunday About 11 set off for home – went by Spondau – a better road – i.e. less sandy – go with 4 horses about 3 miles or so an hour. Went regularly 2 hours at every Post for horses. Horses always in ye county. Vile inns. no meat. uncivil people. charge high as dearest tavern in London.

17–19 August, Monday Arrived at Wansbeck – at 9 in ye morning never lay upon ye road, or stopt more than for a change of Horses. The distance is 30 German miles or 120 English – perhaps 150 English– or even 165. We were 70 hours performing it yth 4 horses (at 2½ English miles an hour without stopping 175 miles. I take 175 or 180 English miles to be ye distance. This makes 6 Eng. miles to 1 Ger. of this country.) From London to Bristol with 2 horses the same distance we go in 16 hours. Therefore in England, we make the expedition of about 4½ miles whilst in Germany we shall have advanced one. The delays in change of horses is the greatest cause of this – & the sanding of ye roads rending expedition impossible. All I have seen of Germany sandy a good deal of wood still oak, birch & fir mostly Scotch fir.

1–5 September Nothing particular happened during all this time. Lived as before at Wansbeck. Fun & Play consumed most of our time. My employ, when busy, still writing letters – During this period, that Rascal Brown returned; & with him 2 fellows named Wms [Williams] & Langton. One of them called here the very day they arrived. Doubt since whether anything to do in my affair. They went away about Sept. 4th or 5th. [Here several phrases are quite obscured] Not so. We shd think of our good fortune as well as our bad. State our present uneasiness with what it might have been if so & so had turned out. That alone is enough to make one always happy.

6–14 September Still at Wansbeck in the old stile. Nothing material happened except that during . . . [more erasures here]

15–19 September Dr Ross sent for.

20 September In same stile.

21–23 September F. quite well again.

27–30 September Had the affair yth ye Boor. He took my horse by the Bridle because I had given his little girl a little stroke about opening a gate. He w^d not loose. I struck his hand. He struck my head twice with the butt end of his whip. I made 3 great holes in his head in return. Cou'd not knock him down. He drew my horse in at a door too small for me to enter – was squeezed off the Back – much bruised – Had giddiness in my head for 2 or so days after.

1–5 October Mrs Parish came on a visit with her little children. Mr Parish sometimes here.

12 October, Sunday Mrs Parish returned. Went with her to Hamburg – was at the Play. N.B. Mrs P. had rec^d assurance from Wrotzer Silmes, & from the Praetor that we shd not be molested, & that the orders of arrest were withdrawn. N.B. At setting out our neighbour Meyer advised not to go as he said orders were given &c. But this I did not mind.

17 October, Saturday Returned to Wandsbeck.

18–24 October This week at Wansbeck. Mr Parish came here Sat^y & the next day Sunday.

25 October We returned with him to Hamburgh.

26 October At Hamburgh.

27 October Executed the Bargain & Sale to J.M. [John Morris] D^o [ditto] B. [Bargain] to J.P. [John Parish]

28 October At the Play 9 o'c. D^o 30.

31 October Sat. Returned.

1 November, Sunday Mr & Mrs Schaland (& Mrs Campbell) came here in ye afternoon, & we went with them to ye house where we lay &c. N.B. F. & I l.i.s.b.

2 November Returned to Wk [Wandsbeck]. Miss Hudson [Hodgson] came with Mrs Campbell.

3 November Miss Hudson came to stay here for company onto Mrs M. [Morris] & sign'd petition to Denmrk [Denmark] for mar^e [marriage]. Received parcel & magazines from Flexney.

4 November Rec^d 10 dollars (first rent) for one of ye houses bot [bought] here.

5 November   Sold about this time the little grey horse for 9 dollars – he cost 10.

6–7 November, Saturday   Mr & Mrs Parish & children & Mr & Mrs Schaland & little one came here to dinner & staid the night.

8 November   Mr & Mrs Schaland went home – & so did Mr Parish.

9 November, Monday   Mrs Parish &c went home.

10 November   Went to Hamburgh

12–21 November   Returned from Hamburgh. N.B. Fr. 13 Mr King. (I first saw at Hamburgh. He came with us to Wansbeck.)

22–24 November   Got up at 3 to go stag shooting but it rained & did not go & next day Mr King sprained his leg.

25–26 November   Pero lost

27–28 November   This is the dear F.'s Birthday – But she had kept me rather ignorant & made me more believe it was Nov. 30 – for which day I had invited company. Music struck up (by accident) at 12 at night of Nov. 27 – which I turn'd into a felicitation of the Dear little Girl.

30 November   We kept this day for F.'s Birthday.

> Company was
> Mr & Mrs J. Parish
> Mr & Mrs Schaland
> Mrs Campbell
> Miss do
> Mr King
> Captn Wolfe.

We had Mr Schnude ye dancing master, by way of setting us out in ye dances. And we danced several minuets, cotillons & country dances – both before & after supper. Broke up about 3. Past a very pleasant agreable day & Ev^g. Everything very well conducted – A very well set out table & Desert, by Miss H.'s assistance. F. as chearful as ye day was busy & danced a great deal with a great deal of spirit.

1 December, Tuesday   Mr King I c^d not persuade to stay longer, thinking himself obliged to set out without further delay for Hanover. He seemed to quit us with regret – & we found him very agreable. Mrs Parish & her little ones stay with us for some time.

2–3 December   Dined at Mrs Schaland's. Went to the English Ball. Great civilities from Mr Evatt. Everything very well conducted. Ladies handsome & well drest. Pretty girls. Miss Poole. Hess (from Berlin) Mathieson agreable – Bielefeld. Most spoke French & many English. Baron Curlzroh – Count & Countess Holstein (White Ribbon) Danish nobleman Baron Burtzrock called so though his father alive, with same title. Most of ye

Danish nobility of the King's Bed Chamber, or Household. Keys at Pide – Batton.

4 December Came back to Wansbeck. Had a sack of Potatoes cut off from behind the coach as we past through the town. Heard that some of our linen were given to a Callico-Printer here by a maid (Mary) whom we turn'd away, for suspicion of stealing; & that she pretended we had given it her – particularly a great number of white Cambrick Handkerchiefs &c.

5 December Frederic shooting in ye garden, 2 shot took a direction though 15 or 20 yards off by striking upon a stone to rise about 4 foot in ye air, & enter the Glass window of ye parlour. Ladies were in ye room no[t] hurt, but forbid shooting any more.
Mr Parish & Mr & Mrs Schaland came here.

6 December Mr P. & Mr & Mrs S. went home.

8 December No mail.

9 December Set about making my will. 2 men found in ye garden about 11 at night. Run away at ye sight of ye boy Nicholas.

10 December Finished & executed a fair copy of my will; witnesses were Miss Elizabeth Hodgson, Franchois [sic] Raisin & John Frederick Siltze. N.B. I first made 2 fair corrected copies. N.B. Forgot. Thursday Nov. 26. Paid. The experiment upon a horse. Gave a Holland Ducat. Le Sieur Tunecliffe drove a nail 8 inches deep middle between ye eyes into a horse's head. He used a balsam. But I think the horse w^d have cured without. Horse seemed not hurt.

6 December Pero brought me back —— was kept up at a house in the Foresetten. Gave Holland Ducat reward. Whole cost 11 marks.

*11–12 December** Walked to Hamburgh. Mr P. came back with me. yth difficulty got out of ye gates.

13 December Mr P. went home.

14 December Went to Altona to see a house wch Miss Vaughan lived in last summer. Won't do – Better be in town, than there.

15 December 2 mails arrived. None now due.

16 December Mrs P. went home. Had been here 11 days. Promised a month – owes 17 days more.

17 December This night an attempt to break into the house. Open'd the kitchen latch wch Frederic heard. He lay in ye wood loft in ye kitchen. Called out to them saying – who is there – in German – They run away. As for Pero, he is lock'd out every night. But he is quite a Coward – He bark'd much at them, as I heard from Fanchon – and they came up, &

* Wilkes wrote to Robert and a letter was sent to Lord Mayor Townsend.

beat him well & then he was quiet. Fanchon heard them walk upon ye sand or Gravel walk in the Garden. None came to call me. Nicholas & Frederic lay together. They got up, but the Coast was then clear. I am told, that by Law no right to kill Thieves breaking into your house. May shoot them only in ye Legs with Bird-shot. This quite ridiculous! Yet it seems ye Law. Perhaps you w^d not be hanged, but you must pay a fine.

18 December, Friday I was mistaken as to the night the house was attempted to be broke open. It was on Wensday night. Decr 6 – Same night the 3 Crown's Inn was broke open. The man who did it, was taken ye next day by the Revenue officer going in with the things into Hamburgh. His punishment is only to work in the Spin-house for 2 years – though he actually broke a hole into the house & robbed the people of all the Kitchen furniture.

19 December Rec. [received] ye Commission* from Cop$^{h.n.}$ [Copenhagen]

20–24 December Walked with F. to Hamburgh. just got in before the gates shut – which is now at 4 (this is ye soonest shutting) – longest in Summer is 9½ – ¼ of an hour diff^e [difference] from time to time as ye days lengthen – is a Frolic of F.'s – know nothing of it, till after walk begun.

25 December Came back from Hamburgh. Had to dine with me Mr Parish Mr & Mrs Geo. Parish & ye little boy George – 8 – Mr & Mrs Schaland & ye 2 boys Frank & Bill – 10 – Mr Domberg & son (Mr Parish's apprentice) – 11 – Mr Thomsen (Mr Parish's Clerk.) 12 – Captn Woolffe.†

26 December Company went home, except Mr & Mrs Schaland ye 2 boys – Mr Thomsen, & Mr Domberg jun^r.

27 December Mr & Mrs Schal: and y^r [their] boy Jimmy went home.

28 December Mr Thompson [sic] & Mr D. jun^r went home. So did Frank Schaland in ye evening.

29–31 December Went forth to Mr Schaland's – lay there.

So ends 1772.

* The King of Denmark's licence to marry in a house at any time.
† The group he invited to witness his second marriage ceremony.

1 January, Friday   At Mr Schaland's, St George's [Hamburgh Suburbs.] In the Evening went to Mr Parish's yth F. & Miss Elizabeth (Thomas) Hodgson, who lives with Mrs M. [Morris] as companion & house-keeper, N.B. She came Novr 72

2 January   Returned home after dinner.

3 January, Sunday   Went in 2 Coaches & four to Ahrensburgh. $2\frac{1}{2}$ hours going – about 10 or 12 English miles called 3 German ones. Got there by $\frac{1}{2}$ after 12. Company in 1st Coach. Self F.M. [Frances Mary] Mr Parish Miss Hodgson.

2nd. Fanchon. Captn Wolffe. Mr Geo. Parish. Mr Thompson Mr Domberg junior – servants – Frederick (on horseback) Nicholas – John, Captn Wolffe's man. Christopher ye Noter's son at Hamburgh. Here we were married* again by special licence, from the King of Denmark – Gave the Parson a fee of 5 Ducats. Dined 11 at Table. The Baron's Secretary of that place dined with us. An extremely good dinner, German drest – at $3\frac{1}{2}$ marks per head for 12 (42 M.) Wine 20 M. Got home again by about 6. All safe & well & God prosper us upon it.

4 January   Fanny a cold & hoarseness. At night Headach. Found it also so myself, a little.

5 January   Both well but F. still a cold.

8 Friday   F. had a very bad night violent reaching & pain in her bowels.

9 January   Found F. a good deal better about 11 – when I first heard of her having been ill. However thought best to send for Dr Ross – but not being at his house, till too late for ye Gates to return, did not come. F. lay abed all day – good spirits & well – but no appetite till towards night. Her illness was certainly occasioned by making sops in the pan in ye kitchen yesterday, & mixing up nasty stuff called Pap – eating this, then no

* At an inn.

appetite for dinner – then eating some wild duck at Supper. N.B. Purged a good deal after reaching. She lay abed all this day; & eat no meat.

10 January, Sunday F. to my great comfort & Happiness quite well. Dr Ross came about 12 – left a composing draught – containing 3 drops (I think) of Laudanum – to be taken upon another such attack, after the vomiting well over – & a cup or two of tea, taken down.

N.B. F. wanted much to drink some Lemonade after her vomiting yesterday – & also cold water – wou'd not drink anything warm. Dr Ross said neither wou'd have hurt her – if Bile in the reaching, the Lemonade or acid good for her also water – if chill a little taken off – it w^d have been very well for her – but small draughts at a time.

N.B. The Necklace that was lost at Mr Parish's was stolen by his Cook maid. Came out thus.

The other maid's mother (i.e. Katherine's) was speaking of ye necklace stolen in Mr Parish's house, before a Jew woman who mentioned that necklace was sold to one Keil a Jew for 16 Dollars by the Cook's sister. She being questioned said as usual she found it in the Street. The Cook finding what was going forward run up to her box, & threw out a pound of tea, desiring the other maid to hide it. As Mr G.P. [George Parish] deals in tea – & she had stolen this – being askt, she said, she had bot [bought] the tea & knew nothing of her sister & the Necklace – Turned off Necklace & Heels but not thought enough to convict either. Necklace not yet recovered.

11 January F. continued to be without appetite; in other respects well.

12–13 January F. now quite well.

14 January Trunk & ale arrived from Swansea.

15–19 January, Sunday Mrs M. gave Fanchon her dismission. Fanchon behaved extremely well, 'till we were settled at Wansbeck: that is, she took her share in our travels & adventures yth chearfulness, & seemed very much attached to Mrs M. As soon as we settled at Wansbeck, some persons began to make love to her, & from that time she has never behaved well. Frederick pretending to court her went something towards spoiling her. But then she is so idle, that she was resolved to make herself no use to us. Mrs M. grew very fond of her . . . seing that Fanchon w^d threaten to go away; knowing her own consequence, though treated all this time as a gentlewoman. Mrs M. tried all persuasions to keep her; she even cried before her. Fanchon was unmoved by Tears, or anything else. She never cried at the thought of parting. Frederick however at our instance persuaded her to stay. Mrs M. then in a fit of fondness, & generosity promised her £30 a year wages.

Frederick's influence over arose from ye amour between them. Fanchon was such a fool, as to believe Frederick w^d marry her. She said to Mrs M. that Frederick promised it. I believe the truth is that Frederick wanted to debauch her, & so might have promised anything. He told me at ye time he had no design to marry; for I thought right to ask him, & to inform her of his answer. He said the girl was such a fool as to think everybody is in Love with her. I fancy one design she had in threatening & I believe intending to go away was to put Frederick's promise of marriage to ye proof.

Frederick's intimacy yth Fanchon for a long while continued; & I verily believed he had lain yth her. About December, a visible coolness seemed to come between Fanchon & Frederick & they shunned each other, as much as the contrary before.

Frederick grew violently melancholy & discontented in his mind. At last he told me, he wanted to go away to his father; & did not like a Domestic Life but chose to be a travelling servant. I agreed he shd go, when his year was out.

Mrs M.'s fondness for Fanchon continued till about the beginning of November. Mrs M. about this time beginning to pay visits at Hamburgh, became less fond of Fanchon at her return. Soon after she had Miss Hodgson with her; & then in a little while more her fondness for Fanchon seemed quite expired.

Before Mrs M. had a young girl called Ellen Cornelison, & afterward, Gosling's young sister. But she did not in ye least take to them; & by that means became the less [?more] fond of Fanchon. Indeed her partiality to Fanchon was at one time carried to a very great height.

Fanchon was always intolerably idle; running away from any work Mrs M. put her to & after her intrigues yth Frederick she shunned Mrs M.'s company whenever she cou'd – seemed to take everything a task, where Mrs M. was to participate. Wou'd run away & hide herself, rather than play at cards yth her. She was an eternal gadder out; & w^d for whole evenings together be running to Mrs Meyer's or another place, rather than be of any use or entertainment to Mrs M. at home. Neither did Fanchon continue during all this time so good tempered as she seemed to be at first.

I am certain, she had not the least affection for Mrs M. She parted from her with^t [without] a tear or regret, & therein indeed Mrs M. was at least even with her. I think the Ladies in general find it more easy to give cause to a servant, than we do. I cou'd not say, 'Get ye gone' to a Post that I was used to, without compunction. It is certain Mrs M. had provocation enough to part with her.

During this time Fanchon was with us, in two matters she behaved very ill.

1. Introducing a blackguard Frenchman, called Vittal, to the Civilities of ye house as her cousin; which she solemnly affirmed to me, though it was an abominable lie, as she afterwards confest, when it was proved against her.

2. When Mrs M. went to ye first play at Hamburgh yth Mrs Parish Fanchon with another whore of a maid, called Mary, run immediately to Town, & went also to ye Play, where she was seen by accident by Mrs Parish. I take it Frederick was concerned in this matter, & they all together spent a jolly evening at Gosling's; our quondam writing master's house. Where they lay too; but who together in a bed, must be left for guess.

Frederick at the time of informing of his wishes to go to his father, told me, that it had given him concern, to think he had displeased his mistress about Fanchon; That he had never lain yth ye girl; & had only said to her what he did, in order to persuade her to stay yth Mrs M.

Fanchon constantly continuing to lie yth Mrs M. 'till Miss H. [Hodgson] came, was a principal cause of keeping her importance & riveting Mrs M.'s attachment. When Mrs [Miss] H. did come Mrs M. still continued a little while Bedfellow yth Fanchon, soon after she had both for her bed-fellows an affair which I took great pains to break through. This ended in having Miss H. only for ye Bedfellow; & Mrs M.'s fondness for Fanchon, almost directly began visibly to abate. She never never grew so fond of Miss H. But her finding Miss H. so much more sensible & useful a companion, was one principal cause of it – of her eyes being first opened towards Fanchon.

Fanchon used to recommend herself by bearing to have anything done to her Mrs M. pleased – by being always ready to go to bed, night or day; to sleep or get up when Mrs M. chose – to do any foolish thing, Mrs M. pleased, of any sort, without remonstrating, & whether to [go] & pick Currants, run in the dirt, or hide themselves from ye Writing & Dancing Masters &c.

Besides that, one talent of pleasing lay in teaching Mrs M. some foolish little French songs, & telling her some foolish stories.

All the use she has been of, was at first to keep up Mrs M.'s chearfulness, & to teach her by ye necessity of conversation to speak French. In both which she served very well: And therefore I don't, if it was only upon ye latter account, begrudge her the cost she has put us to.

At Lille I gave Fanchon a watch wch I paid 10 Guineas for.

Mrs M. gave her innumerable new Clothes & Linnen. In short she has never been put to buy anything for herself, since she has been with us. Besides this, she has had a great deal of money as well as other presents from time to time from Mrs M. & me.

At parting Mrs M. paid her £20 – which is at ye rate of £30, for a year, she having been now with us 8 months. I think this money enough for her, without farther presents for any journey to Calais, or on any other account. She seemed to insist upon Mrs M.'s unwary promise of £30 a year wages; when she ought to have had only 10 or 12 at most. This was an¹ [another] cause of Mrs M.'s farther inclination to part yth her at this time. She very prudently saw it was saving £10 between this & May next.

22 January Fanchon went off this morning. She never asked for me to take farewell, & was quite merry & brisk when she parted with her indulgent Lady; who no later than the day before had given her one silver tablespoon and one silver Tea spoon. Then indeed she made some sort of pretence to squeeze out a tear; but it was soon wiped away. I am satisfied the girl has not the least principles of regard for either of us. She seems in no hurry to return to Calais. If she chose it she has surely money enough in her £20 for wages & journey both – But if she wanted even more money for ye journey I shou'd not [have] scrupled adding it, that that might not be made a pretence for staying here. I think it is but just to send every servant back free of expence to their own country from whence they were taken. But if this Girl will not go, I can't help it. I believe it is convenient for her to go in consequence of her amours. She seemed to be rather rotund about the waste [sic]. . . Some time back she was very ill; & from what I have since learnt, I think she had a miscarriage at that time. She had an extra ordinary flow of —— Mrs Parish learnt Mrs M. from relation of it to construe it as a miscarriage. Qu? [Query.]

2 February, Tuesday Went to Hamburg

3–4 February Went to ye Play.

5–6 Saturday*

7 February, Sunday Went to ye English Chapel

8 February At Mr Wrotzer (i.e. Senator) Pope's about ye stolen Necklace – Well furnish'd house. One Room hung with 200 Scripture, glazed & framed Prints – most of them out of sight – a Frequent & great Absurdity. House put all in mourning as far as a Brush or Broomstick for ye Loss of the Lady of ye house – as is usual for Master & Mistress at a vast expence. In the examination the Praetor seemed to have no rule of evidence & admitted Hearsay & set down particulars intirely inconclusive, as well as irrelevant to ye present matter. What persuades the Judge's own mind is

* Ahrensburgh marriage registered.

suff: [sufficient] evidence – However He acted only for examination & present Commitment, not for punishment. Cost £30 to prosecute a Felon & his punishment at last only a whipping & a few month's imprisonment. Town will pay these charges if a Burgher is Prosecutor & gives it up to them, provided the Praetor thinks there is reasonable ground. This was the present inquiry. Supt at Captⁿ Wolfe's. His father an old Boatswain-voiced fellow of 80 – hates to be told he is old. Went to Wk [Wandsbeck] in a sledge & back – a fall in ye town.

10 February   At ye play

11 February   Again at ye Praetor's, one goes out of office each year – so each is Praetor 2 years. Present at a small manufactory of Chocolate. One man can grind down 8 lb in a Day. Nuts are small, like Cashou nuts. Black kernel with taste of Chocolate – Burnt like Coffee in a Roaster turning about. These nuts bot from 12 to 28d per lb. Common People make a Beverage, like Coffee from the burnt husks, which are rubbed off – give 4d per lb for it perhaps our English Drink call [called] Cocoa. Chocolate sold from 8 to 6 mark per lb of ye manufacture at Hamburgh. First Spanish Chocolate sold there at 9 marks pr lb.

Frederick paid off everything & discharged. Was I believe honest – but is not an useful servt [servant] – Neither is he a chearful one & he was always troublesome at acct [account] ye maid. He was extravagant & wasteful – proud & forgetful. I question his regard for me.

12 February   Masquerade at ye Playhouse – very pretty – must break up precisely at the Blowing of a Trumpet at 4 Because there are Church Prayers at 6 & the pius people were offended at meeting the Masqueraders return home in their Dresses. The Dresses were very well – But no other fun than Dancing – people are such fools as to give willingly 12 D. [?dollars] as much to sit down in ye Boxes & look on, as to be in ye Ball. Might have cold Chicken &c – But the Germans all provide themselves yth supper at home – Tea gratis – Coffee Punch &c as paid for.

15 February   Return'd to Wansbeck – Mrs M. turned away Margaret, who behaved ill – About Frederick & the Cook – & was impertinent to Mrs M. when she spoke to her.

16 February   Found 2 large pieces of Beef (16½lb) salted & concealed by one of ye servts in Frederick's Room – Have reason to believe Frederick gave away victuals of ye house to some of his shooting Comrades – & introduced & countenanced rascals such as Vittal, & Louis (Berlin) to come in for regale &c against my express order – No reason to be sorry he is gone. Maid (Margt.) hired for 6 months, served only 3 – Besides wages for ye whole 6 – Notwithstanding her misbehaviour, she requires

Boarding & Lodging found her till time out. Also stole a considerable part of a Tub of ye Ale.

18 February, Thursday   This day Frederick taking his leave of us, parted yth regret & tears. He expressed much gratitude for my kindnesses towards him. Said, whenever I cou'd command him to anything he w^d obey it & that if I travelled he w^d attend upon me for nothing. I told him, to take care how he took notice of such persons as Fanchon & Margaret. He said, he was satisfied his character was hurt by it. I told him I hoped his character was too good to be hurt by that. Our 7 Pidgeons flew away.

19-22 February   Employ'd these days in packing up our things, & preparing to leave Wansbeck.

23 February, Tuesday   Left for ever that cursed vile village of Wansbeck. Came the same night to Mr Toderhosts' in the Wantrahm, where we had taken lodgings at 30 Dollars per month from yesterday ye 22nd. Very good, & well furnish'd – Civil, & genteel people.

28 February, Sunday*   This day our Term expired at Wansbeck. N.B. The Professor Noelting of whom we hired the house, went today to Wansbeck with a pack of notaries, Carpenters, Upholsterers &c to the number of 8 or 9 & behaved very meanly in his pretended appraising of damages to his furniture – appraising as low [?high] as 6 D. [Dollars] damages to the stairs – 2 D. to a door – in short about 50 of these articles – charted 7 marks for wooden spoons lost in his kitchen – which might have been in number – half a dozen & wch one might buy for 7 marks —— 140 spoons. Charged 42 for 2 quilts which Mrs Toderhost saw & said she cou'd buy new for 20 & so on with other articles. Mr Vaughan, Miss V. & Mrs Ross drank Tea yth us.

1 March, Monday   Mr Parish & family supt yth us.

5-6 March   Supt at Mrs Parish's.

7 March, Sunday   Was at Church. Note – Bot a fine set of Dresden China last week – 140 Dollars, at 3 $ each. An airing to Staffen Hoffe Altona – pretty steep hillside woods – by ye Elbe. Miss Poole there – pretty – F. observed her pale & paints at Balls. Young Schaland I kept from Church to Dinner.

8-9 March   Supt at Mrs Parish's yth Mr & Miss Sadleir (Linnen Draper) Mr Rieswater Capt Painter of Falmouth.

11 March   Mr Hodge of Manchester. Mr P. Capt Wolffe dined yth us. Supt at Dr Ross – met Mr P. &c.

14 March, Sunday   At Church.

15-20 March   Nothing happened worth putting down.

* Robert received a letter from Henry Harford.

28 March   Dr Ross &c Mr P. &c supt yth us. Captn Mingie sung very well – fat –

30 March   Supt at Mr Parish's.

31 March   Met with at the Boomhouse an East Indian. His acco^t [account] of himself was – that at 11 years of age he was stolen from his parents – & sold by Count Lalli to a Portuguese merchant – that he was afterwards presented to Mme Pompadour – who put him in the military Academy at Paris, where he was 7 years & had perfectly learnt, every part of ye art of war. The military exercises for horse & foot – fortification gunnery – the making of gun powder &c. Having a genius for painting he had adopted the profession of a Painter of Portraits in oil Colors. That he had been 14 years in France & had also been in the year 1768 in England, particularly that he was at Vauxhall, that he knew Lord Berkeley & Lord Spencer Hamilton – spoke highly of the English nation – as to the manners of ye noblesse – but for the lower sort – they were un indigne peuple &c – that his sister was the wife of the Nabah [Nabob] of Goleondra – that he was going there by the Russian Caravan, was in a few days to go to Lubeck, thence by sea to Petersburgh then to Astracan – there joining ye caravan & in 5 months hoped to be in his own Country – that his brother-in-law c^d arm 200,000 Cavalry that he shd teach ye people ye art of War &c – talked of always inspiring them with amity towards ye English & that he prefer'd that Nation to the French. I invited him to dine with me in company with a German Baron. But he said he was going over to Harburgh for a few days – He was very polite & very intelligent – spoke extremely good French & knew something of everything we discoursed upon – He said his name was Porus – or Porah as it w^d be called in his own country – I mentioned Porus – ye celebrated antagonist of Alexander ye Great. He said the same name and he was from the same country – & knew ye history very well. He had forgot to speak his own language; but c^d still understand something of it – when others spoke. He cut no great figure in his appearance; but was drest in good clothing enough (A great coat & Coutteau de Chass) had no servant – but did not want for money to perform ye journey he was going upon – & had letters of Exchange wherever he went.

The Baron dined with me. He is said to be an odd character – I found him tolerably intelligent. He is said to have lived a year or two wth a girl he kept in a Ship of his own – His family there; & no other abode. (Fishing for ye livlihood of ye family) Has a small estate down the river near Cookshaven; some expectations upon ye death of others his relations. Shd then go, he said, & live in England for some time. Play'd very well on ye harpsichord. N.B. He saw Count Lalli's execution. It was at the place de Grieve at Paris – at 5 in the afternoon in May – not at night by Torch light, as I had heard. It was true, he was gagged – He met this fate, with firmness & a cool indifference.

1 April, Thursday　Mr & Mrs P. supt here.

5 April　Mr King came from Zell.

11 April, Easter Sunday　Was at the Rabe.

12 April　Dined at Mrs Calvert's – on Capt Mingies' Beef Steaks.

14 April　Went yth King to Harburg. 4 hours going. Wind & tide contrary. Lay at Harburg this night – the first night absent from Mrs M.'s home. King learnt more German in 4 months than I in 10. In the 1st place I believe he may have a better memory for languages, & more facility in speaking them than I; in the 2d it must be considered that he had also more advantages in not being yth any English companion. Supper & Breakfast & bed cost 2 a piece.

15 April　Return'd back in 1½ hour. Mrs M. lay at Mrs Schaland's.

16 April　Went down River with Captn Mingie.

17 April　Lay on board Captn Mingie's Brig. More beefsteaks underway there.

18 April　Went ashore at Cookshaven. Lay on board a good Natured Dutch Hoyman.

19 April　Went aboard a Collier – Big – Captn Hayman – Lay there.

20 April　Came back – as far as from Stade in a Fisherman – The whole 5 days & 4 nights cost me 10 shillings – & Mr King as much who accompanied me. Pompey lost.

22 April　Mrs M. went in ye evening without giving me any notice to lie at Mrs Schaland's, from wch I was lockt out by the gates. I suppose it was out of a piece of fun – or to serve me tit for tat, as we might think for leaving her, but I was very much chagrined about it, & c^d not help writing her a letter to be sent to her in ye morning, & going low spirited and supperless to bed.

23 April　The Letter not sent to F. She came home about 1. I was quite overjoyed to see her. She went out of a piece of Fun & by way of Reprisals for my leaving her yth Mrs R. [Ross]

24 April　F. Miss H. K. [King] & I set out for Lucksleid. Went first in a boat to Schlafenhoffe – then another to Blankenesse. But first we saw Mr Bouy's Gardens at Schlafe Hoffe. Lay at Blankeness.

25 April　Went in ye Ferry boat over to Buckstahoo – Along ye Krance in a stool waggon (3 German miles) to Stade. Lay there.

26 April　Stade a very pretty town. Strong. Yet commanded in one side by a Hauteur – went back as far as Altona in ye Post Boat, Hamb[r] gates lockt. Lay at a good house at A.

27 April Came home. An expedition not very pleasant – saw little & it cost in 3 days & 3 nights 4 Gns.

2 May, Sunday Was at Church.

11 May Set out with Mr King for Zell. The same night about 10 went in ye Post Coach from Harbourg.

12 May Arrived at Zell about 7 o'clock in ye evening. Good Post Coach built on English principles at Hanover; holds six: much such another as ye Exeter coach. Goes 12 Dutch miles i.e. about 60 or 70 English in 19 hours. Saw ye Queen of Denmark. Every night sups in public. A handsome Schloss, or Palace. Schloss properly a fastening. Moated round. Princess of Brunswick there.

13 May Went to Hannover. Palace indiff[t] [indifferent]. D[o] that at Herrenhausen. Gardens there large & fine for ye old taste. As handsome very near as Versailles.

14 May Saw Gen. Spurcken's Regiment reviewed. Set out same evening a horseback, for Brunswick &c. Hired a heurs, un bischen aus die doer spatzieren gehen. Mr King saw me a little way out of the town: c[d] not attend me, & I was resolved not to desert my resolution of seeing the country, so I went alone. Lay at a little village called Peina, in ye country of ye (Catholic) Bishopric of Hildesheim.

15 May Went to Brunswick – dined there – with Captn Langdale by King's recommendation. A Catholic in the Duke of Brunswick's army. The Duke told him first that he was as good to be shot at as another man. Same night to a little village called Hessen.

16 May Came to Ilsenburg. Great civilities from the Graaf of Stolberg, living there. An Iron work. Ascended the mountain, called Blocksberg. By [?far] the highest in this part of Germany. 3 hours up. 6 hours down, another way hills over hills. Lay at Yagher's (or Huntsman's). Guide (or Boden) with me. Quite knock'd up. Likely to have lain in ye woods. Never underwent such fatigue before. Boots worn out. Feet sore. Saw the Print of wild Boars in ye Snow – also Dung of wild Stags.

17 May Set out on foot – afterwards in a waggon to Zellerfeldt, whither I had before sent my horse. A Saw mill. Saws across a piece of thick fir (Than) Tree in 5 minutes – 2 lengths of such a tree in 10 minutes. They said 2 men w[d] be 2 hours sawing one. Saw the mine works at Zellerfeldt & Clausthall. Hundreds of boys crying Herr Vetter (N'oncle i.e. Netter) – gave them nothing, though I was told at Brunswick that I must change 2 guineas into small money to get quietly through them. Returned to Coslar, an ancient free city – situated at the foot of an amphitheatre of hills, a fine meadow before it, in the midst of which is a Cloister. Saw some Sulphur works. N.B. It is extracted out of some Lead ore by burning it in stifled heaps, piled up with wood mixt – & about 9 holes or Chimneys left in ye midst for ye Sulphur to run down – whch is afterwards boil'd in small coppers, & purified. Lay at a little village 2 hours off, where I got about 10.

18 May   Came to Zell. 12 Dutch miles – wch I believe to be 72 English (or even 84) Arrived at 9 – out at 5 – 12 hours a horseback. Greatly tired – 4 hours in ye heat of ye Day & no Wirtzhouse to hide my head in, going over a common. N.B. Made this Journey of 5 days, all alone – except with the guide over ye Mountains – Cost only 2 £ – People civil, & not imposing. Mr King & I very glad to meet. A Dog follow'd me today & yesterday w^d not come over a piece of water, & lost near Zell.

19 May   At Zell – saw Prince Ernest's new Garden – English made – very pretty – Little of English at Brunswick Carolin College – Captns Speke, Dalton, Biron Pierson – all military – & some more. A very idle, dissolute place, tending to no improvement. N.B. Captn S. Speke is a son of ye Brave naval Captain commemorated yth another son in Ives's voyage. He does not show or did not to me, anything worthy of such a father or such a Bro^r. [Brother]. Set out in ye evening for Hamburgh in ye Post coach. Accompanied there by an English Gentleman, who had travelled all over Europe. I take him to be a person who hires himself out to accompany others.

20 May   Came to Harburg, about 7 in ye evening – But no crossing over.

21 May   Arriv'd about 8 in ye morning at Hamburgh. Found ye little F. well & happy. This day spent in receiving our friends, to a little entertainment we made at home upon occasion of this Anniversary of our happy union.*

24 May   Supt at Dr Ross. Mr & Mrs Stevens there. Mr S. seems very fond of his wife who is about 24; he about 50. He said to me, 'All my wife's family die of consumptions: I dare say she has not above 2 years to live'. Mr & Miss Vaughan also there.

25 May   Supt at Mr Parish's.

30 May   Din'd 7 o'c at Mr P.'s Went to Schaffen Hoff.

31 May   Weather for 4 days very hot, turn'd cold & used fires.

5 June   Dined alone at Mr P.'s

6 June   Still using fires. Poor Poodledy killed dead by a coach going over his body, just before ye door of ye house. That little dog I was very fond

* Of the marriage at Ypres.

of – I brought him from Berlin in August 1772. Cost 1 Ducat – spent a dollar in advertising him once when lost. He was often my bedfellow. No dog had more names. Juliet his first – then Caccad – Caccâc – then Powdledy-Poppie. I loved him. Yet I had rather he was dead, than lost; and when dead I c^d not much grieve after him. This is nothing particular, yet I believe it may [be] accounted for on good principles – or good for such as a man need have towards a dog. I only said, when I found him dead 'that to grieve after a dead dog were to be too much a dog oneself'.

9 June Mrs M. executed her will. Dr Ross & Mr Toderhost, witnesses. Mr P. Mr Vaughan & ye 2 above supt & play'd cards here.

10 June Wait'd upon Mr Matthias, & deliver'd in ano^r memorial of complaint.

11 June Republish'd & added a codicil to my Will.

13 June At Mr Schaland to Tea yth Mr Parish. In ye morning at Church.

14 June Packing up & settling affairs.

15 June, Tuesday We left Hamburgh having been there a year & 9 days. We did not leave Hamburgh till 7: & did not reach Harburgh till 11 in a small boat, 2 oars. Row'd myself very hard to gain time. Kept unawares so long in ye Evening at Hamburgh, not knowing how late it was. The Post Coach staid, for us. Its usual time 10. W^d have staid till 12. Had ye whole coach. Mrs M. slept well all the night, on one of ye sides to herself. One jolt threw her at full length down upon our feet in her sleep – not hurt. Quite pleased with ye Coach. At 9 arrived at Zell on Wensday May* 16.

Zell.

17 June Went to our lodgings at Mr Ribenstein – 5 minutes walk out of Zell. The situation like Turnham Green – Excellent house, well furnish'd – large Garden. Mrs M. quite delighted. 22 Dollar per month of which 8 D. reckon'd for ye Garden stuff & fruit – that is altogether 3S per Day – £1-1-0 per week without ye Garden stuff – 2/- per Day – 14/- per Week. To have it either way at our option. For ye present took it at ye first. Ribenstein a curious old fellow – once in higher life – A Commissary in ye War, & rich. Now half a madman & poor. His wife clever but canting – 2 Daughters, useful good girls. From Friday June 18 to Tuesday 29. When we had been a fortnight at Zell things gone on very well. All our goods safe from Hamburgh. Whole journey, goods & all, may be set down at 10 or 12 guineas. The Queen of Denmark desirous to see Mrs M. sending enquiries after her. King we found at Zell – always with us – & always fond of his Company. A sensible worthy prudent & chearful man.

* Robert's error. The month was June.

Mrs M. grown fatter – & looking much better. Always running about & in high spirits.

30 June Mrs M. gets a Music Master (Beckman) & ordinary Master (Horn). N.B. to mark ye days they are to begin at & continue.

2 July Mrs M. went to Mme Ompteda who after all the messages, that had passed, told her, she c^d not be introduced to the Queen without recommendations. This appears very extraordinary as well as very ill usage. The Queen had made many enquiries after Mrs M. Mme von Wolmeda had ask'd through Mr Ribenstein whether she did not intend to be presented. I had informed Mme Ompteda through Mr Ribenstein that the visit to her was in order to be presented. She had appointed the time for this visit, saying, that it was to present her: And after all, when Mrs M. comes there, she brings out her inquiries whether she was a daughter of Lord B. wch Mrs M. saying she was, as she c^d not say otherwise, she then replies, you cannot be presented without recommendations or a ticket of rank from some of ye English nobility. Now Mrs M. had never claimed to be presented yth ye rank of Lord B.'s daughter. Perhaps it w^d never have been mentioned on ye part of Mme Ompteda had not Miss Hodgson foolishly answer'd to ye inquiries of the Queen's footman, who we were, that Mrs M. was ye daughter of Ld B. But Mme Ompteda had no right to take notice of such subordinate inquiries: she shd have taken Mrs. M. as merely a gentlewoman, 'till she had announced herself as something more. And it was very cruel & impertinent in her to suffer ye appointment to be made with her for ye presenting: at ye same time resolving to ask such questions about being the daughter of Ld B. wch she knew by ye answer wd prevent ye presenting from taking place. Perhaps from other reasons, relating to our particular story, the Queen chose to decline receiving us: & this was an afterthought for excuse.

3 July I desired Mr Ribenstein to call on Mme Ompteda to say that I thought it was very extraordinary she shd suffer the appointment to go so far before she proposed any difficulties & to inform her that Mrs M. did not ever desire to be introduced with rank, as Ld B.'s daughter, but only with the common rank of any other English Gentlewoman. I was in hopes she w^d have said to this that as such Mrs M. might be presented; that she might have ye satisfaction then of refusing. She only answer'd, 'It was very well.' Which was an answer as extraordinary as her behaviour.

4 July Mrs M. having taken notice of a little girl about 6 years old, part of a large Family poor proud & idle, who almost starved this little fine Child, resolved to take her to herself while she staid here; and today she came for the first time. She is a pretty child. Mrs M. part clothed her out of some of her old things. Her name is Carolina Wolffe. At Church. Revd Rocque preach'd French Reformè. Dined at Stolson's.

5 July Young Mr Rocque dined with me & so did Mr Cook. Mr R. now a common soldier, as all must be in ye Hannover Service till they are officers. He is never to a Commission first. They serve as Common Soldiers, about 6 months & as Bas Officers Corporal & Serjeant about 6 months more. N.B. I have gone into ye River to swim about 6 times & do it now pretty regularly. Mrs M. goes in to a Bathing tub every day. Mdme Ompteda sent for Ribenstein & said she was sorry she c^d not present Mrs M. till she had ascertained her rank; He answer'd Mrs M. does not desire to be introduc'd yth any other rank than that of a private Gentlewoman: & that was what I was commission'd to tell you on Saturday. She then said, 'She w^d take a little time to reflect upon it.' Ribenstein preparing his garden for a Vauxhall. The Queen, as he says, desirous of it & lending him money. Gave King silver-mounted gun wch cost me £7.

6 July Mrs M. dips Caroline every day. Ribenstein goes on yth his Vauxhall; to be ready by ye 20th.

7 July Wrote 19 letters to go by Mr King. Supt at Stoltze's. King set off in ye Post Coach for Hamburgh upon ye expedition of fetching my sister Jenny here from Swansea. Strong mark of his friendship. Advanced 10 guineas for this journey & —— besides wch he is to replace to himself for ye journey, when he gets to London.

8 July Spiltz* left yth us. Went into ye River yth Mr Welch the young English painter here. Saw ye Prince's House, all over. Fine Pictures; fine Dresden Porcellane: same curious turning of ye King of England in Ivory. N.B. A good Painter at Hannover called —— A good Picture of Prince Charles done by him at Prince Ernest's: The Prince paints very prettily himself. Met ye Queen walking with one Lady, & ye little girl she takes care of, something in ye stile of Caroline. She said, She w^d not prove a Stepmother to her. Alluding to her Husband's Stepmother in Denmark. 20 Servts of her own in Livery. Allow'd only £4000 a year – being an annuity from ye King, for £40,000 repaid of her fortune from Denmark: N.B. Spent last year £18,000.

9–10 July The English Mahler went off & left his Coffre behind – Nobody knows where to. Yet I believe he is an honest fellow: seems sensible: I dare say a good genius for painting – but too modest to push himself. His terms here indeed a little too high. I took a long walk, 2 hours, down ye side of ye river till I came to a bridge, & then back again, ye other side. Supt at Stoltze's. N.B. Caroline's Mother came to see her go

---

* Probably Spitz, the dog who died in Marseilles.

into ye bath (a large tub) – so frightened at the sight, or pretended so, that she took her child off with her directly, with nothing but her shift on. Afterwards she & all her family came here to scold. Poor, so as to be without victuals: yet proud, as the richest Noblesse. Mrs M. resolving not to be without a Child set out forthwith into all the little Boor-houses to find one: at last she did to her mind: the Mother of ye Child, crying out immediately, 'It was good luck, that was come to her' as soon as ye matter was proposed. This Child is called —— and is —— old. Her mother was an Amp's daughter i.e. a Justice's (having about 2 or £300 a year from his place) married (what they call beneath her) an honest young Boor. The Child is fair, with flaxen hair, Blue eyes – as ye other was Brown with Brown hair & Black eyes. N.B. This Elizabeth seems rather clumsy about ye shoulders: T'other very finely shaped.

11–12 July Went with Mr (Stallmeister) Elderhorst to Hannover in his little Wagen, in 6 hours, 1 pʳ good horses. At Smith's Schank. Went to ye play for a quarter of an hour – tired of it. Went out to walk round ye walls, & then to their little Vauxhall. Only lit on Sundays – then about 250 people there on a full night.

13 July Went on a hired horse, to Pyrmont – from 10 in ye m. to 9 at night. This road, English fashion. Milestones, turnpikes – found by this time, that 1 German measured mile is 5½ English. Ham-eln 5 G. miles off, is a very strong little fortress – too near the hills – which are very high. One very near is fortified. So ye whole Strength of ye place must depend upon that fortification upon ye hill. Here first askt, since I came into Germany for a pass. Was obliged to go to ye Commanding Officer – Askt usual questions, & he wisht me a good ride.

14 July Pyrmont very pretty. Many broad walks – double rows trees – sans Level – some easy ascent – some steep. Houses like in Herefordshire. But all white without. A good deal of Company there. Come usually about May, stay till end of July or as fine weather last: The Place is open from April to Michmasse &c. Music – Ladies dancing Allemandes in ye Walk – Supping publicly, as Vauxhall. No lights. Traiteur's houses to eat at, by the sides of the Walks – Shops on each side. 2 Public Rooms yth Biliard tables & a Pharo table. Play'd low at ye Latter. Blackguards – like Barbiers standing about, & putting down as low as 3 Grossens on a Card. Lay at a nasty house called Steinmeirs. For self & horse (tho' I had nothing in ye house but 1 glass of Brandy) to pay 2 Goldens S5.D2. Went off again at 9 quite satisfied – I shd think it to be compared to Tunbridge. About 5 wells there all close together. I think ye same qualities – as ye had ye same taste. One Boil'd up, as if over a Cauldron. Here the Fashion for a pack of Blackguards, men & women to sit, facing each other, on a double row of Benches, over ye water, wch keeps bubbling up under their feet. This water is however quite cold. It is taken in carts to ye houses; & some people Bathe in it, upon made warm either their whole Body, or any particular parts. They report great cures of Contractions. It is droll to see all the Blackguards, men women & Children – mixt yth ye Gentry – drinking ye waters – well or ill if commanded – some washing ye Eyes &c. The Prince, as he is called or Furst von Walbeck, lives in a moated Chateau just by – keeps a small guard – perhaps altogether, of 50 Soldiers. No great beauties. Drest a good deal English – Ladies yth morning sticks – Young Ladies catching hold, in ye German fashion, of old men's hands to kiss. Return'd through Hameln. Dined at a good ordinary yth ye officers. The Landlord, a civil fellow – called Klein-Smith.

In my return, at Springen – saw Captn Weiss there (an English Captain) whom I had before seen (May 19) at Zell – Spoke to him civilly – he seemed shy. Therefore afterwards past him several times, lookt at him, & spoke not a word, or moved my body – particularly when he went farther on in ye way, in ye Post-Coach, he had hired from Hannover. In this with his Dutch Leader, he went one day, as I did, to Pyrmont, & return'd the next. This is the most sensible thing I know of him. He was yth us when I saw (May 19) Pasteur Rocque's collection. He then said a very uncivil thing – for the Pasteur going to show him some philo-sophical Instruments & Experiments – He said he had seen so many of them he had no need to do so. This fellow travels about with the ridiculous character, which he publicly gives himself, of travelling to forget the loss of an amiable wife. N.B. Saw ye Amptman's Bustman's pleasant retreat near a fine Spring in ye wood near Springen. Had inscrib'd in a Grotto, Ille terrarum mihi praeter omnes Angulus ridet. Return'd to Hannover.

15 July Set out at 10 in Post waggon for Zell – Arrived there at 6. Fellow travellers an upper servant of Mdme Walmodin – Took upon himself all ye airs of a man of distinction – & a poor stinking devil of A Jew. Dined well on ye road at Engessen – Dinners there always pro-vided. A good roast Turkey. Found F. surpriz'd & overjoyed to see me. N.B. It was yth ye greatest difficulty she had let me go. N.B. This Eve^g Mr K. sail'd for England from Hamburg. Found Fan. had taken another little child about 3 year old / or under / call'd Maria Elisabetha —— daughter of a very poor woman. Mrs M. had had a Contract drawn up by a sort of Lawyer to bind ye bargain – sign'd on both sides – & in each possession – whereby Mrs M. is to keep ye Child for ever, & the mother parts yth her too.

16 July Mrs M. does not like Miss Edelmann at Stoltze's house – I shall therefore take very little more notice of her – She bears a good character – was very great yth King. I paid what ye English painter had left of Debt here – Hol^d [Holland] Ducats & 4 marks – & had his things immediately sent off to him at Hamburg, whither he had gone for want of money here – & he was too modest to ask me, or anyone else. Swam in ye Broad river. Stream quick, but pleasant still to swim there because so easy, & one can swim so far. Mrs M. goes every evening into ye wood to drink tea, crossing ye river.

18 July Dine in ye wood yth Ribenstein's family, when Mrs M. invited – & old Jacobson who lives in ye house: But Jac^n did not come. N.B. The chest of Lemons from Hamburg turn'd out. 435 good. Cost 16#. Car^e [carriage] 2#. Sold 210 for 12# to Stoltze.*

19 July B. [bathed] 1½ H [hours.] Not in ye wood.

20 July B. 1½ H. Sent Mr Pasteur Rocque a present of 6 Bottles Welsh Ale. He came aft^ds [afterwards] to see me in ye afternoon. Made a present in ye even^g to Mr Elderhorst of 12 B. [bottles] Ale. He askt Mrs M. to go to Hannover today to see ye fireworks, & w^d lend a coach. But N.B. must have hired horses. After some intreaty agreed – But afterwards finding Mrs M. rather indiff^t [indifferent] inclined her not to go, when I came to consider of ye Exp^e [expence]. I then presented her for her own use yth 20 dollars, wch I told her was her due, as being saved by not going. I had other reasons for not going; though I hated to check Mrs M. in any inclination to move about or to take pleasure in ye world. For I thought it w^d be better to see Hannover in our way from hence, when we shd not return: & that there we c^d see it yth my sister Jenny, & Mr King too. Besides when Mrs M. went to Hannover she w^d be for seeing ye Vauxhall, wch is only illuminated on Sunday nights; & that w^d take us up 6 days to stay for, & be a very great exp^ce, as well as inconvenience.

24 July Dined at Stoltzen's to meet Mr Higgins. A Brute, but not so bad as I expected by relation. N.B. He drank tea yth us.

25 July At Church. French Reformès – Pasteur Rocque, Professeur royal. Stipend from ye King, & another Pension he has, £200 per annum. Whole service lasts an hour. Begins yth Prayer, then Psalms. Then Sermon. Prayer & psalms again, to end. A sensible mode of worship. No mummery. Edifying & not fatiguing. Higgins & Komp dined yth us. Komp a worse Brute of ye two – But well match'd.

26 July In ye wood in ye even^g. I swam across ye river as I do sometimes.

---

* Morris therefore had 225 for 6#.

Pero goes as well into water. Today he saw a sheet of Paper swimming. He went into ye river a long way, & bro[t] it quite to land.

27 July The time seems to be near at hand for our leaving this place. Mrs M. displeased yth Mrs Ribenstein. They will want some of our accommodations, when ye Vauxhall begins & Mrs M. will part yth none. My plan is to set out in one of the large Bremen Boats – In 3 days at Bremen. Then by sea round to Hamburgh. There meet my sister; then off for France.

28 July The Queen came to see ye Vauxhall preparations. Mrs M. & Miss H. playing at See-Saw. Queen admired Pero. Translated a letter of Higgins to Marckholtz ye Ober-Stall-Meister & Land-Schaft directeur, conveyed by Cook [an enemy]. Dined at Stoltzen's. Drank some glasses of my ale, of wch I gave to Mr Elderhorst 12 Bottles, at his house.

29 July Had ye Bricklayer Fencing master for he is both. Give 6 grossens an hour. Tolerable master. Strong arm – quick. No Grace. Mr Ribenstein askt me to lend him 3 Louis d'ors, wch I thought proper to refuse; nor did I chuse to pay it him in advance of rent, because I thought he might afterwards being sure of his money, become encroaching in his behaviour.

30 July Went to see one of the Bremen Boats here. Good accommodations, though not used to passengers. Weather squally & rainy – as well as cold.

31 July Employ'd the day, as I have done many others in writing letters: as well as I did yesterday. Had a little fencing in ye Even[g]. The pretended Master & Bricklayer a poor hand. I can hit him often often [sic] in plain Carte & Turee [?tierce].

1 August, Sunday Work still going on in this Vauxhall, weather indifferent. At night came I guess about 120 people. Very little eat or drink. Showery sometimes. Lights went out. Queen came about 10. Walk'd 3 or 4 times round ye Garden as if she was walking for a wager. Droll to see our Caminer Ymfers stretching y[r] [their] limbs after her. Then took a little Dance. 5 couple in a little room, flagged yth Stones. All gone about 11. There won't be half ye people come here ye next time. I believe everyone in Zell came.

2–3 August Fine weather again. Wind turn'd to the N.E. from the contrary points.

4 August* Fine Day. Mrs M. another quarrel yth Mrs Ribenstein, about wanting ye carpet. The people here seem desirous we shd quit their house, as since their Vauxhall, they want so many of our conveniences. They talk of serving us notice to quit; & so we might as well prepare to

* Robert's 30th birthday.

move. Mrs M. had a foolish quarrel too sometime ago, about ye little girl she first had, called Caroline. She had a sister married to some sort of a Police-Commissaire: He sends to me today, a ragged devil to tell me my dog had bit somebody, must therefore be tied up, or w^d be killed. This By ye Bye, a mere lie – & so I told him: At same time putting my hands gently upon his shoulders, & pointing at ye door, telling him to go about his Business. The fellow grew into a Passion: I went away. It is a mere spite of that pitiful petty commissaire – because he thought it w^d vex me. I had thoughts of sending ye Dog off for England, & so I shall. In the afternoon came a written order from ye Amptman not to let ye Dog appear out without a muzzle, under penalty of being killed &c. Mr Elderhorst, Mr Cook, 2 officers drank Punch &c with me at night.

5 August Mr Cook went with me in ye morning to ye Enterfangen, or Duck-decoy, a horseback – lent me by Mr Elderhorst. Dined at Stoltzen's. In ye afternoon, went again in ye evening to ye Duckery in Mr E.'s little waggon, yth Mrs M. &c. Saw one Duck caught. About 100 Decoy Ducks to catch this one. They said they had 200 Decoy Ducks in all. It is no great mystery for all these Decoy Ducks returning from ye great Lake, at regular periods (or pretty nearly regular) into ye Gut or decoy (cover'd over at top & ending in a hoop net); They are fed at ye furthest end of ye gut. But when they come there, the first disturbance, or ye sight of a little dog, frightening ye Stranger Ducks, & they fly forward into ye net. They cannot fly Backwards because ye Disturbance comes from thence. The rest used to have food, stay for it; & are afterwards fed. Mr Cook supt yth us.

6 August The mystery about ye Excisemen asking how many Lemons we had, in number, explain'd. For they w^d not believe it was lemons we rec^d, but more wine. At last we assured them of it, & then found, no excise was to be paid for Lemons tho' before yth [they] s^d [said] there was. It seems no one must open any package rec^d till he has sent for the Exciseman, & he present. Diff^t [different] duties payable here, & 3 diff^t Collectors.

8 August A very fine day; pretended to be 400 persons at ye foolish Vauxhall. As soon as ever Church is over of ye afternoon then goes a Drum about yth a Sergeant, or Corporal, & after a tattoo, He cries out, 'Tonight will be a Vauxhall'. Few people eat or drink; No sitting down heartily to table: only a Butter-bread & a glass of punch & away. Some Dancing: Poor work on ye sand. Several Gentlemen eat a flying supper yth Mrs M. Called at ye Amptman about ye order he had sent that my Dog Pero shd not go about without being muzzled. No evidence before him of his doing mischief, as pretended: only that foolish Police

Commissaire told him so. I said it was only malice. He promised to inquire of him, what proof he had.

10 August Determined first to go off directly, for France, to meet my sister at Spa, without staying in this country for that purpose, or going to Hamburgh.

11 August Another Vauxhall – few people they said, 154.

12 August Saw here Mr Macdonall, a handsome tall well behaved young man . . . seem'd of noble family, about 20. Had travelled in Italy – saw there Musgrave, Seward & Graves. I had some little conversation with him, in ye Garden, & in my Apartments.

14 August Bid adieu to riding & dancing any more here. But rid this morning to a Protestant nunnery at Winchausen, 2 G. miles off yth Mrs. M. & Miss H. – set out at half 6 return'd by 10. Left my Boor's knife by forgetfulness at a Boor's house, which I had found a little before, in riding.

15 August The weather very hot, for this week & more. This morning my poor faithful great mastiff Pero set off by a waggon for Hamburg & today at night they brought me an acc^t [account] that he was dead 2 or 3 G. miles off, by the heat – But note, I had given him, a dose of nitre, the Sat. at noon – too much, I fear, yet he spued it all up directly & seem'd well after, & eat & drank heartily: I also had given him all. Farewell with the gentle Spirit, Poor Pero: & may I see thee again, in another Life.

16 August, Monday Zelle. Notwithstanding ye great rain of last night, as well as of Thunder, Lightening [sic] & Wind, the Weather continues monstrous hot, though a little cooler, than before; which was really too hot to breathe in. We dined Sunday in ye Cellar. I was very ill Sunday morning; partly by the weather, & partly by drinking nasty Frantz wine at Stoltzen's house though only 5 Bottle in 4 hours time between 4 of us. Continued ill all Sunday. Continue Packing up. The Storm yesterday knockt up ye Vauxhall; But tonight ano^r [another] in its place. I intended to have taken a German Boy from Stoltzenhause with us, but his mother being a poor old sick woman who lives partly upon his Bread I determine to leave him, or if I take him, to pay as much to ye mother, instead of ye Boy, for wages, as she gets from him, which is about £28 per annum to which the Boy is very willing to consent.

17 August, Tuesday Shan't take ye Boy. Drank tea at Mr Rocque. Rec^d great civilities of him & his family. Mrs M. had not ye civility to go – for wch I was very sorry, but c^d not help it. I believe, one reason weigh'd yth her not to make any visits at Zell, the affront she rec^d from Mdme

Ompteda. Mr King,* & Mr Schauroth stay'd the afternoon here, & play'd at cards. I still not quite well. Pain in my back. Sleep ill.

18 August   Weather now pleasant & pretty moderate in warmth.

19 August   Prepared for going. Bought a coach.

20 August   Packt off heavy & household Articles for Bremen & London. At 8 in ye Eve^g set out in ye Coach we bought & 4 Post Horses for Brunswicc. Self, Mrs M. Child & Maid Louisa.

21 August   Arrived at Brunswick in 14 hours only 6 miles, each 2 Leagues. Put up at Angot's Kellar – tolerable good house.

22 August, Sunday   Went about Brunswick; & to the Princess's new Summer Palace, yth Mrs M. &c. A trifling Vauxhall at Br. too.

23 August   The Fair. At ye Play.

25 August   At a masquerade, given by the Duke. Gives 4 in ye year, each costs £100 – or perhaps only £50. Very pretty. In the Opera House. Hire a good Domino for 1 Dollar – or about 3/6 English being ye 6th part of a guinea, as it goes there. Bad custom not to unmask. I did so however, spoke too; but did not mind that. Court gracious; affable; convers'd yth Mrs M. The Dutchess, sister of the K. of Prussia, very like her brother.

N.B. Was at ye fine Gallery of Pictures at Salts-Dahl Palace, about 1 mile from Brunswick. Also at ye noble Library at Wolfanbuttel. Inside an oval. Ratcliffe Library seems taken from it; & so they there said it was. A Collection of Bibles in all Languages. Saw 2 in Welsh. All write their names down, who visit it. Read Voltaire's, in his own hand thus – François de Voltaire, agé de 47 ans né à Paris. 21 Octr 1743.

26 August   Saw the Kunst Kammer, trifling as they all are in Germany. A Pack of Ivory & Amber trinkets: a mere Don Saltero.† Set out at 10 at night for Hannover.

27 August   Early in the morning, past through Hildisheim. Roman Catholic Bishop's State in ye midst of Protestants – Country fine. Town & people miserable. 30 stout fellows singing vile nonsense over & over again ye same in Latin, in a Church. Indignation, not to be refrained, whenever I enter into a Priest-govern'd Country. Arrived about noon at Hannover.

28 August   Cou'd not persuade Mrs M. to take ye trouble of going to see Herren-hausen, any more than I cou'd at Brunswick to go to see Salt's Dahl, which I visited alone a horseback. N.B. I also went a horseback with

---

* Edward King left for Swansea on 7 July.
† No. 18 Cheyne Walk: Don Saltero's Museum. Salter, a servant of Sir Hans Sloane, formed his collection from the overflow of his master's curiosities.

a young Captn Speke, to see ye Duke (or Prince) Ferdinand's Palace, one mile towards the direct road to Hannover through Peina. Full of Prints every room – Some elegant rooms; but small. Wilkes's Print. Many English Engravings. All sorts of stile. N.B. Saw also 2 of Wilkes Prints in a Book of Prints (of which there are many Books) in ye Kunst Kammer, Brunswick. There was written under one 'Flattering Likeness of a bad man' the other – 'a worse print but nearer resemblance'. Not exactly those words, but such a meaning only express'd in coarser language, & bad English. They said, it was written by ye person, who sent it over from London. Probably the minister from Brunnore Court. Mr Cook came from Zell. Brought me some letters. Resolved to set out that night; & so did.

29 August On the road. Came up with one Baron Klopman – who had been acquainted yth Ld. Baltimore at Mittau in Courland; and knew Mrs M. He came from Hamburg, was going through Frankfort to Studgart, the little Court of the Duke of Wirtumburg. Travell'd genteely in a good Chaise, 2 servts. Joined company. Supt at ye Crown Inn Gottingen.

30 August Mr Elderhorst's son & his Tutor – Mr Vaughan, Mr Boyé dined yth us. In the afternoon set out for Cassel (3 o'clock) arrived 3 in ye morning, at the Hoff d'Angleterre.

31 August 2 good rooms, but was obliged to pay a Ducat a night for Lodging – askt 1 Louis d'or – & afterwards 3 dollars. Never to recommend ye house.

2 September, Wednesday Saw the Khunst Kammer (or museum) trifling stuff. Saw the Model house – or Elevations in miniature of several buildings (Lustor) & pleasure houses of the Landgrave. This more trifling still. Picture Gallery & Palace – fine. Collection good. Cassel - fine town. Many new buildings, which called the French new Town. Fine Parade in the Orangery of the Park. Curious marble Bath – as fine as from the noblest Grecian or Roman model. Landgrave, a proud silly fool: He, like his Ancestors makes more expence than he can afford. Then the cry is, He is ruin'd – But the fact is, His subjects are ruined. This Landgrave married a Daughter of George 2nd. Took an Italian or French mistress, & turn'd Catholic. Since married a Protestant princess, of the house of Brandenburgh – But still continues Catholic. Has built a fine new church for the Catholics; to remain as an immortal standard of his folly, which he expects will be of his honor. Has country, & wants subjects. Gives good encouragement to new settlers at Cassel – Yet he is obliged to build houses, which remain without inhabitants. His subjects like all other Germans fond of Coffee. He makes a Law, None shall drink it, under the severest penalties.

Qu. [Query] the reason or policy of this? The less Coffee they amuse themselves with, the more Beer & Brandy. His subjects, like most of the other in Germany, ruined by the little Zahlen Lotteries; by which as small a sum as 3d or 4d is taken for an adventure. Was also at Wassenstein – an immense unnatural cascade – 2 English miles, or less, off Cassel. Building at top, Grand, curious & fine. The fellow who show'd it off, play'd some water in my face for which I gave him a kick of the Breech & a beastly dowse in the Chops.

2 September We had all the time with us here, at Cassel, Cap^n Sr James Murray (a sensible modest young man) & Lieut^t Speke (an impertinent fool) At night set out.

3 September On ye road towards Frankfort.

4 September Arrived at the Hotel de la Maison Rouge at Frankfort. Country on ye way Romantic. Hill & valley – wooded properly & cultivated. Only 20 German miles required, with stoppages 48 hours. The Inn here at Frankfurt – new & superb – as fine, & as good to live in as any in England.

5 September, Sunday Went about ye town. Concert. Madame Sirmen plays excellent violin.

6 September At the Fair wch begun this day. Every night to ye Play.

7 September As yesterday.

8 September Mr Boulanger, a young Captain in the Dutch Cavalry, with his travelling Companion, Mr . . . . . a Swiss Gentleman came here from Cassel. We had proposed going together down ye Rhine to Spa; but they brought me some letters,* wch had been sent to Cassel for me, that my sister & Mr King arriv'd at Hamburgh Aug. 29th. This alters our Course – and we now shall go to Geneva direct & so I have written them.

11 September From this every night expecting my sister Jenny & Mr King.

12 September, Sunday At a Concert. An old fellow Marchiani sung – Good voice & power. Yet to me disagreable. I hate ye mere execution both of ye voice & Instrument.

13–14 September As before: Tormented with this momentary expectation of my sister. Play'd a joke upon Mrs M. by sending her a billet at ye play, as from her, being come to ye inn upon wch she set out Post-haste – But I interpreted ye matter & brought her into ye Box again.

15–17 September Went in ye Mayence Market Boat as far as Hucks – 2 hours down ye river – $\frac{1}{2}$ way to Mayence. Then walkt knapsack on my back – i.e. a wooden Flashen-kellar slung to my shoulders by my handkerchief wch contain'd a Bottle wine, meat & bread. Went to a salt work.

* One from Jenny to Mrs M. included.

Saltwater spring (not very salt) pump it 2 stories high – then trickles down
through 4 thicket of small sticks – incrustates on these sticks – collected off;
& afterwards boil'd up – Went over a very high hill called Altkonig.
Dined at the very top of it – near 5 hours walking from Hucks – went
through great thickets, but clear ground underfoot. Good walks made to
lay snares for Cranz Vogel or blackbirds – A twig growing from the
Bush or tree, is twined round in a circle – in ye middle of this circle are
two ringole or knots of horse hair – like the sort of wire rings for Parrots
to swing in – underneath from the ring of twig hangs a bunch of Haws –
wch in ye Country grow very large – this Bunch they cannot well reach
either from the Twig, or ye hair nooses. Put a stone in one – a stick in
another – money in a third & fourth at ye nooses – told this Below to a
man – who said the people w^d begin digging where ye [they] saw the
money thinking more must be there – & that Witches &c put it there.
Great fatigue ascending ye mountain top resolved not to eat till I got there
– left the empty bottle & the Fleigchen-Keller behind – name in ye Bottle
– found it late & towards dark, when down ye hill – hired two horses –
for 2 Goldens – home – came home ½ after 9 – Did not go to Mayence as
I intended, when I set out, because I had not left Mrs M. in good spirits in
ye morning. At ye top of ye mountain they say stood once a Palace or
Castle of an old King. 'How long ago?' said I – 'It may be 200 or 2,000.'
'Aye', says she, 'thereabouts.' There seemed remains of a wall, & Ditch
round – or it might be remains of a volcano – The Top of ye mountain
seems to have been thrown up by a Volcano.

19 September, Sunday   Was at a Concert. All the other nights at Plays
where we pay a Golden a piece for ye Boxes & Parquet – i.e. of this
currency – to ye amount English of ye 11th part of a Guinea. £0.1.11.

20–22 September   Sr Jas Murray came here – Had seen my sister & Mr
King at Zell. Went there himself (out of his way 12 German miles) merely to
pay his respects to ye Queen, as some other Englishmen had been foolish
enough to do – e.g. Mr McDouall. N.B. Was in ye Garden house here, at a
foolish dance yth Mrs M. to give her a little pleasure. 3 other ladies there.
The men ill-behaved low creatures – half drunk so soon went away.
Miss H. had her cloak stolen.

23 September   Instead of going to the Play tonight I took a pleasant walk
out with Mr Morse an agreable sensible young Gentleman, Stuff-manu-
facturer at Norwich. Mrs M. at ye Play, as usual. Sr Jas. Murray to conduct
her to her Chair home. N.B. Saw ye young Hereditary Prince of Darmstadt at ye Play last night. A handsome young fellow – Rich fancy
uniform, of stile of his Father's Horse Guards. At Darmstadt the Prince

has a room, supported without pillars, for ye purpose of exercising his soldiers, & big enough to exercise a whole regiment together. That Prince keeps 14,000 Good Troops – Best improved exercise – Partly Prussian, partly French Manoeuvres. Ruinous to him to keep so many. Yet reckon'd as powerful a Landgravate as the other Hesse (Cassel) The Foible of this Prince is ye perpetual exercising his Soldiers, himself, from morning to night – & sometimes they say, he calls them up in ye middle of ye night for this fun. N.B. Hanau guarrison'd by a Regiment of Hannoverians, though a Town belonging to Hesse Cassel. It was design'd the residence of the late Landgravine upon her seperation. Prussia, Brunswick & Hannover were the Guarantee of this seperation; & they say, they drew lots, who shd keep ye Garrison. It is now ye residence of ye Hereditary Prince of Hesse Cassel – a week-man – about 32 years of age. English Strangers well rece^d everywhere. One Alexander here, an insufferable tiresome Scotchman, teaches English which he cannot speak. Music always at the Table D'Hôtes in ye Fair time. After Dinner, ye room itself, ye same as a Fair. Give ye Musicians 1 Baz or 6 Creitz. All the Plays acted here, translations from ye French & English – mostly throughout Germany. Very few original German Plays, as I can find, either ancient or modern. The best set of Actors & Germans, as I have seen; & these not all super-excellent.

24 September   Best hock sold here 2 Goldens – £0.3.10 a Bottle – made in ye vintage of 1729 or 1749 – that the oldest wine talk'd of as being to be had here. 1764 reckoned a good vintage, & good wine now. Took a walk in ye Evening instead of going to ye Play, & so did last night.

25 September   Have been here three weeks; weather mostly good. T.G. [Thank God.]

29 September   This morning to our great joy Mr King came yth my Sister to us, so long expected; safe & well. They had waited at Hannover for ye convenience of y^r [their] Post-Coach: otherwise they had staid as little upon ye way as they cou'd, considering they were ill at Zell. Bought a poodle Black Dog Cartouche. 3 Goldens 6 sh.

30 September–20 October   These days we amused ourselves a little altogether.

3 October, Sunday   Set out at 5 in ye afternoon.

4 October   Having passt through Mayence arrived at Manheim, at 11 in ye morning. N.B. Past over the Rhine twice, over Bridges of 30 or 40 Boats. Fine view of ye Rhine. Set out in the Afternoon for Landau where arrived Tu. 5th – 6 in ye morning. No entrance sooner. Frontier of Alsace. May be strong: are improving ye fortifications. Same night, came close to

D

Frankfort by about midnight – Shut out by ye gates – Lay at a little village, about an English mile off. There found my sister's trunk had fallen off, & was lost. Immediately sent off, an Estafette to Landau, to enquire all upon ye way.

6 October At the Hotel d'Esprit (Ghost). In ye afternoon set off with Mr King Post after the Trunk. Great uneasiness to us all. Never more dejected. Lay at Hagenau. Publish'd everywhere 10 Guineas reward.

7 October Set out farther on: Accosted everyone we met on ye road, still inquiring after the Trunk. Got to Landau this night; so far no news.

8 October This morning opening of ye gates came ye Postmaster of ——— to inform us there was news of our Trunk. Recovered the Trunk to our great joy about noon. Had been found by a Jew; a Butcher saw him pick it up, & so the secret c^d not be kept, though they concealed it 3 days. The finders had only 2 guineas; But we were obliged to fee others; viz. – that Postmaster who came to us at Landau &c so that the whole cost in Expences & Rewards, amounted to full 15 Guineas. However joy enough for us to return yth it. Came to Strasburg by 9 at night. All gone to Bed – But we roused them with our gladsome tidings – & Mrs M. w^d get up & make us welcome.

9 October, Saturday At Strasburgh.

10 October, Sunday Set out about 5 in ye afternoon. N.B. The Duke of Cumberland yth his Dutchess at Strasburgh. Great honor done him. N.B. a Corsican Regiment of horse at Strasburgh. Little men.

11 October Came to Basil in Switzerland, but one in ye afternoon. Fine view of the Rhine here. Romantic Situation. Duke of C. to pass here. In France travels at Fr. King's Exp^{ce}. Found difficulties about horses, as no Post for Horses in Switzerland, so set out again for France. Shou'd have got in quiet days journeys to Geneva yth ye same horses to Geneva in 5 days & it w^d have been best we had gone on to Basil through Berne &c.

12 October Lay outside town of Besançon. Romantic situation; fine views. Cheap country.

13 October Went through a long defile of Rocky mountains – Tops of ye mountains steep rocks, like a fortification of art.

14 October Having lain at the Posthouse (good & reasonable place) at Pontarlear last town in France, set out with horses hired to Geneva: Romantic view all ye way. Walked a good deal. Lay at ———

15 October Dined at Morge: fine situation upon ye Lake of Geneva. Had a view for ye first time of ye Alps – took for Clouds, & by way of Joke had a mind to pass them off upon Mr King for ye Alps. Lay at Aignon.

16 October   Arrived about noon at the Balance d'Or, Geneva.

17–18 October   Geneva: Agreed for Lodging & Board at Mr Mussita's derrière le Rhone. 2 & 3 p^r [pair] stairs – Italia Master.

19 October   Came to our Lodging. Mrs M. discontented yth Geneva – Has no taste for ye Beauties of nature therefore no pleasure in ye Prospect. Longs only for Plays & Balls – Taste vitiated by wrong mode of life.

24 October, Sunday   Lost my Topaz Arms, seal – fancy motto 'Trial by Jury & the Law of the Land' fell out of ye setting. N.B. Only pay 1 D. or 2 D. for an advertisement put in ye feuille d'Avis.

25 October, Monday   Having purchased 3 horses altogether for 18 Guineas – Begun to take some rides.

26 October   Went up a high mountain in Savoy – where dined at ye village. Left the Horses at ye foot of ye mountain by themselves for 2 hours.

27 October   Rid out by the Duke of Hamilton's; pretty view from the Back of his House over ye Rhone: He's a boarder there. (Jacques came: a new servant)

28 October   The Tour de Jardinage, a pleasant walk by the Rhone, conflux yth ye ——

29 October   Mrs M. never walks out but to a Millener.

30 October   Everything prepared for a little tour for Mr King & me. At night call'd upon Mr Groteheuse, at Ld Chesterfield's Lodgings – Ld C. affable & lively enough. Has 3 Servts – to each of wch he must talk diff^t Languages – German, French, Italian – as they know no other.

31 October, Sunday   Bad rainy Day, or shd have set out early this morning for Turin. Mrs M. got up at 5 to Breakfast yth us at our intended setting out. Rain all day. Lodges & boards in our house, a young Mr St Leger – Irish – A young Lad agreable enough. He sups mostly yth us – But we are boarded by ourselves. I never knew such a town as Geneva for playing at Shuttlecock — Young men & maidens – Old men & Children all together in ye streets – Sides of some of ye streets, have a high Piazza overhead – high as ye 3rd story. Dirty town; few houses yth any view. The most chaste town in ye world as Mr King informs me. Made an Uniform, of Blue & Red, steel Buttons – Gold Epaulette – Buff waste; & Breeches – to travel in. Duke of Cumberland gone into Italy by Lucerne. N.B. Wensday Oct. 26. My new servant lad Jacques came. His wages – 10 guineas a year – to give him Livery – morning Clothes – Hat, Boots & riding Breeches – & $\frac{1}{2}$ a guinea per week, whilst I chuse to leave him upon Board wages – N.B. Here to find him in Lodgings; which he hires, at 4 Geneva sous p^r night.

1 November, Monday   Set out for a Tour into Italy. Mrs M. encouraged me to it. Besides I felt chagrin in observing her discontent at Geneva, which for ye present I cannot remedy. She had seem'd discontented. I prest her to acknowledge whether there was not something more than ordinary upon her mind. She said at first, that there was; afterwards she discreetly past it off, as a joke & said otherwise. Yet another time to ye same question, she said 'She shd be less uneasy, if I loved her less'. This struck me; & it hurt me: But I thought that there might be no more in it, than that I was only troublesome to her for ye moment. Yet again other thoughts wou'd come into my head; that some impression might have been made upon her by the giddy gay young fellows at Frankfurt & she, for want of company had been mostly with. Yet I resolved to set out for Italy because I thought, as She had before rec^{ed} me with greater affection upon a return from absence this might again be the case. Besides, she had sometimes said I was jealous; & as I knew it was impossible for a couple to be happy, where either party was so, I resolved to give her occasion to see that I was very far from being jealous of her, by trusting her so much alone. (One time when she said to me, that she c^d not bear my jealousy of her, was upon occasion of her calling out of ye window to Mr St Leger, & talking to him so, hanging their heads out over the street – that I said, it was improper & begged she w^d not do so. I explain'd to her, that it was not through fear of her virtue I said so much, but that I thought it was a proper concern I shd have for her character to give that advice, because all men were intruders, & she might not see what little beginnings led to, or the impropriety the world w^d attribute to giddiness alone, though it was not guilt.

Well then it was upon Monday Nov. 1 1773 that I set out from Geneva for Turin, thus attended & equipped. King – Jack (the new hired Swiss lad) 3 horses – Mirabaud (excellent, but old) cost 7½ guineas – White mare 6 guineas – Besançon – for the Portmanteau – mare 4 guineas. All good. Lay at Chamberley – Future Countess of Artois (daughter of the K. of Sardinia) there on her way to Paris – Illuminations. Wet through, & rid ourselves dry again. Tired – Went as far this one day as the Voituriers do in 2.

2 November, Tuesday Lay at Modane. Had been told this was half way, between Chamberley & Turin – but it was not so much. Rather the foot of the Mountain (Mount Cenis) is so. Excessive cold. Fortified ourselves a good deal with Liqueur agst ye Evening. People surprized to see us ride so hard, keep out so late, & drink so hard – Went into farther excess merely to surprize them more. They said of us, that our horses were made of iron & ourselves of Steel. They were surprized to find what even their own horses c^d do. They thought they must be English horses. They have no idea of anything in travelling, but a regular plodding perseverance. Up early & abed soon – a mere jogtrot pace – & to go about 30 English miles at most in a day upon ye finest road. The roads this way we found admirable good – all new made. Did not reach the little village of Modane till 11 at night – fine moon light – past by a smelting furnace of Lead & silver ore, just before we came to ye little towns. Took a very comfortable warm there en passant. Everything barren about – All the road we came, was no more than a winding path up towards the foot of the Alps.

3 November, Wednesday Left Modane at about 8. Came to ye foot of Mount Cenis. Dined. Surrounded by a dozen muleteers – show'd the King's tariff for ye payment of ye muleteers & Mules for assistance over the Alps. Mules for ourselves. Muleteers to guide these mules & again other muleteers to conduct our horses. 'If any traveller, for his farther security choses an additional guide, he was to be had for such a price.' We attended to all this very patiently. The Consequence was we laid our heads together – & resolved to cross the mountain without any guide at all. So we mounted. Clapt spurs to our horses, & can be almost said to have past the Alps at full Gallop. It was $\frac{1}{2}$ after 2 we set out from this little village at the foot of ye mountain. At that time these guides had never been used to conduct any. They had only been asking us at what time we chose to set out the next morning. In $4\frac{1}{2}$ hours we got to the other side; but that had left us an hour in the Dark. We had got from our horses – they pickt out their own way very well along a very good beaten track. I think I have seen worse mountains to cross in Wales. I am sure I have [?seen] worse ways across some of our Welsh Hills. I sometimes walk'd at a distance following my own inventions. Had a whistle with me, to recover my company by – Once out of a hearing – lost the road; grew dark & thought I shou'd have lain on ye mountain. After we had descended it; still went for an hour or so farther on to a town called Suza – where fine quarries of green marble. A very pretty town – Romantic View of the Alps round it. N.B. I never saw a marble quarry whilst in Italy*, for which I am sorry. I must take notice of a Piedmontese officer coming on ye same road – He journey'd very slow. We had a little talk with him, telling him how far & how fast we had come. He cried out, 'Oh, Quels Gens' & beg^d us for God's sake to go on, he c^d not wish to be with us – Yet with his perseverence & getting up at 4 or 5 in ye morning, He past by us. We are chagrin'd. But in passing him again, I told him, that he put me in mind of ye story of the Hare & the Tortoise – & so in taking my 2nd leave of

* Robert made a Grand Tour in 1769.

him, I adieu'd him, with saying, Votre Serviteur, Mons. le Tortoise. Yet this same Tortoise overtook us again, as we were going to ascend the Mount Cenis. In the wildest part of ye Mountain, I turn'd about & exclaim'd to him, This is just such a situation as I fought the wild Indians in America. Which he swallow'd very well; & I said it to aggrandize my Character as an English Officer.

4 November It was an easy half-days ride to Turin – But as it rained a good deal about noon we did not get there till about 4 o-clock. The Country was very pleasant we past through – Some very picturesque old Roman Ruins on small Prominences. Remarkable ruin of a Temple on ye wayside. Fine Pillars lying on the Road. Piemont – Speak all Italian this side the Alps. The other side in Savoy speak all French. These call the King of Sardinière Duke (of Savoy) here Prince (of Piemont) The Alps has a large foot; all to go under the name of Piemont. Lodg'd at Boeuf Rouge – 2nd best house – But good enough. A Table d'hôte. At the Burletta. Good female dancer.

5 November Saw the whole of Turin. At a Bourgeois Play – Lother & Holofernes. Burlesque stuff – then more burlesque Piemontese (Mock Doctor) farce. Saw the King's Palace. Pictures of the King's victories. Blanks left for the victories of the present King. Some Battles fought in ye late reign (in Savoy) in places similar to ye Battle of Quebec. In the large square – fine Exhibitions for the populace. Woman through a speaking trumpet telling fortunes. Man showing off a ship. Quack Doctor acting Punch. Fine Piazza's &c. N.B. Never knew it more bitterly cold.

6 November Set out in the afternoon. Hotel at Turin cheap. Rode 5 hours. Dark – fell into a Ditch whilst I was turning my head aside to crack my whip. Lay at Hedge alehouse. Askt whether we w^d have Black wine or white; I askt what sort of wine the white was. 'Sir, we have only black!' I ordered a Pint of that, thinking just to taste. The Pint was as Big as two of our quarts, & did not cost above 4 pence English & was most excellent strong bodied wine. Here I first found the necessity of talking Italian; & even in one night pickt up a good many useful words.

7 November Past through Alexandria: Beautiful Country; a large deserted Town. Past full drive through a village about Church, I had my nightcap on my head, & having lost my hat did not perceive it. The people all cried out, 'Cappello, Cappello'. I thought they meant to upbraid me for not going to Chapel. I answered Cappello is for you & not for me. And so rode off, leaving my hat behind. Got to Nuovi, by 9 at night. Quite dark. Took the advantage of following a Post-Chaise, by which we obliged ourselves to keep up well & saved missing the way. A rough

Butcher for our Landlord: We askt him what sort of a road it was to Genoa. Tout Carossable Mons. [Monsieur.] The first time I had heard the word, & spoke in a very hoarse voice it made an impression upon us. Such a Tone of a voice. I call the language of my rough Dog Cartouche; so that when I have a mind to talk to him, I call up as many of such expressions as I can recollect. 'Venez chauffez tous les Deux' is another instance of words which I heard in that tone of voice; & were urged to Mr King & me, as we were passing one Evening through St Honoré Street at Paris, by a poor old nasty devil, who I suppose had the impudence to call herself a Lady of Pleasure. Our Butcher Landlord wanted to persuade us we had a very fine road for the rest to go to Genoa. C'est tout suite Pavé. He said it was as plain as the Table: It was but 10 french Leagues, & we c^d easily go upon our own horses to Genoa in 8 hours. Then the road was so well guarded, we might go with a hatful of Louis D'ors openhanded. Chapeau plein des Louis. There were 14 companies of Marechaussée always upon Guard for that road.

8 November We set out at 8 in the morning. The road indeed was sur le pavé, but such a pavement, that the worse road I ever travel'd I w^d have rather gone. It was all paved with round slippery marble pebbles. We cou'd only go a snail's pace; the road being perpetually up & down very steep: Yet we saw a Courier & a Postilion with a monstrous large Portmanteau go on a horseback full gallop. It rained incessantly. We were wet through: yet rode on till 12 o'clock. Stopt at a Hedge alehouse. Immense underground stables full of mules; to the number of 100. Stript to the skin & dried all our clothes. Mounted again about 2 or 3 still in the rain. Soon wet through: yet rode on without stopping till 9 at night; and even then not at Genoa: for we Lay at Campa d'arena within an English mile off Genoa. During our progress this day Mr King was riding on a brisk trot, leading the way. We heard the fall of a great Rock: Jack informed us what it was; I desired King to get off his horse & walk a little way, to see if we were right, it being quite dark. In 3 or 4 yards he came to the top of a very deep precipice; which was in no other than a marble quarry. We hastily returned, finding ourselves upon observation in a very narrow path, & the ground on one side very steep below us. We were afterwards obliged to knock up a fellow in his house to come in and put us into the high road; which for ye value of a shilling he did: But not till we had got into some other intricacies, before we got this guide, having once or twice been upon the point of crossing a very rapid river, thinking Genoa was upon the other side. No fireplace, at the Inn where we lay. Only stoves in the Kitchen. There had been a fireplace upstairs, but it was turn'd into a cupboard. When we askt for a fire, they made us one by bringing some chips & shavings in an old basket, then setting fire to the Basket & all, they put it down to burn in the middle of the room, leaving the door open for the smoke to go out at. Having no means of drying one's Clothes & sitting up, I supt in bed & was waited upon by half a dozen pretty little girls & boys, who vied with each other in assisting me, & were very well contented with a few chicken bones I gave them to pick that night & a few pennies to put in their pocket the next morning. The Hills between Nuovi & Genoa called Apennine mountains are worse to cross than the Mount Cenis of the Alps.

9 November Rode into Genoa to Breakfast. Struck with the grand & beautiful appearance of the Town, the bay & the Hills. Palaces superb: elegant Italian Architecture. Profusion of Marble. Streets clean mostly narrow; not above 2 or 3 streets passable for carriages. Many chairs. Ladies of certain rank allowed to keep their own chairs, with a Portes for footmen before them.

Cost Mr King & me, with Jack, 3 horses 9 guineas to come from Geneva, & be 9 days. Put up at La Sta [Santa] Martha, which is the Posthouse; a most imposing place. Askt for lodging 6 livres Genoese (i.e. 9 pence Eng. a-piece per day) & took 4. Hired a Lacquais de Place, who had served in that capacity in that place to Lord Baltimore: said, he thought he was mad. I askt why; he answered, 'because he gave 2 guineas to the postilions, who conducted him from the last stage to this place. 'A pretty fellow, said I, are you, to say a nobleman is mad who gave away 2 guineas which to him were as to most men are 2 livres.' Out of respect to Ld B.'s memory I turn'd him off. Went to the play. Begins late i.e. after 7. A remarkable capering girl; Dancer. Brava Lamberti. Only applauded when she whisk'd up her petticoats over her hips.

10 November Left the Santa Martha, on acc^t of its dearness & imposition. Our horses still remain'd at the stables belonging to it. We now went to the English public house, kept by one Welsh & his wife – Irish – honest, good sort of people. Here we were lodged & boarded (breakfast, dinner & supper) at 4½ Livres each apiece per Day – 3 — 4½ Eng. Found in this house Mr Wm Munro, Birmingham, merchant – and a Blackguard Fellow miscalled Grace, son of one Grace a Buckle-maker in Newgate Street.

This was such another house, as the resort of the English Sea-Captain at Hamburgh: & we had several here. Father Hutchinson always coming backwards & forwards. A good natured poor Irishman – searching to do an office for one & for another by way of picking up a little trifle for himself. He was born of Irish Parents at Genoa. Serves in many capacities; among others as a Pimp. There is a celebrated Abbé does the same at Venice, to whom many of the English have letters for that purpose. This Father has 2,000 Genoese Livres per year i.e. about £35, with this he maintains his mother & sister. Every evening we used to play at penny unlimited brag. Grace suspected of marking ye Cards. Upon the whole I won, I believe, a guinea or two; which I afterwards lost, & more to it, by cutting in at Whist & having that rascal Grace for my partner. Our penny we called, as it is at Genoa, a Pop & a Pop-over; used to be always coming in a droll Irish tone out of the mouth of that poor innocent fellow Welch, which kept the House. Other Irish Fathers. One fine Paddy-whack, fit for the plough & about 35 years of age, with whom we drank Chocolate at a fine Convent, where he was residing, as he said, *to finish his studies* – I saw no books in his Chambers, but about St Anthony of Padua, or some such sort.

11–17 November   At Genoa. During all this time I staid at Welch's. I shd have gone away much earlier; (For my intention was not [to] stay at Genoa above 3 or 4 days.) But the wind prevented us from going either to Leghorn or to Marseilles. On Friday 12th I sent Jack off with the horses over the hills to Nice, & thence to Marseilles – a journey he performed with ease in 6 days – There went with him upon one of my horses a Mr Guillaume, a genteel young Scotchman, whom we made acquaintance with at Welch's. Time towards the conclusion of our stay began to hang very heavy on our hands. King grew ill; & seemed to have caught a sort of ague, with which he set out at last, & it did not leave him till he got to Marseilles. I never went more than twice to the play. Saw a very foolish Englishman acting the nobleman, crying out at every spring of Lamberti, the Dancer – Damn ye Body, what a fine strong woman. Damn my body! Damn my body! Got acquainted at Welch's with the following sea Captains: Captn Gray, Captn Elles – one Captn Palmer (once in ye Hamburgh trade, who abused Mr Parish, for wch I took him down.)

Took our passage to Marseilles, aboard a French Tartar (Gracopello). He disappointed us, great difficulty in getting our earnest of a guinea Back – Battle royal between our Boatman (from an English ship) & his crew. He wou'd not sail because of ye threatening appearance of ye weather; yet we immediately ye same day hired a small boat from Genoa, to the astonishment of the whole harbour; for the wind blew very hard. My chief employ, when I was taken with a fit of tediousness from my long detention at Genoa was to write long and affectionate letters to a young wife, from whom I begun to regret exceedingly my absence, vowing therein never to leave her for so long again; who I then thought loved me in return with an equal affection.

Genoa. Churches superb. An elegant one after an imitation of St Peter's at Rome. Fine prospect of Genoa & the country round it from the Top of that Church. The Town & situation put me a good deal in mind of Bath, only that Genoa had the advantage of the Sea. A theatre of hills environs on ye side of the Land: Those hills interspersed upon its' declivities with superb palaces: The Hills themselves very rude & romantic at the tops. Weather extremely cold during our stay at Genoa. Lived at Welch's quite in the English fashion. Punch & Porter. No hams at Genoa; or as I heard of in Italy. Famous for cheap work & muslins & Cambricks: Umbrellas: a large Parmesan cheese worth £3. Turkish slaves, chained together going about the town selling of Slippers, night caps & Footmats.

Saw all the Galley slaves; Turks & Culprits mixt together. One Irish Rogue told us a long story, of his being condemned for 5 years for running a little Tobacco: The truth was: he had been condemned at the Gallies for some offence: but he was then there from having sold himself for a trifle after his first time was out for a longer term: The Turks keeping their shops, for the other slaves, sailors &c to buy things at – Some of them had Cook's shops – Many so rich, that they might thus purchase Liberty, but do not chuse to return home.

At noon, every one at Genoa, & qu: if not all over Italy, falls down on their knees, wherever they happen to be, when they hear the clock strike: Here everybody knelt down at the change at that hour; when they say some prayer by way of thanking God for another day.

However we walked across ye Change at that time with our hats on, & nobody said anything. Another time I walk'd across ye change with a Portmanteau upon my Shoulder wch I had just been buying; but this was not at their noon prayer: However this was enough to astonish all Genoa; for it soon went about the Town, that a gentleman of a thousand guineas a year in England, who had also married a Lord's daughter with £30,000 besides, had deigned to carry his own Portmanteau. The Truth was, I did it partly out of fun to create this astonishment, & partly because having just boᵗ ye Portmanteau there was no one directly at hand to carry it home.

One Nobleman at Genoa, had a Playhouse, a Church, & a College for students, all built by his ancestors, & still parts of his own Palace.

At some Church I saw some people kneeling by turns very fast one after another, to whom a Priest presented a relic to be kissed, muttering at the same in an odd gabbering tone some latin words; I knelt down in my place & rec^d the relic to kiss: This was also soon over Genoa. Fine Figs. Grapes not so fine. Fine flowers, Arabian Jessamine$^{(yn)}$. Went several times aboard English ships in ye harbour; made heartily welcome. Aboard one from Newfoundland, was a little Esquimaux Indian, with his Canoe, just like what is hung in the Boomhouse at Hamburgh; I went into it myself: I sat in such a hole that if it overturn'd, I thought I c^d not get out of it: I therefore did not chuse to quit hold of the ship; but I tried myself in the Canoe. The little Indian c^d only answer to the Question in English, what his name was. John Strong Longcock – which he spoke yth a remarkable deep voice; as if the sound came from his Belly.

One morning being in a Boat yth Grace, who was a remarkable noisy bullying fellow, always pretending to have ye ability of taking others in respecting their Cash, I said to him what will you give me to jump in the sea now: He said 2 french Crowns (i.e. $\frac{1}{2}$ a guinea) Done, sayd I; & in I jumpt Cloaths & all: I found it easy enough to swim to ye oars of ye Boat again – though I had my Great-coat on. One Crown I gave immediately to ye Boatman, & the other I kept.

18 November, Thursday   We set out for [from] Genoa. Self. King, Munro, Grace in a small boat; about 2 in the afternoon; 4 men: Agreed for 5 Guineas to Marseilles, or 2$\frac{1}{2}$ to Nice. Stopt this Evening at Pagi: a pleasant village: Grand & curious Orange Gardens: Multiplicity of Orange & Lemons. Some almost ripe: Eat one or two of the China Oranges; Water works – water coming out of the Branches of Trees: All Water works I think contemptible; these as good as most: reckon'd fine.

19 November   One of our Boatmen, quite a Robinson Crusoe in his Look – talked English – Had served aboard an English Man of War. Came at night to Porto Maurizio. This is a little Genoese Village close by a very pretty Town, in the Piemontese territories, though that Town is nearer to Genoa. Bad lodging, & worse supping. Askt for a Reckoning; the answer was, 'It's not necessary to make any reckoning: Bed & supper together is 2 Louis d'Ors.

I was pitched upon to extricate our Company from this imposition. We had far'd better at Pagi, & had paid only half a Louis – & they had askt but 2 french Livres more.

'What, says I, is the Reckoning?

Duoi Luigi.

'Then, Ecco duoi Scudi di Francia'. The man of the house attempted to lay hold of me: I drew my hanger: & he soon kept his distance; but he ran upstairs & fetched a gun: We called to Arms; & we were arranged Battle array; However we marched off in triumph to our Boat: & paid no more.

We had some Chance of being overset in ye Boat: the wind was squally. I was not quite sick, nor quite well: As for ye danger I did not in the least attend; & when the wind was highest I did not think it worth my while to lift my head up from where I was lying by ye side of King at the Bottom of the Boat.

20 November Past by Monaco; a little Town on a Rock. Country along the Coast, is the declivity of high Hills; beautifully interspersed with villas, Orangeries & Olive Trees.

Came to Nice; just a little after Sunset – Bribed some fellow to get us a Pratica as they call it. i.e. permission to Land, upon the Commissioner of health coming down to inspect our Bill of Health. Lay at the Hotel de Grance. Saw Guillaume, Dr Durell Principal at Hertford then resident at Nice for his Health. Seemed to me to be as cold here, as any where else, where I had been, & the Climate not better. The Town miserable: Enough to inspire any one with ye Hip. No house yth any prospects: only one part of the Town any pretence to Elegance & there is a sort of a square of new buildings. N.B. Past the Var, the next day, which divides France from Piemont: a small stream very rapid: the bed of the river wide: some parts wide, These are shifting: yet I refused a guide, & past safe.

21 November Set out on Bidet, Post about noon – Rode continually till Mond. 22 at 7 at night; except 2 Posts, I went once in a Cart & the other Post on a Dray, being obliged to take my turn to do so – And 2 hours in the night, I stopt, at King's earnest request to give him a little rest, being ill. Not near so much in ye danger of passing ye Varr as pretended. One of our little Portmanteau lost on ye road: whole value about 2 guineas: No chaises to be had, & as Munro had a large Trunk we were obliged to hire what sort of Carriage we cou'd get, which were never better than a sort of wheel barrow on 2 wheels, & sometimes were literally on Drays: the former they called Tambourets: the Drays were much ye easiest; Grace & I get on a horseback a good [?way] before King & Munro, who being left behind us, were detained in searching after the little Portmanteau, which they then began to discover was lost: One of the Tambouret in which it was, with Munro & Grace, for one stage that night, had from being loaded too heavy at night, tilted entirely over, throwing Grace, Munro & all the Baggage entirely out & at which time probably the little Portmanteau was lost: I askt Grace, whether he had put in all things particularizing at ye time of ye accident; he said he had, & mentioned expressly the little Portmanteau: But he was a Lying Dog at all times, & I ought not to have believed him. We made search & inquiry; I also advertised the Portmanteau in the Marseilles paper; but no intelligence ever received on't. I tried all I cou'd to outride Grace, & leave him behind; and so I shd have but that once I took pity on him, because he complained of being ill, & in another stage the Postilion w^d not leave him behind for fear of the horse.

Rode the last 15 miles to Toulon, over execrably stony rode in an hour & a quarter. Came too late for ye gate & obliged to return back for one League to a village to lie at: Yet I learnt the next day at Toulon; that they w^d have open'd the gate, if we had called to them.

23 November Walked in to Toulon. At the Croix de Maltha. I run on before; & past in without being noticed by the Guard; Grace coming after, being drest in an odd Sailor's habit was soon snapt up, & conducted by a Sentry to the Commandant. I follow'd laughing: He begged me to accompany him to the Commandant after I had joined him in the Town: I c^d not help laughing in the Commandant's presence at Grace's odd appearance: The Commandant asking me, where I came from, I told him from America, that I landed in Holland, & having mistook my way had rambled all through Germany & Italy: We past muster, after a good deal of apparent suspicion, & were dismist.

Visited in a Boat the Harbour: No ship of war ready for sea; & only one Frigate: Many laid up, which they said c^d be made ready in a month's time: i.e. about 16 of ye Line, & several Frigates. Was aboard one Frigate just ready to sail for the Coast of Barbary. The Harbour seems easily to be forced by a Fleet of English ships, being very wide, & not intricate from ye sea, but there afterwards a turn in towards the Town, where ships lie very secure.

Toulon seems strong by Land: Lately a new fortification on a rising ground towards ye Entrance of the Harbour. This day to dinner arrived King & Munro.

24 November Munro & I set out about 10 in ye morning on Post-horses to Marseilles: The road lies through a very barren Country: the part nearest Toulon, full of Olive Trees: The way all hilly: Seems a country full of mines; Coal near some part of the way; saw waggons of it coming to Marseilles. The French have a great notion of Coal smelling very ill, when burnt in houses: Some English I found at Marseilles declare, that the French Coal did smell bad, but some English burnt by them sometimes there, they allowed not so. I have observ'd many persons from Coal countries become converts to wood fires esteeming after experience the latter much pleasanter, but I never knew yet one of a wood country become a favourer of Coal fires. For my part, after all the experience

I have had, & I have experienced a good deal of Wood-fires, I prefer Coal infinitely, both for warmth, chearfulness & smell.

Put up at Marseilles at the Croix d'Maltha; Good table d'Hote; Dinner & Supper: Everyone putting up there must pay about 4 shillings a day, which includes his bed, dinner & supper, whether he partakes of them or not.

25 November Marseilles a fine Town: Streets Broad: Good houses: Fine Harbour: very inaccessible to an Enemy both by Sea & Land: Fine broad pavement walk by the side of the shipping. The Galley slaves in their little shops on one side exercising all manner of trades: I went to be shav'd by one of them, out of Curiosity, by way of opportunity to give him a shilling. Drank Tea with Mr Bierbeck, the English agent; his Lady of North Wales; knew many of my acquaintance: Lady Stepney was travelling that way with her daughter & publickly with her Paramor Morgan, at the time Sir Thos Stepney died.

Was at the Playhouse here; full of the filles de joye, said to be 3,000 of them in this Town; Saw none pretty, none anywhere, such as in England. *26 November* King by this time was recovered of his illness, which took him a couple of Days before he left Genoa.

Poison laid in the Streets for ye Dogs on account of some pretence of a mad wolf having bit some Dogs in the Country. Spits, Mr King's favorite Pomer & indeed everybody's favorite lickt some in a corner; I observed it the very moment & chaced him off; I therefore thought it w^d not hurt him; yet in 5 minutes or so, without any warning, I saw him [in] the agonies of death at my feet, in a Coffee house, where I was drinking some Coffee: I tried every remedy in vain: In 3 minutes after he was dead: This gave inexpressible Concern both to King & me.

I saw at Mr Bierbeck's a young English Girl, Daughter of Mr Roberts of the Union Coffee house, about 13, just come out of a convent, very ill; seemed to me in a Consumption: Mr B. said she was in one of the fevers of that country & had been so for 35 days. They usually last 50: No danger till Belly swells: There had been great difficulty to get her out of the convent, & interest necessary to be used through Ld Rochford to effect it: a greater difficulty was at that time subsisting concerning Miss Macnamara an English young lady at Nice; whose parents had been long in vain endeavouring to get her out; & about which there had been messages & disputes between the Courts at London & Turin. If the people of the Convent can make any pretence for these young School Girls to be turned Catholics & to have an inclination to become Nuns, they will not let them out.

27 November We set out from hence on our own horses in the afternoon; & lay at Aix.

28 November Munro & Grace had a great quarrel with their Voiturier: I put on my uniform, & with that made sufficient interest with the Commandant of that place to release them from him, though I had tried before in another dress in vain. This being my . . . . wife's Birthday, we did not forget to celebrate it as such: Little did I think how different her sentiments were towards me from mine towards her.

29 November Grace & Munro came a horseback; & today we got to Avignon early in the afternoon. A pleasant Town Avignon: the country towards it forms very fine approaches. King & I missing the way had like to have rid on to Spain: It gave us pleasure to think we were in ye high road to that Kingdom. Something new or something strange were enough to carry us anywhere: We did not hear Egypt or Arabia mention'd without wishing to be there.

A fine Carthusian Monastery near Avignon most delightfully situated on ye Banks of the river.

This evening at 8, we set out again on our way to Lyons.

I had conceived a disgust ag^{nst} Grace; from some discourse he had held; about my marriage; or rather about my wife; I had had great mind to punish him; I was resolved to take the first opportunity to resent: He used some practical wit towards me with his whip; I drew my hanger & made a cut at his arm.

30 November I had a terrible fall yth my mare, by crossing a rut in the night time: She lay with her leg in ye rut so long, that I thought she had broke it: The force I came with to the ground was so great, as to break into pieces a powder horn in my Pocket: I greatly hurt my thigh & lamed myself. However I was resolved to ride on without stopping to Lyons: which I did, though for ye last 3 stages greatly fatigued, & vastly inclinable to sleep even in the cold night upon my Horse: I did not get to Lyons Gate till ½ after 12 this Tuesday night. I only rode my own mare the first stage from Avignon: the rest by Post upon Bidets. The very first stage from Avignon, Grace was knockt up, & went to bed. Some few stages afterwards Billy Munro was sadly knockt up, sick, & desired to lie down in ye Stable. We consented to wait for him a little while, because he seemed a spunky fellow, and wou'd if we had insisted upon it have come on with us sick as he was: We did not however come into this compromise, till after King & I coolly laid our heads together whether we cou'd justify taking him on with us, & riding him to death; which was determined between us in the negative, because he possessed a young wife in England.

About 10 or 11 this morning King received a sprain in his foot by dismounting from his horse, so had come on no farther: So I then left both him & Munro behind because having gone on then so many stages without stopping, I was resolved as well from a desire to return with all expedition possible to the *fickle ingrate* at Geneva, as from an inclination to find out how much I cou'd do in ye article of riding Post without stopping.

I rode from Avignon to Lyons (which I am satisfied is near 200 English Miles – the Leagues & Post in that country being very long) in 28 hours, in which time I only made a delay of 4 hours, except the necessary time of changing horses, which is usually done very quick (at most in a quarter of an hour) & riding always as fast as the horses cou'd go, I reckon that I went 10 English miles an hour, whilst upon the horse's back. The last stage of all, only within half an hour of Lyons, I found myself rather too far gone in fatigue, even to attempt that little distance. I condescended to ask for a Bed, & they saying they had none, raised me sufficiently not to think of resting there. I had rid all the way in a heavy Genoese Sailor's Grago, to keep me warm, but it contributed to fatigue me exceedingly, & the fall I rec^ed did not assist me. I cut such a figure in my Graigeau that the people took me on ye road for ye Spanish Courier, & were often asking me what news from Madrid. I lost my hanger on ye road by its flying out of the scabbard in the night time.

1 December Put up at Lyons at the Hotel d'Artois. King & Munro came in to dinner. Found myself much tired, lame & had a sad cold.

2 December About noon Grace came at last. At the Play. Wanted to raise 20 guineas for the accommodation of Mr Munro; which I askt for of the Master of the house, received, & lent to Mr Munro upon his bill; which was duly paid in London.

3 December Jack arrived, with the 3 horses. Sold Mirabaud to Grace for 10 guineas; he purposed taking him to England; but using him improperly on ye road he was obliged to sell him at Paris & thinking himself well off, for 2 guineas.

I bought at a Bijou shop, a Tortoise shell Toilette Box, for rouge & Patches, inlaid & set in Gold; taking it home found the representation on the lid to be the device of a Cock treading a hen: Saw it was a fit present for a fille de joye, but not for my little wife, as I intended it. With some difficulty I got the man to change it me for another.

At 7 at night I set out on Post-Bidets to return to Geneva. King had a terrible fall, in which his horse almost cut his Eye out. The Post-Bidets very seldom fall: never knew it but twice: Road steep & slippery: some part of the road nothing but a sheet of ice, yet always went full drive.

NOTE In our way between Lyons & Geneva, when we approached pretty near the latter place, we had to pass through a very ancient fortress situated in a most romantic spot formerly belonging to ye Savoyards, now within the Territories of France. The road which was necessarily very narrow led through the Gates of the Castle, at the Bottom ran the river Rhone, in each side high steep impassable rocks & mountains: Art did not add much to the strength of the fortress & it was only guarded by a few old miserable invalids. Here we were asked for a Pass, & in default of having one call'd up before ye Governer, whom we found an old gouty fellow in a greasy nightcap more like —— than an General [sic]. But we were still more surprized to find this renowned Veteran to be an Irishman who insisted upon it we ought to have a pass because he was sure he had one when he went from London to Dublin: *that is to say, a pass for a Vagrant.*

'Now, do you know, my dears, says he, if I were to do my duty, I cou'd keep you here for a month.'

'However, as you are *Countrymen*, you have nothing to do but to mention your name to me, & whenever I hear it, it shall serve as a pass for you next time.'

Teague was as good as his word; for when we past by Paddywhack's Castle at our return I only sent up my name, & though it was night, he immediately ordered the Gates to be opened, & let us through.

4 December Having rode all last night & incessantly this day, I arrived at Geneva about 3 in the afternoon. Fanny ran from my sight; conscious (as I was certain afterwards) of her treachery & ingratitude towards me. Little did I expect to be so received from all my pains & dangers in returning with [the] expedition I did: Cold reception for all my anxieties.

5 December Fr. continues to conduct herself towards me in such a manner, that though I c^d not now help being convinced that are [her] affections were not warm towards me; yet the total change of them I did not yet find out.

6 December Spoke to F. about having another marriage celebrated between us. I put it on this footing; that though I knew our marriages already had were good, yet I desired another at this time, when she was older, as an argument & proof to the world that I was equally her choice, when she was at a more advanced period of her age as [than] before: She put off my request under pretence of trouble & inutility. I did not yet find her out.

7 December I spoke about a marriage with the Clerk of the Parish of Cologny, about a league off Geneva; easy to be had at any day. F. still

103

puts off her answer about another marriage, under pretence of time to consider.

8 December I prest F. to the possession of her person; & from that moment soon discovered the whole secret of her perfidious heart. During my absence in Italy she had writ word to her Brother that she could not love me, never had done so, wished the marriage set aside, & was resolved at all events to desert me. I was shocked; beyond expression shock'd. But I summoned up all my fortitude, upbraided her nothing & bore it with a tolerable degree of manliness.

I informed King & my sister of what had past. It was to Mr King, as great a surprise as to myself: It was the last thing he c^d have suspected.

9 December F. seemed herself miserable & I gave way to weaknesses. I had slept very much disturbed; & no rest for mind or body after 4 in the morning.

By this time I became more reconciled to the change, which had happened in my domestic fortunes. I wrote my sentiments to all parties about it: F. wrote again to her brother: & wrote also to that piece of a mother of her's, & to Mr Parish. Seeing how determined she was I thought it best she shd be conducted to England by others, than by myself when I was certain to be basely betrayed & abandoned by her upon arrival there. I therefore desired Mr Prevost either to come abroad to conduct her, or send somebody to receive her at Paris. Besides, upon discovering her mind to me, she had made me give my honor, that whatever she was going to say, she shou'd be equally soon permitted to return to England; & never having forfeited my honor to her I was resolved not to do it at the moment of seperation. There were also delicate circumstances between us: Some might have esteemed me in the light of her Guardian: I c^d justify nothing without her free will & consent, having brought her abroad entirely with that I was resolved not to detain her a moment about it; or even to disguise a moment my intentions or dispositions towards her.

11 December Found myself much easier in mind: I had suffered a good deal by a Cold upon my return to Geneva in the manner I did at this inclement season: but by this time I became better.

I begun to think since F. showed herself to possess such a mind, that this matter must have happened sooner or later; & better now than afterwards. F. had said, before I went to Turin, when I prest her for the cause upon some occasion of her being thoughtful 'that if I loved her less, she shou'd be less uneasy.'

I c^d not help now interpreting the pain she felt to arise from the struggle between gratitude & depravity. She prest me to the Tour to Italy. She also destroyed her will made in my favour, before I went. All this convinces me, that she had her whole conduct in view, before I set out from Geneva.

The affectionate letters she in such numbers received from me, during my absence, she hardly gave a perusal to. One, which I had outrid, coming to her after my arrival, she threw into the fire before my face, on pretence of being disgusted at finding it so dirty.

The first time I believe her mind admitted a change to me, was I believe soon after I came to Mr Mussita's, when upon her improper romping freedom with young Mr St. Leger, who boarded in the house, whose only room his bedchamber above stairs; she once ran up to play some trick yth him & was always calling out of the windows over the street to him, whilst he was in his own apartment above; I thought it just, from my regard to her, just to hint the impropriety: She flew into a passion; called me jealous: And I resolved, & kept my promise of saying no more to her, let her romp or talk as she pleased. Yet I believe, the idea of my being jealous now began to rivet itself in her mind: and in consequence she formed a disgust at me: wishing to have the opportunity of being married to another; that she c⁴ have the marriage already past set aside; that I had injured in marrying her so soon, by debarring her of a more mature choice: that her fortune was so great, she cou'd have married a Lord: that her Brother had an income equal to L⁴ Chesterfield, who lodg'd at the next door; therefore it was an injury to her consequence to be seperated from him; that what had past relative to my possession, she cou'd either deny, disguise or have excused her from her youth; and in these notions she was encouraged by that infamous vile malignant, foolish Creature, Miss Hodgson. The flattery F. had met with at Frankfurt did her no good. She now appeared to be a perfect composition of pride & vanity. She wanted Miss H. to deny, & even upon oath, that I had ever lain yth her. 'Pooh, says she, what signifies an oath?'

AN ADDITION   My sister overheard Miss Hodgson (in discourse before begun between Miss H. & Mrs M.) in an adjoining room say to Mrs M.

Lord, Madam, how can I say so: and if I were to say it, who wou'd believe it?

Mrs M. What signifies what is believed as long as it cannot be proved?

Miss H. But Madam, if I am put to my oath, I must then say the truth.

Mrs M. (mocking her in a whining tone) Put to oath . . . . Pooh. What signifies an oath?

My sister directly after had an opportunity of asking Miss H. 'What was

that loud conversation she had with Mrs M. about an oath. Miss H.
answered her, It was, that Mrs M. wanted me to swear, that Mr M.
never lay with her, which I told her I neither wou'd nor cou'd do.
N.B. I intend to write down separately the distinct proofs which I have of
cohabitation, which are as decisive, as ever were in any case. In p. 37 of
this journal* is a particular of all ye times I ever lay with her. Miss H. has
seen us in bed together; particularly at Frankfurt. Fanchon has lain in ye
same bed with us at Wansbeck: & can say even more than that. Miss H.
& her sister knew that Mrs M. miscarried at Hamburgh. Mrs M. even told
my sister so herself at Geneva, during my absence in Italy. A proof she
had not then everything in her mind, which she formed afterwards. But
she was changeable in this respect.

12 December, Sunday Prepared for ye journey to Paris. N.B. In my
absence from Geneva Mrs M. had much employ'd herself in writing verses
out of books. Sought to be alone. Talk'd of madness. Said she thought she
shd go mad. Askt how people lookt when they were mad. Miss H. did not
hesitate to tell us she thought she was mad.

13 December, Monday Set out about noon. This morning Mr Mussita came
& told me, that all the disagreement between me & F. came from ye Gouvernante (Miss H.) that he had pickt up from his servants, that she had held
this discourse in the kitchen: that Mrs M. was too young for a wife, that
I had seduced her from England, & that when we return'd there the
marriage w^d be broke. 'I taxed this Creature yth this, & she denied it in the
most solemn manner: Nay, she had the impudence when I came to Paris
to deny that Mr Mussita & his wife had supported ye assertion in her
presence & mine, as they did, of her having said so. This occasioned me
afterwards to write to Mr Mussita, that I might [have] his assertions under
his own hand; which he accordingly sent me.

Till Mr Mussita had told me what he did, about Miss H. I had thought
her to be entirely innocent in the matter: and she herself pretended to be
intirely on our side, laying the whole to F.'s natural fickleness, & even
saying, that she thought her to be out of her senses. She afterwards denied,
she ever said such a thing. She also amongst other charges she chose to
make agst F. said, that she had proposed very early to Fanchon at Wansbeck to run away with her. I charged her with having said this, when
I came to Paris; she denied it, & offered to take her oath though Mr King
& my sister supported she had said so, & declared themselves ready to take
their oaths of it, if it became them. F. was always ready to excuse Miss H.
in everything we c^d urge against her; though these articles plainly

* Volume 1 of Morris's Diary.

convicted her of acting a double part. Miss H, had the impudence to tell my sister upon this matter at Paris, that what she said was false; & so F. told my sister she thought it: Though I had proof from F.'s own mouth afterwards that she believed this creature Hodgson had said so but laid it to the natural levity of a woman's speech.

In short I never saw any instance of any woman's mind being under so manifest a prejudice, as F.'s was, in regard to every matter which concerned that poor contemptible Toad-eater of hers, Miss H.

14 December At 4 in the afternoon arrived at Lyons. Obliged to sell 2 horses to the master of the Hotel for 5 guineas: & had 2 guineas out of that money to pay for their keeping.

15 December Set out at 3 in the afternoon. Hinder Axle broke short off close to ye wheel about 9 or 10 at night: Kept 3 hours in the high road, sitting in the Coach, till assistance came: Patcht up a temporary Axletree for ye wheel broke off & got to Villefranche, about midnight.

16 December Delayed all this day in getting a new Axle Tree made. Cou'd not set out sooner than one in the morning of —— [sic]

17 December Road bad & heavy.

18 December More accidents to our wheels. Pickt out of F. something of her mind. She said, she knew her fortune was great & that if she had not been married to me she might have married a man of larger estate & with a title too. (The title, the title it is that sticks yth her.) That I had therefore done her the greatest injury by marrying her so soon; which she never could forgive me; that she only accepted from the first of me, because she wished to get away from the disagreeable restraint of school, & that she w^d have run away for that purpose with anyone else as soon as with me; & gave a hint, if she thought I had on purpose pickt out the most disagreable school for her, that I might succeed in my views of possessing her fortune; that I had access to her when no one else had, & therefore she had none to chuse but me; not that she ever loved me; & that she did not at that time know what love was. F. was now no longer inclined to consider the sacrifice I had made of everything for her sake; the unceasing attachment I had shown to her: She was freed from disagreeable restraints, but her pride w^d not suffer her now to consider herself under any obligations to me, as her deliverer: She wou'd not conceive, that she might have made a worse choice; she wou'd not think, that it was her smiles that bewitched me, & that it was her own conduct that inspired me with a resolution to make the proposal I did; which I shou'd not have made, but that from ye particularity of her behaviour towards me. I thought I saw in her an equal love to what I possessed for her. She now wou'd not

allow, that there ever was a time in which she certainly loved me; yet she
bore the appearance of doing so, & I am convinced had the reality of it,
till very lately: To this all her great pretences were, that she had not time
to think, till she came to Geneva; the futility of which answer as well as
the falsity of it, is known to all who have been acquainted with us both. F.
treated me with such manifest disrespect & even contempt upon ye road,
that I c^d not help beginning in my turn to form a disgust against her: It
was but momentary; but whilst my passion lasted, I cou'd not help telling
her, that she was welcome to go & follow her own vicious inclinations;
for my part I had had enough of her: the possession of her person had
been enjoyment enough to me; that I did not repent of what had past, for
it might have cost me as much to enjoy another. This speech exceedingly
hurt for she pretended to lament her situation & to drop a few tears: the
word vicious was what stuck to her; to her ideas that infallibly meant
lascivious: This matter was made up the next day: for I cou'd not bear to
see her uneasy, or even to live with her for ye few days she was likely to
stay with me on bad terms.

21 December After many accidents to our wheels & delays in consequence of them, we arrived this morning 5 o'clock at Paris, after having
made the most disagreeable journey that cou'd have happened to man.

22 December, Paris I askt the woman of the Hotel de Dannemare, Rue
Jacob, where we put up to accommodate me with 20 guineas for a little
while till I c^d receive remittances from England. The woman's name was
Blondel. She had lived 9 years in England – was much frequented by ye
English & talkt the Language well. She promised me the money – upon
sending to her Banker's. She cou'd be at no risk since I had so much
baggage at her house. Yet after keeping me in suspence several days,
obliging me to send repeted messengers to her, & never coming up to me
herself, in the end, she told me, that she cou'd not let me have the money
not being able to command so much: In which I took care to let others
know, that I thought myself very ill used by her.

26 December, Sunday F. & I during this time were upon tolerable terms,
but not upon the best, or so good as we afterwards were upon before she
parted from me. She had constantly frequented the theatres; amused herself in Shops, given her darling Orders to Milleners. She seemed in better
humor: but still she seemed as to the grand purpose of her heart to desert
me immovably fixt.

During this period I had some terrible inclinations in my own mind to
break off all appearances of friendship yth her. Often times I thought her
even in those few little moments of good humor, which she gave me, &

whilst she had her hand open to receive every present from my foolish generosity, that she still at heart was but dissemble, the more deeply to afflict me. At these periods my mind was upon ye Borders of distraction. One evening that devil Miss H. was cooking up some remedy [for] which she called a pultice for her foot; other ideas rushed into my head, & I cou'd not help expressing a doubt whether that was the remedy it was pretended for. This had like to produce a terrible fracas. For Miss H. did not fail to report everything of that sort, with aggravation, to her young mistress. However it past over, without farther explanations; but F. saw at once what it was that had come into my mind to suspect.

Another time at dinner F. refusing some glass that I had used, I said to her, 'If anything of mine could defile your mouth it has been defiled long ago.' I saw plainly by her eyes, that she well understood my latent meaning.

This day being Sunday ye 26th, we went to Versailles, where we saw ye Royal family, & the Count & Countess of Artois at dinner; But the King did not that Evening sup in public.

Saw in the Palace a fine display of the Royal manufacture of China at Seve, close by Versailles, there by ye favor of the King admitted to be exposed for sale. Fine, but exceedingly dear.

27–31 December During this time several little bickerings yth F. But in general I purposely kept up a Levity of Behaviour, & was upon good terms.

1774

2–4 January   F. & I were by this time got pretty well reconciled together; but still she was fixt upon first writing to her brother, before she w^d consent to live with me. Here it was her grand leading passion Pride interfered: Because the Idea of her Brother's fortune & of her own never absented itself from her mind.

Nothing seem'd to me ever to work such an effect upon Mrs M. as a serious threat I one day when alone by her Bedside made of printing & publishing to the world, in case she shd entirely turn against me in England & the marriage be set aside, the full particulars of the powers she had granted me, & of the intimate scenes that had past between us, in which not one incident shou'd be omitted, that if she was not to be esteemed a wife wou'd not leave her to be looked upon as a most lascivious whore. She took this very seriously; & indeed I meant it. She said, 'If I did so, it wou'd be publishing my shame as much as hers: & that I shd bring all the married Ladies in England upon me, by betraying the secrets of the Marriage Bed. However from this time, she visibly took a turn to wish (in appearance at least) that the marriage might be established. She came to say, that though what had past might be excused her on ye score of her youth, yet it wou'd not be excused her, she knew, that she had wished to have that marriage set aside. She grew fearful after this what might be my vengeance, in case she proceeded to say, & do the worst towards me in London. She said, she shou'd be afraid to speak to a man, without looking to see, whether he had got the pamphlet agst her in his Pocket. From this time she used to say, that I shou'd lose my love for her, when she was absent; & she began to suppose that when she offered to come back to me I should refuse to receive her.

I informed her of my intentions of going into Holland, & my reasons for it. She wanted to persuade me not to go there, saying there was no worthy cause for putting my life to a risk, and added that if I lov'd her I wou'd not be running myself into such danger.

I had previous to this took many steps to ingratiate myself yth her, & to prevent, if possible, a seperation which I was sure w^d be fatal to both of us; & if she were afterwards, to return to me, with the greatest show of fondness, the recollection of it cannot be healed, & therefore it is impossible, it shou'd ever intirely be redressed. In her most favorable moments to me, I tried if it was not possible to move in her the passion that I had often raised before & often gratified: (One day F. had been for some time sitting upon my lap, whilst I was talking tenderly to her, when she started up all of a sudden, threw herself down upon a chair, & seem'd much affected. I askt her what she was concerned at: she said, 'Because I cannot hate you.')

But in vain: she was callous to every sensation, but her own pride.

I probed her upon another score: trying to find out whether she might not have a licentious view in her seperation. I suffered my discourse to lead to this, that a married woman, who was capable of conceiving a passion for others, had this only chance of preserving her reputation by cohabiting sometimes with her husband. 'No doubt, says she, you think this reflexion will have a mighty effect upon me: but all you can say to gain this point is I assure you to no purpose.' And so I found it. Sometimes I thought she was afraid to be left with child: But this she readily denied. Then again I thought she wou'd have submitted to everything, but for the fear of being discovered by me in that respect to my sister & Mr King; of which I always assured her most strongly to ye contrary; but her doubts were not removed.

Yet sometimes I cou'd soften her so far, that she wou'd sit for hours on my lap: play with me as much as I wou'd on the couch, & let me come to her bedside of a morning, & tickle & play yth her in bed. One evening she took off her stays on my lap, shew'd me & let me feel her Breasts, talking of their being grown: but seemed again here apprehensive that I shd mention this indulgence to others. She even told me when last she had her ordinary courses (ses ordinaires) & that they were suddenly stopt, she said, on her journey to Paris by drinking a glass of Alicant wine, which she was told had an astringent quality. To prevail farther with her was beyond my power. Her pretences most uppermost always were, that it wou'd be argument greatly agst her character, & urged to convict her of Lasciviousness, if she granted me any favors, whilst she continued in the mind to separate herself from me. Yet I am apt to think there was still some secret spring she moved by, which I cou'd never touch.

5 January This day about noon arrived Broughton (Late Lord B.'s servant, & now Mr Harford's) his wife, with old Renshaw, famous for being a witness to Ld B.'s will, for having married one of his cast-off whores & for having run away with the money of the Parish of Marybone. These were the Persons sent by Mr Prevost & others to conduct according to her own desire my extraordinary young wife home. It went greatly against me to suffer her to go attended by such people. I put it to her pride; but she was determined to accept of them, & wou'd have gone I am sure, attended by a Thief. Her Brother was now ever upon her Tongue. Yet no Letter was bro^t to her from her Brother. Broughton del^{ed} [delivered] to me, a mere formal letter from Mr Prevost; I askt him if he had any others; he said 'No', yet he soon after del^{ed} to my wife a letter from her poor silly mother, directed to Miss Harford: This she now readily opened, which at Wansbeck, she had too much regard for her honor, not to refuse to do. This letter run in the strain of assuring that there was none, who w^d not at her return both love & pity her: that by her she shd always be well received, whilst she behaved with prudence: & that she might be sure that the whole past, wou'd be laid to the score of her youth, & soon be forgot & forgiven by the world. This letter F. immediately shew'd me.

F. askt Mrs Broughton, whether people were not a good deal surprized at what had now come to pass. She answer'd her, 'It was what everybody expected, & what everybody wished.' I took care to let this good woman know that while she staid under the same roof with me, she must take care to keep her tongue within some decent bounds. I askt Broughton, whether he claimed any authority to take my wife away, if I did not permit it; & he said, 'No'. Yet though I always was resolved to suffer my wife, to return to England when she insisted upon it, I took care to let her know, it was without my approbation she went; I entreated her to stay to the last wch she refused & she refused to let me attend her.

7 January This day F. departed. The day before we dined together at Mr Rosenhagen's, Hotel de Tours, Rue de Paon. F. was serious, but not said [sad]. For a few days, when the moment of departure approached to a certainty she seemed fond of me. She intreated me to keep up a correspondence with her; she promised to write to me constantly of everything that passed. She wou'd not go, as she said, to a public place of diversion without acquainting me; & what I disapproved, She wou'd admit. She had visited with me during her stay at Paris some Jewellers shops, by way of amusement in seeing their goods. There she took care to fall in love with diamond hair pins to the value altogether of 56½ guineas: which

I with my foolish pride & passion of gratifying every wish cou'd not hesitate to present to her. After the possession of these presents she became in appearance a good deal softened to me: But I was cautioned by Mr King & my sister agst deception; and if she acted in this strange matter by any rule or principle, besides Caprice & Pride, I shd suspect her of the deepest dissimulation. F. began also to set her heart upon the wish of appearing in a little white Sattin trimm'd with Sable: and there too I c^d not help, though at the Expence of 20 guineas, conceding to her inclinations. It hurt my sister from her regard to me & my family to see me throw away money (the loss of wch at this time cou'd not fail to distress me) upon so ungrateful an object: but it never hurt me to bestow anything the most costly upon one, whom I had so long so tenderly loved.

Coming back from Mr Rosenhagen's on Fr. ye 7th I stept out of the Coach into the Coffee-house thinking it best to cut as short as possible the cruel seperation that was going to take place. My Eyes cou'd never have borne the moment of her departure. I took no leave, & thought I had fortitude enough to bear what was coming on but I miscalculated my own strength & giving way to weakness, in the midst of the Coffee-house I burst into a flood of tears, I hurried to desire ye waiter to shew me into a private room; he abruptly told me he had none; & shocked at his indifference I instantly recover'd the former possession of myself; & since that have not known any farther weakness on the subject. The waiter hasten'd to feel about my breast to see if I had not been wounded in a duel: the only thought I suppose that c^d come into a Frenchman's head, as I was drest in an uniform. I passed it off as well as I cou'd & pointing to my head rather than to my heart, I laid the cause to a disturbed imagination.

7–8 January At night I lay at the Hotel d'Artois, Cul de sac Coq, near the St Honoré side of the Louvre; where I had taken temporary accommodations. I had resolved to lay abed till Mr King shou'd come & inform the next morning that all was past & over. About 11 (Sat. ye 8th) he came, not to tell me that they were gone, but that having neglected before to inquire after a passport, they had now sent for one to Versailles. The necessity of this had already come into my head: though I never thought to advertise them of it the day before.

This morning arrived letters from Mr & Mrs Parish relative to this unhappy affair: That from Mrs Parish to Mrs M. was sent opened, with an express desire, that I wou'd read it before it was deliver'd, & soften any expressions which the Change of Circumstances might render necessary. I read it, with pleasure & astonishment. It is really divine composition; & coming intirely from ye heart, it is as striking an instance of the Pathetic,

as ever I remember. It came into my head that F. from her natural intention to what was good & serious might give Mrs P.'s letter a more careless
perusal than it deserved; & laying it casually by, it might soon come to
perish, without it making that impression upon her mind, which it
deserved & was so well calculated to effect. I therefore, though I saw
nothing in it to correct & much less to soften, made a Copy of it; which
had been a great consolation to me ever since: Because it gives me ever an
opportunity in my own justification to add the authority of another to my
own assertions, whenever I speak of former transactions between me &
Mrs M. as a letter received from her this morning does of the late occur-
rence. The Conclusions from both most manifest is that the origin of this
seperation is to be drawn from Fanny's fickleness & not my misconduct.
I desired Mr King to deliver Mrs P.'s letter to Mrs M. & at the same time
to add, that it was my most earnest, nay my last request that she shou'd
attentively peruse it; 'saying of it, that there was not a sentence that ought
not to be written upon her heart.' Yet was this request urged in the most
forcible manner afterwards by Mr King all in vain. She open'd the letter,
read 3 or 4 of the first lines then hastily turning over to ye Conclusion saw
there Mrs Parish's pathetic exclamations upon my sister's feeling for her
brother. 'O! poor Miss Morris, indeed, says she, I wonder what Mrs
Parish wou'd think yth her advice' & then she threw the letter without
farther perusal in the fire. Yet, this same young creature, laughing &
giggling at that moment, had been crying most desperately all the night
before after I had left her & had this morning only been addressing me in
the most tender & affectionate manner as the only relief for ye Load of
anxiety which lay upon my mind.

I drest myself, & gave a call upon Mr Rosenhagen; by way of talking
with him over all this affair. Mr Rosenhagen, is a clergyman enjoying
benefices in England, bred at Cambridge & once a great friend & acquaintance of the Rev^d Mr Horne, who had long ago given me an extraordinary
character of his classical abilities. I found him a very sensible man; &
I heard some in Paris give him the credit of having written the celebrated
letters signed Junius; nor do I think the imputation groundless, as well
from some circumstances I can recollect, as from the visible powers of his
genius. My first acquaintance with him at Paris was made at the Winter
Vauxhall. He married in November last at the Dutch Chapel in this city,
to a sister of the celebrated Mrs Garnier, & his Lady I found a very agreable
accomplished woman. I explained the whole [of] my affairs to Rosenhagen, who as a man of the world instantly gave me very wholesome
friendly advice. He insisted upon it, I shd not have let the young creature

go: I shou'd have acquainted him at the first yth ye affair, he with his wife, Lady Lambert & other Ladies, wou'd have come about her & plagued or joked her out of her resolution of departure. If there was doubt of our marriage, he wou'd not have minded any of the censure of discourse, but have married us himself here, & his marriage w^d have been good, he said, for he was a Clergyman. He little knew my wishes or my feelings. I wanted no possession of her, but with her inclination & above all I despised the idea of her fortune. If I had chosen to take his advice or wanted any assistance to detain her, it was not yet too late; for by that time she was not departed. It was only 2 o-clock this afternoon she set out. Mr Rosenhagen, said at the first moment that there must be some intrigue in ye moment, some other whom she liked better. Here again he spoke, as a man of ye world: But I won't be so blinded with prejudice to my own hopes & wishes to say positive that he spoke wrong. Rosenhagen offer'd me every assistance in his power; but when I informed him afterwards, that I was a good deal distrest for present cash because every demand was now coming upon me since Mrs M.'s departure he took care to tell Mr King, that 'this money was a devil of a thing: and no man thinks of ye necessity of it, till he finds it.' 'Why, do you know sir, says he, that there is no man in the world, that will lend ano^r a guinea.' However I have no occasion to quarrel with a man who refuses to lend me money; nor did I ever ask Rosenhagen to lend me any; though I did ask him to indorse a Bill upon Mr Parish for ye sum of 200 guineas; which at first he promised; afterwards retracted; & again, when he found I cou'd not get such a bill with his name negotiated here, he offered to do so. However we are upon very good terms together; and his Lady is very polite & obliging to my sister. N.B. Mrs M. took ye little child from Zell yth her & talked of leaving her at a Convent at Calais.

9 January After F.'s departure.

10–13 January This time I spent at the Hotel d'Artois; in a most recluse way; but in good spirits. I lay abed every day till about noon; then King came to give me a call. My time was always employed in writing accounts to my friends of the late strange event which had happened. I wrote particularly a very long account of everything to Mr Parish. To many I enclosed Copies of Mrs Parish's letter & of Mrs M.'s. I never went out in ye day. Towards night I began to creep a little. I had some reason to be afraid of creditors, as Mrs M. had run me into such great expences during her stay here; and now upon her departure they were all coming upon my back. One, for the Sable, I was obliged to appease for ye moment with the delivery of my Watch & my Gold Stock Buckle into his hands. We had but a few guineas left for our ready cash; & we were almost reduced to our last guinea before I rec^{ed} a supply from my Brother. Sr Jno Lambert refused to advance me any, either by way of Loan (in advance of the expectation of remittance) or upon my draught, in London or Hamburgh. Yet Sr Jno Lambert knew a good deal of me. I had £500 credit upon him, at first coming abroad: And when I came here first this time he did advance me 30 guineas, till I c^d receive a remittance; wch I soon did of £50 from Mr Thos. Lockwood & thus he was repaid.

I now took heart to quit my retreat at the Hotel d'Artois, & returned to the Hotel Dannemare where Mr King & my sister were left but where I own I had a great dread of returning because I had also left another there, who was now no more to be found. Fortunately I did not return to reside in the same rooms, which she had inhabited.

14–15 January In these days I called upon ye several people I owed money to; by my appearance & discourse made them pretty easy.

16 January, Sunday Today, to our great relief we rec^{ed} a remittance of £100 from my Brother.

17 January Now made all my creditors at Paris satisfied paying several of them in part or in ye whole.

18 January I went with King to Odineau's the spectacle of young actors – excellent little Harlequins.

19 January Was at the Italian Comedy, once more to my great satisfaction to see that most excellent actor my friend Carlin, the speaking Harlequin.

20 January Went to see that fine piece of flat-arched architecture the Bridge of Nieully. Went yth King, Mann (the King's Messenger) & one White, a poor thievish rawbone Irishman. We dined there, & Paddy-whack, after drinking a Bottle of wine almost out, filled it up with water, insisted it was bad, & changed it for another. I saw the Paris Vauxhall in my way: & a very pretty elegant place it is.

21 January Dined at Mann's Hotel Victoire, upon an invitation we c^d not avoid. Never knew such Blackguards as he & all his company.

22 January This day I finished the journal here kept which had not been regularly carried on ever since I left Geneva, though some few memorandums I had preserved. I have nothing to add relative to Mrs M.'s desertion of me, than that at her going away, she said to Mr King, who handed her to ye Chaise, 'Well, if I ever do live with Mr Morris, which I think I shall, I do declare I will never have anything to say to any of his family, who are a set of —— I won't say what.' This was to justify herself, for having for sometime behaved ill-mannerly & untenderly to my sister.

23 January, Sunday   Still employ'd in writing letters. It was a great task to me, the copying over so many times as I did Mrs M.'s letter to me, & Mrs. P.'s to her.

24 January   Only trifling matters.

25 January   Have got up constantly very late of a morning, since F. had been gone. I have had myself sometimes happier moments, when I c^d doze away my reflexions. In the day time I have been usually industrious enough: Since Mrs M. has been gone I have had a great occasion to write, and a great deal I have written. Today I wrote some letters; & I prepared some Papers for Holland.

26–27 January   Employed much in the same manner, mostly writing. Translated Mrs P.'s letter into French. Thursday begun fencing yth Mr Parquier, Rue Fromanteau, by ye old Louvre. Went to his school at night. Fence there with Iron cage masks to prevent accidents to the Face. Pay him 3 livres a lesson.

28–29 January   Called upon Ldy Lambert. She knew Ld Baltimore well, & said, if any man was ever mad he was. She thought Mrs M. appeared so too. She farther acquainted me that Mrs M. had now upon her return to England, declared that I had never lain with her. She showed a disposition towards that malice & falsehood before she went. She said to Miss Hodgson, when she was dressing her, to swear I had not, What signifies an oath? These words my sister overheard from an adjoining room at Geneva: And soon after asking Miss H. what they were about she told her, that Mrs M. has been pressing her to swear that I had never lain with her: but wch she told her she never cou'd nor w^d do for her. I told Mrs M. the last thing almost before she went away, that I w^d forgive anything but never supporting such a falsehood, when she came to England, because it was a falsehood no man w^d bear. She made no reply.

30 January, Sunday   Went yth ye fencing master to ye Convent of Carmelites (Les Carmes) said to be rich. Large Garden in Paris near Luxemburgh: piece of ground in this part of Paris occupied by Gardens. Convent mean & insignificant in appearance. The order make a vow to eat only fish & vegetables: i.e. maigre yet make great Debauches in y^r maigre. Wine to excess; for that is still maigre. Have 3 or 4 courses & eat maigre as much as they please out of ye Convent: In it when they want to regale they sham being ill, & feast away, according to y^r own fancy. Walkt in ye Luxemburg Gardens. Large & fine. Much company. I knew ye Luxemburg Palace again from what I had remembered of it in Jan. 1769. There is a noble gallery of Paintings there but I never saw it. Went this evening to see Wildman exhibit his bees – Hotel Bayonne Rue St

Honoré – As soon as I came into the Room, I boldly handled ye Bees, taking them up as so many flies – & in that way they did not hurt me. Wildman soon came, into ye Room, with ye Bees on his arm; afterwards yth a swarm on his face & head. He had Barnacles* on; pretended only; that they might not tickle his Eyelids; not y^t [that] he was afraid of stinging them. He shook them off his head upon a table, by giving a jump, & at same time forcibly shaking his head downwards. He put them on his head & arm, in another room out of our sight. Will not let anyone see him take ye Bees out of the hive. He did one Experiment, of putting them upon any person's Hat, from a hive; before I came into ye Room. I pretended to doubt the Bees c^d sting & to surprise the Frenchman was resolved manually to prove it. I took one, & handled him roughly till he stung me. I saw Wildman's Mahogany (Glass) Boxes; for Beehives; very curious. Also ordinary hives, to stand upon another yth a trap Door, & so take ye Honey without destroying the Bees. This Wildman set up for a Conjuror, in Competition yth Jonas & others in London. He has some of his Conjuror's actions about him relative to ye Bees; for when he pretended, that the Bees w^d not go into ye hive, when he ordered them not, he turn'd & put the hive in a different manner, than when they afterwards went in: yet he pretended it was ye same. He has lately travelled, over a great deal of France. About 8 or 10 spectators. Goes out to exhibit in private houses in ye daytime. I bro^t by accident in my Cloathes home a Bee, & an hour after, putting my hand upon my thigh, & pressing unawares ye Bee, he stung me very violently; much more than ye other had done at Wildman's. Others of ye Company had shown themselves fearful of carrying home some of ye Bees; yet Wildman had ye assurance to insist that if they did the Bees w^d not hurt them. I put ye one that stung me under a glass, took care it should have air: It died in about a couple of hours. I tried after it had stung me, whether it c^d sting me again, which I found it c^d not. They have this sting behind in ye skin.

31 January, Monday Consumed the day in preparing for our journey from Paris. Cou'd not settle ye price of the Lodging at the Hotel. Mrs Blondel a damned canting Bitch – offered me at 4½ Gs per week, for ye whole 2d floor: declared I w^d give no more than 4. To induce me to give 4½ had the impudence to charge 5. I left at the rate of 4½ yth Mr Pasquié, Sr John Lambert's Clerk to pay them. The matter they agreeing to have settled after I was gone. They supplied us yth some infamous Bourgogne wine (for it does not deserve to be called Burgundy), at 2 livres a Bottle, which was not worth 15 sous. Mr Pasquié told me that nowadays no

* Spectacles (slang).

prudent regular people ever put up, at Hotels & that at any future time he c^d take me a very good Lodging in a private house at one guinea a week. This Pasquié offered me every civility. Refused to take a present of half-a-guinea, which I presented to him, & even prest upon him. Wou'd not let me leave money in his hands for future portage; & even offered to pay several small sums to the amount of about 4 or 5 guineas for me, wch I c^d not settle before I went. He declared, he shd have a real pleasure in serving me; & so I do believe: yet why I cannot tell; unless he had conceived a prejudice in my favor by report. His master Sr John Lambert seems to me to be as arrant a Jew as ever I met with in my life. Rosenhagen called in the Ev^g – Said, he w^d soon go to London if it was for no other cause, than to call to account that impudent Printer who had inserted a paragraph of his being the author of Junius. Yet to me, he seemed (notwithstanding all the bustle he made) inwardly pleased with the flattery of that assertion.

We finished all our packing & went to bed at 2 in ye morning.

1 February, Tuesday I awaked myself at 4 in expectation of ye Coach, which soon after came. About 5 set off. Past through St Germains; but was asleep. Heard there are still many Irish families there; who came to take up their residence yth James the 2d. Sister very ill yth a swelled Jaw. Country nothing remarkable. Lay at a village.

2 February, Wednesday. Candlemas day. Le Chandeleur, ou la Chandeleuse. Set off this morning at 4. Sister very sick. Past through no great Town. Country began to be pleasanter. A fine River (le Dure, ou la Rivière d'Ure) on ye right hand; running at the foot of some steep Chalk hills – to ye left a pleasant Bottom. Much overflow'd. My sister's face broke on ye inside, & she was much easier & better. Had formed to herself great apprehension of its breaking on ye outside; and these apprehensions made her lowspirited, & so greatly augmented her illness. Arrived at Rouen about 7. Put up at the Hotel Vatel. Seems good hotel & reasonable. Cost a guinea apiece for ye Diligence; which they call a Berlin; & holds only 4, which places we filled. Had our own keeping to find; which in some part of France is found for the price paid for ye Diligence. Distance from Paris 14½ posts . . . 29 Leagues. 2 days, same horses. Coachman had the impudence to expect & ask 3 livres apiece from each of us for Drink money. I gave him a Crown of 6 livres; & think I gave him too much. Cold & wind high.

3 February Had a good deal to do to put all our things in order. One Trunk packt off for London per ye Mary, Brigantine, Captn Dunn, directed to me at Mr Symonds together yth a case containing a gun & silver sword. Called upon Mr Louis Durand to whom address with a small credit from Sr Jno L. Received us very civilly; & willing to assist us about ye convent for my sister. Rouen presents a fine prospect to ye River side. River rapid & wide. A good many ships. Fine Gothic Cathedral, in ye Canterbury stile. The Normans architecture very similar to many instances in England. This is a Cyder Country; & the houses, built much with wood, & puts one much in mind of ye houses in Herefordshire. A maskt Ball here at a shilling a head entrance. Weather cold & wind still very high.

4 February This morning Mr King & I called upon Mr La Fosse (Moisson) at the Poste Royale Hotel. Yesterday he had run purposely agst me, on the street, as I was standing still with Mr King & talking to my servant. I askt him what he meant by that, & if there was not room enough to pass. He said something about affronting a Frenchman: & putting his hand on his sword, said, 'Voulez vous venir?' He was at this time so exceedingly drunk, that he c^d not speak plain. At first I was in a passion at his putting his hand to his sword, & had great mind to have drawn mine: wch Mr King seeing he said to me 'Laissez-le, il est Sou.' [?fou]'. Then he turn'd to King, & askt him what he said. King replied, 'Je dis que vous etes sou. Allez.' He retorted Allez with an angry tone of voice; However he went away as we walked on. It wou'd at that time have been a pity & almost a shame to have drawn a sword upon him; so drunk he was: However since, I am sorry I did not; as he showed by his subsequent conduct he w^d have deserved it. In the evening of yesterday we went to the Caffe de l'opera: We had [not] been there long, before in comes this drunken fellow, though at that time, not so drunk as he was. The first of us two who struck his eye was King. To him he immediately says 'Estceque c'est vous qui m'avez offensé dans la rue?' Upon wch King said, 'Monsieur que voulez vous?' And at that time ye other replied nothing; but he went & spoke to one of his acquaintance in the coffee house, one almost as drunk as himself & then he came back to Mr King, put his hand upon his sword & again said, 'Voulez vous venir.' Mr King told him, that if he had anything to say to him, let him learn his name, & he w^d give him his. They mutually did so; and this morning we called together at his Hotel; when we found him abed: but we had inquired first, at the Coffee house, whether he was a Gentleman, where we were assured he was so, though a drunken one. In short we found his character to be just as King said it was: a young fellow of some fortune who was now spending it as fast as he cou'd among a set of Blackguards.

When we called at his apartment in the Hotel, we found this young fellow abed. He said he knew what we were come for, though he had lost the direction we gave him. He got up, & seem'd still drunk. He cou'd not say whether we had offended him, or he us: however he wou'd give us satisfaction: & a little bleeding of a morning wou'd not hurt either of us: I askt him, whether it was me or Mr King he intended to go out with: He said Both of us: I askt him: what both at a time? He said, as we pleased. Since then he neither wou'd nor cou'd particularize either, I proposed to King to toss for him; He that won upon the call of a Crown, being to have his life. It fell to King's share. Being always convinced it was a foolish matter, & that no real offence, worthy of the least consideration, had past on either side I now more than ever thought it incumbent upon me to have the matter accommodated; yet so as with honor. I said that as the Lot had fallen upon my friend, & I was no longer concerned in it, I cou'd now more freely speak my sentiments, that it was a foolish affair & did not deserve a duel. This young Frenchman however kept talking on in his old foolish stile; so that King thought it best to put a stop to this conversation by asking him, whether he meant to joke with him (badiner). You shall see that soon says the young Frenchman, still almost drunk & apparently affected by ye Liquor of yesterday. 'Non, je ne changerai jamais.' He begun to sing, as he had done the night before at the Coffee house: At which he took his sword up from the Table, & walk'd out. King followed him: I came after, & so did a most blackguard thief looking dog, who we found in ye Room, as seconds. This fellow had quite the appearance of a shabby whore's bully, & another fellow, whom we also saw there, seemed with him to be preying upon ye foolish extravagant drunken young fellow. Whilst we had been sitting in ye room they had begun a conversation upon Gaming, which undoubtedly makes a principal part of their profession. In walking out of the Town, this shabby second to the Frenchman askt me, whether my friend c^d fence well. I told him, he understood to manage his sword, but nothing extraordinary. 'Because I assure you, says he, l'autre tire joliment.' 'Cela se pourra.' I replied.

Finding this did not take he soon after said to me, 'Have you a mind that you & I shd put an end to this affair.' 'Yes says I, I have, being of the same sentiments from ye beginning, that it is a foolish, groundless quarrel, & does not deserve the risk that both are going to put themselves to.' I said no more, & was resolved not to interfere again; because I began now to suspect, that it was never designed by ye young Frenchman's friends that there shd be any duel in ye matter. The intended combatants took their ground on a very retired spot at the Bottom of a Bank. The Frenchman stript; & opened his breast, to show he had no false cover there:

King prepared to do ye same. At that moment up comes the young Frenchman's second between them with a handkerchief tied with a knot, into a round, the meaning of which I cou'd not then nor since comprehend: He then askt them, whether either had cause of offence agst the other (whch he long before knew neither had, except that his principal had given ye Challenge). They both as they cou'd not help, were ready to answer no, they acknowledged each other for Gallants hommes shook hands, & there was an end of the Duel: But it was very observable, that the young Frenchman was much more reasonable at the moment than he had been before. I cou'd not help soon after forming an idea, that the young Frenchman's seconds & friends were in perfect understanding together, that there shd be no duel; and that the whole was contrived with a design to flatter this young Fellow, that he was a man of courage, & with a curiosity to prove ours. We adjourned from this bloodless field to the Coffee-house; when the young frenchman in his usual stile, treated us all, with preserved Apricots, which or something similar, smacking of the Brandy, I suppose his usual breakfast. He askt us to dinner; but we chose to decline the invitation. His name is la Fosse, Moisson; and he & his family of Caen in Normandy. We called again afterwards in the Coffee-house; & met with some fellows who w^d have talked to us upon the morning's affair: But we shunned their conversation; however they w^d force upon us to hear them say, that our adverse party acknowledged us to be very gallant young fellows, & that they were very well contented with us. Packt off a trunk & ye Gun, per Capt. Dunn for England. Was obliged to pay at the Customhouse, 5p^r Cent, upon ye value we set upon the Gun; which I put at 50 livres: & also a smaller duty of so much, in ye pound for what it weighed, amounting in this latter charge only to 8 sous in the whole for the permit to about 4 or 5 livres.

Enquired & found there was no permission to go out shooting near the Town: Two English Merchants (Mr Morris of Manchester, Qu? and another) keep a pack of hounds, & with permission of the Lord of the Seignory go out hunting twice a week. Mr Durand supt yth me. Were at the Play, to see the Frenchman in London. One Character called Jack Roastbeef. In that name seem'd all ye joke of the Piece: altogether very foolish.

5 *February* Frost decreasing. Wrote Letters; & did not go out till the afternoon.

6 *February* Fine day. Yet staid at home, writing till one o-clock. Then walk'd out. After Dinner the streets, Bridge & walks, full of Masqueraders in low life. Good Figures: Crowds of people. Finished today the great

concern of settling all my affairs in case of Death. Sister went out for ye first time.

7 February Wrote some matters in ye morning. Dined at Mr Louis Durand: well & civilly treated. French Ladies familiar; & too much so; Conceived the idea of disposing of my sister there. Was at a lowlived Play in a Booth; Harlequin. Sister dined yth us; & now may be said to be well again.

8 February The morning employ'd in writing: & I may add the afternoon too. Mr Durand & his Clerk a Spaniard supt with us.

9 February The morning employ'd in writing. Entred into a Discourse with Mr Durand about accommodating my Sister at his house; which he & his Lady agreed to; but we did not enter into particulars of the charge.

10 February Wrote a little in ye morning. Dined at Mr Durand's. Went to Mr Picard's Fencing school. Very good master. Agreed for 24 sous (1 Shill^g Eng.) a session; both of us.

11 February Wrote in ye morning. Fenced at Piccard's an excellent Master. Bought a Black Wolf Dog yesterday of a Routier of Lyons, for half a guinea, who, after he had sold him me, cried, & begged to be off ye Bargain. The first opportunity this afternoon, he run out of ye Door, & took ye high road to Lyons, after his former master, who set out last night an hour after he sold him me. It rained so exceedingly hard I c^d not instantly follow him, & afterwards c^d not find him. I sent after him & he w^d not let the man pick him up, & he escaped again; never to return. He was very like Spits. Such a faithful Dog ought to be yth his old Master.

12 February King went out a Hunting. Mr . . . an English Gentleman keeping hounds here; 18 couple; good ones. Fenced again. Packt up partly ye Trunk. My Sister went to Durand's. We supt there.

13 February Wrote a long Letter to Geo Jones [his solicitor] & sent several of my Matrimonial papers. Walkt out: Fine walks & prospects near the Town: The most agreeable place I have yet seen in France. People foolishly mad after masquerades in ye Street; these latter days of Gras. Made a present to Mrs Durand of a fine Pheasant: Cost 6 livres. A Holland's Captain & his Interpreter call'd in the Evening; Half drunk, when they came, we afterwards made them quite so. The Dog, Loup, Spits, Wolf, whom I thought set off for Lyons, found again. Supt at Durand; When [went] to the Masqued Bal, at ye Playhouse. Great number of good characters. Quite full – & the best Masquerade I ever saw. Staid till 6 or 7 in ye morning. Had a dispute with a French officer. I happen'd lightly to hit his tie near ye Fireplace. I begg'd excuse: He seem'd to scan me over yth his eye, in a manner that made me resolve to try, whether he w^d be civil to me or not: so I took occasion to observe to him something about a mask, when instead of answering me upon it, he begun to hum a tune. So I askt him, whether he sung to affront me. His answer was that he sung: which put me a good deal in mind of ye Quarrel in Shakespeare, about a man's biting his Thumb. We had a little conversation, but I soon afterwards left him; when meeting yth young De la Fosse, I took him for my Counsellor, who, as is his usual way has but one advice to give – 'Il faut lui faire foutre le Champ.' Accordingly I went again to him, & told him, if he sung to affront me, I was come to ask the reason of it. He begun explaining, & addressing his Companions about; & our conversation some[how] or other had a pause: However the Commandant of ye House interfered; & no more came of it.

14 February Mr La Fosse, & a friend of his, a Lieutenant in ye Marechaussie dined yth us; & we afterwards supt with him. Continued fencing. It was Wensday or Thursday last we begun. I improve a good deal. Piccard ye best master I ever knew. Mounted the top of the Cathedral. A very large bell – a foot thick in metal. People here tell you a foolish old tale, of a Jay, that used to steel silver cups &c from a Silversmith in ye Churchyard, & carry them up to the steeple – upon suspicion of ye theft the Silversmith's maid was hanged – Afterwards things still continuing to be missed, the Pie was watched & discovered. Upon wch ye Silversmith founded a perpetual Mass called La Messe de la Pie, which is still continued to be celebrated under that name every day in the Cathedral at noon.

15 February Wrote a little in ye morning. Vext yth ye receiving of Letters* – am resolved to retire from them. Mr Urrar a young Merchant (with his father) at this place, called in the Evening with some Magazines. A very good natured young fellow: indeed too much so to be to me agreable. Walkt together up to the Gallows: 3 skeletons hanging. The Wolf Dog's collar lost: pickt it up himself at returning & we found it in his mouth. La Fosse supt yth us, tired of him and went to a Ball. My sister there. Home by 2 in ye M^g.

16 February Sister not well. She staid up too long at the Ball. Fenced as usual. Smoked in ye Evening. Am resolved to learn to smoke by degrees that I may not be put to inconveniences in that respect.

17 February Went to y^r [their] English Chase, by Mr Lally's house, brother or Heir of the unfortunate Count Lally. Handsome convent of Carthusian monks. How it makes one's blood boil to see such vile dogs live in Palaces. Mr Holker – a partner yth Garvay in ye hounds – both

* On 14 February one from Miss Hodgson. Not answered.

known figures. This Holker, has set up the Manchester Cotton Manufacture here, & employs 900 hands. Lately established for his son Vitriol manufacture. Has ye Croix de St Louis having served a very little while in ye Army. Is Inspector of all the foreign manufactures in France. Came to Rouen yth only £10 in his pocket: was patronised by Choiseul.

Saw a little run after hare. Left them to return home to write & continue my Fencing. King stay'd & saw a Fox killed. Towards the latter end of the Chace, there were 8 or 10 English there. Patrick Blake was one, who married Miss Garland, & lives in a village close there – near Rouen: his Lady with him, till she comes of age: Said his Lady knows me (as she well did) & wᵈ be glad to see me & Mr King. One Mr Biddulph (a good natured young fellow of Sussex) out too: One very intimate with Urrar. The cook of this house, who knocked a Louis out of Jack's hand condemned by ye Lieutenant de Police to make it good. Sister dined with us. She is now well again. The Loup (Dog) becomes acquainted, & now follows well. Sent off this evening all ye copies of Mrs M.'s Mrs P.'s, & my letters. Smoaked a bit of Pipe in ye Evening. Out of sorts & spirits for some time. Jack not ye better for gaining his cause of ye Louis agst the Cook: the Law too expensive to be put in Execution; & the Cook only answerable by his goods, of wch he has none.

18 February Fenced as usual & wrote. All writing Business now pretty near done; & I must decamp. Mr Hurard [?Urrar] Mr Biddulph & Mr Bellesta (the Spaniard Clerk to Mr Durand) supt upon my invitation here. Called upon the young Mr Bachelier – acquaintance of Chalman's, to whom I had been civil in London. Left my name, but no return of visit from him. Executed my last will – Messrs Hurard, Biddulph & King, Witnesses. De la Fosse also supt here. Wᵈ give me his sword.

19 February Went a hunting. Rode as madly as I cᵈ with de la Fosse, through the streets &c joining our hands, on purpose to try his spunk. Garvay knew I had executed my will last night; & upon seeing me ride my Brute of attack horse over a Ditch, where he came down, upon his belly, he said, I had good reason to execute my will. Good hunting the year round. In May leave off Hares for Foxes. Then the Chevreuil or roebuck for ye summer – this Chevreuil common in Scotland & well known in Darbyshire. There is an original race of Norman Hounds, very good at Staghunting. We took a hare today; which was given to the Dogs because it was Lent time. Called at Mr Blake's, but he & his Lady were walk'd out to Rouen. Biddulph who supt yth us last night an English Roman Catholic: as the other English at the Hunt were. Wᵈ not for ye world touch a bit of meat in Lent: & make a rule to eat no breakfast.

Prepar'd again the Trunk for setting off. After dinner Captn Osborne, whom I had seen in ye summer of 1772 at Wansbeck call'd upon me: He has been resident here 6 months – Had his wife yth him: now sent her to England: Expects to go out a Commissary in ye East Indies. And as to the Bill he had given Woolfe, for many advanced to him, of wch I went part, he said it had never been presented in London or w^d have been paid so c^d still whenever Captn Wolfe w^d send the Bill for payment, together with some things which he left behind with him upon his saying he shd bring them to London: of wch I think he mentioned a sword for one: I askt him if I shd write as much to Mr Parish, & he said yes. Was to have supt by invitation yth La Fosse; but he disappointed us, & did not sup at home. He has my sword wch I begin to fear for. Will have nothing more to do yth him.

20 February, Sunday Packt up the Trunk & deliver'd this book with my will & some other papers into ye custody of Mr Durand, for fear of the dangers of the Seas.

Huzza!

F.'s Sayings &c; & mems. of F.

1773

*7 January** I said, 'Your Mamma when she sees you will say, "How cou'd you think of marrying at your age?" Then I wou'd say to her, said she, "How cou'd you *not* think of not marrying at my age?" '
N.B. I qu: if Mrs H.† was much older when first connected with Lord B.

11 January Observing me buried with my papers, all lying about me – She said, 'You men, have your amusement in papers, just the same as we have in Laces, Blend &c.'

I askt her, which she thought the rational & useful?'

She answered – 'Perhaps one as much as the other.'

7 February A secret‡ – Now I can b.y.c.e. This is meant as a Mem or ——.

17 February Burst into Tears, & shed them a long while upon recollection of ye loss of her father – as she had several times done before. Bless her feeling heart.

19 February I said to her in fun, 'Let you & I disguise ourselves as Pilgrims, & go about the world seeking our fortune.'

Her answer was, That wou'd be silly, to be *seeking* our fortune, when we have *found* it.

28 March 'Said she had been talking to Miss Hodgson about religion.' I afterwards took occasion to say to Miss H. thus – 'Don't talk to Mrs M. about religion. She is young. Your conversation will not instruct. She does not want to have her mind improved by you. If every old woman, or young Woman – are to give lectures upon religion, what is the order of ye Clergy set apart for? What you can say, may only fill her mind with vain superstitions; But if you are unavoidably led into ye discourse – Say no more than this – 'Read the Scriptures: & follow what is there directed. For the rest go to Church: & do as other people of good character do.'

In this I hope & believe I was right.

May Upon asking me which was ye most chearful of my sisters, I answer'd, 'None of them were very chearful'.

'Oh that is a pity, said she; *young persons shd always be chearful.*'

June Having seen the Madhouse at Zell she said to me the next morning in Bed, 'I think I shall sometime or other be mad, & pray do not let me be put in such a house as that, if I shd be so.'

I said, that she shd not allow herself to speak of such a thing: But if the misfortune was to arrive, that her condition of life w^d put her above that: And that besides, I did not believe that by the Laws of England I shd any more have ye power of putting her in such a place, than by my own disposition I shd have the conscience of doing it. To one part she replied that where we are intimate, you know, we like to mention every thought that arrives.

July F. is much afraid to be alone in the Dark. Of this she was speaking one Day

---

* Four days after the second marriage.
† Fanny's mother.
‡ The day after registration of *.' Now I can *bargain ye certificate entry*'.

saying 'I cannot conceive the reason, why I am afraid: I do not believe in Ghosts, yet when alone in the dark I cannot help filling my fancy with them. That guilty people shd apprehend the sight of apparitions, is no wonder: The Ghost that troubles them is their own Conscience. But thank God, I am not one of those guilty people, & yet I am afraid!' I thought, this was a proper opportunity for introducing, what Burke has said in his Essay on ye Sublime upon this head, deriving very truly the source of this fear from the natural effect which the absence of Light produces on ye human frame, upon which the mind naturally runs into a melancholy association of ideas. But I was fearfull, that I shd be obliged in explaining this, to introduce terms of art, that w^d render my discourse a little too intricate. Perhaps to get rid of this fear, it requires as well a strong frame of Body as a strong mind.

July I said in Joke to her, as is often said 'Do you know who is Lord & Master here?'

'Yes (says she) it is you: and I am Lady & Mistress.'

We were alone – & I was speaking of ye little girl child* we had – So I said, 'I can make a better child than that of a piece of Stick.'

She retorted very jocularly & well, 'It appears you can make a better one of Stick, than you can of flesh.'

23 September She held a most sensible & pleasing conversation yth me: in which it was doubtful which was most conspicuous, the sense or the beauty of her expressions. Her task was to give me lessons of improvement in behaviour. A sweet instructress I thought her. Whilst she spoke it was impossible not to be of her opinion, & afterwards one w^d be so, but for ye weakness of one's nature. One of her expressions was – 'From being rough we become *rude*; so that no friendship will justify the excess of familiarity.'

1774

8 January Parted from my dear Tormentor; Received her affectionate though unaccountable Letter; with the inclosed Card of direction; communicated to her from that Creature Miss H.

Mr John Morris, Chinaman, N. 42, Great Queen Street Lincoln's Inn Fields.

N.B. Besides the letter from F. wch I have copied there was a Postscript thus:

Don't forget to send me your picture. The enclosed is the direction. The letter was written at Paris from the Hotel Dannemare. Jan. 1774. The same day F. set out for England.

I was then at another hotel, having lain there the night before.

21 January F. appeared before the Chancellor in Lincoln's Inn Hall. Was quite composed.

List of all the books read by F. Before F. came with me abroad:

1 The seven champions.
2 Arabian nights.

* Probably Elizabeth mentioned on 10 July 1773, whom Robert thought 'rather clumsy about ye shoulders'.

3 Persian Tales.
4 The Bible all through.
5 Some Grecian History.
6 Some Roman d°.
7 Some English d° in one thick Vol. 8vo.

After she came abroad has read:

8 Robinson Crusoe.
9 Clarissa.
10 Joseph Andrews.
11 Don Quixotte.
12 Tom Jones.
13 Amelia.
14 Pamela.
15 Sterne's sentimental Tour. (part)
16 Gay's poems. (part)
17 Reliques of Ancient Poetry. (part)
18 Rowe's tragedies. (part)
19 Roderick Random.

N.B. Perhaps it may here be observed that the second collection of reading is not so good as the first: Yet the second is not bad, being all the best models in this kind. F. has a vast appetite for stories. This proceeds from lively apprehensive imagination. I never knew anyone read yth more attention than she does; or read quicker. She hardly ever stops till she has read a book through; & make[s] nothing of reading one Vol: of Roderick Random in a day; or I believe I might say both Volumes. At present she only reads for entertainment. As she grows older, I doubt not to inspire her with a taste of reading for instruction. She says she is fond of History; I shall endeavour soon to put some history into her hands.

15 January 1773

F's reading in French books:

1 Contes Arabes. (part).

F's English reading continued:

February

20 Devil on 2 sticks.
21 Marmentel's Belisarius.

22 Shakespeare's K. Rich. 3d.
   & afterwards many others of Shakespear's plays.
23 Gil Blas.
24 several odd plays as
   Provoked Wife.
   d° Husband.
   Beaux Stratagem.
   Wonder.
   School for Rakes.
   Way to keep him.
   Conscious Lovers?
25 Otway.

July

26 Pope's Odyssey.
27 Tales of ye Geniis.
28 Mdme —— Fairy Tales.
29 Count Fathom.

German Obs. & Mems.

1 No pretence of accusing K. of Prussia of unnatural crimes, as I have heard in England, from any report current as I cou'd learn abroad.

But the Prince of Prussia – who had one wife divorced from him, is said to be accused by both his wives of attempts to have other connexions with them than he shd have.

2 Have 50 Holidays at Hamburgh – so great a place of trade – kept as strict as Sunday – No work, no Change, nothing sold, Everybody dresses fine, makes carouses in ye country &c. Lady Day & many such holidays among ye 50.

One good that Struensee did in Denmark was to abolish all Holidays – None kept throughout those dominions, but 1 at Xmas and Easter & 1 at Whitsunside.

3 Altona – a pleasant town – almost as well situated for trade as Hamburgh. But much less trade there though they have few or no taxes, – great fredom of Commerce. This arises merely from ye want of repute abroad – not being known enough.

4. Hamburgh is in a decaying state. The Exp^es of ye government greater than ye revenues. The Senate want to impose taxes, which ye Burghers won't agree to, particularly a Poll Tax, & Stamp Duty. Have very few & small taxes at Hamburgh. Free liberty for everything to import & export. Goods not consumed in ye place only pay a small passage money i.e. ¾$ per £100 of value & some goods as Copper, Lead &c none at all.

5. Denmark – All people in ye Danish dominions Rich & poor, young & old pay 4D a month Head-money which is found a very oppressive tax, & what is most grumbled. Yet qu: For I did not pay this at Wansbeck – nor any other tax – But for Beer; Tis paid at Altona.

6 *July 1773* I have seen as yet no summer plough'd fallow in Germany – & I

am told they sow their plough'd grounds without intermission ev'ry year. But I believe they observe regular courses. The chief produce I met in Hannover is Rye – some Barley – good deal Oats – a little wheat Beans Peas Potatoes a great deal Buckwheat. They called wheat by ye German name for White & that is probably ye meaning of ye English word.

7 Sept. They grow Indian corn; & make Brandy mostly of it: The Bread made of it is stringy. Tobacco grown. Salt springs not very salt to ye Taste; the water pumpt up 2 Stories high then let to trickle through a thick pile of Sticks where the salt collects, by the water evaporings. These piles of sticks all under the range of a long cover'd Barn. Plow near Frankfort, & draw Burthens on ye road with Oxen, by the Horns. The oxen seem to work well by the horns & have no disorders at their horns.

8 Sepr. A pair of Oxen draw a waggonload of Hay – 4 wheels – drove easily by a small whip.

9 In Piemont, the Oxen all of a Fawn color, strong & well made: used much for draught; yet draw by their horns, & their heads are held up by the Team bending upwards very high, to which their heads are tied.

Names of Relations. 1772

x mark on those that deserted me or took not my part.

1. Mrs Margaret Morris (maid: name Jenkins) Swansea.
2. Miss D°. D°. (sister at Mr Lockwood's, Mortimer Street, London.)
3. Miss Mary D°. Swansea.
4. Miss Jane D°. D°.
5. John Morris Esqr (my brother) Clasemont, near Swansea.
6. Miss Bridgeta Lockwood (my niece) at her father's, Mortimer Street.
7. Miss Matilda D°. D°.
8. Thomas D°. D°
9. Mary D°. D°.
10. Mrs Jane Morris (aunt) Forest, near Swansea.
11. Mrs Jane Lloyd (aunt) i.e. my mother's half sister, Aberystwith.
12. Miss Bridget D° (1st cousin) D°.
13. Thos. Lloyd, Esqr (D°) Carmarthen or Abertrimary Cardiganshire.
    Rev. Richd D°. Warwick.
14. Miss Ann D°. Aberystwith.
15. Charlotte D°. D°.
16. The Edwards of Machynlleth in Montgomeryshire. My mother's first cousins & their several children – in all a great many. I may mention – Edwards of Talgarth & his children.
    Dr Edward Edwards of Jesus Coll: Oxon.
    Mr John Edwards, Att^y at Law, Machynlleth.
    Mrs Owen of Llunllo – & her Daughters, the youngest married to Mr Anwyl, Att^y at Law, Machnylleth.
    Mrs Annwyll near Machynlleth & her daughter.
17. An abundance of 2d Cousins on my mother's side – as Mrs Gwynn of Garth, formerly Miss Parry &c.

18. The children of Thos Lloyd Esqr. my second cousin.
19. The Rev^d Mr Severn of Abberly, my father's 2d cousin & his children.

Names of Acquaintance in London when I left it on May 15, 1772

Of the Law – particular friends.
 x John Bicknell Lincoln's Inn.
  Thos Morgan Gray's Inn.
 x Thos Lloyd do
  George Jones Lincoln's Inn.
 x Samuel Pairlement do.
  Richd Jones, Castle Yard, Holborn.
 x Watkin Lewes, Cecil Street.

Names of Barristers (my friends)

  James Poole Red Lion Square.
  Richd Cocks Temple.
  Henry Howarth* do.
  Robt Comyn Linc. Inn.
< Edwd Bearcroft L. Inn fields.
  Mr Serjeant Jephson – Serjeant's Inn.

Law Acquaintances &c

  John Lloyd, Lincoln's Inn.
  —— Ingram do.
  Walwyn Greaves ⎱
  Richd Musgrave ⎰ Temple
  William Seward, Esq. Lincoln's Inn.

Particular Friends in London

  Henry Norton Willis, Kensington Palace Green.
  Mountagu Wilkinson, Clifford Street.
< Edwd Boughton, Berners Street.

Families – intimate with in London

  Mr Thos Lockwood – Mortimer Street.

* Of Mitre Court, Inner Temple, where Robert lay hidden in 1774.
< Half-turned?

Revd Mr Edward Lockwood, Welbeck Street.
Mr Gowlans, Harley Street.
x Mr John Lockwood, Harley Street.
x Mr Symonds, Salter's Court.

Particular Political Acquaintance

x Mr Townsend, Austin Friers.
x Rev. Mr Horne, Vine Street, Piccadilly.
Mr Wilkes, Prince's Court, Storey's Gate.
Mr Oliver, Fenchurch Street.
Mr Sawbridge, New Burlington Street.
Mr Robert Bernard, near Hyde Park Corner.
Mr Wm Davis, jun^r, Piccadilly, Books Mer.
Wm Ellis, Esqr. North Street, Westmr.
Mr Tooke, Serjeant's Inn, Fleet Street.

Acquaintances in London

Mr John Lewis, stockbroker, Temple or Garraway's. Coffee house.
Mr Wm Tolson, Mercht, n. 54 Houndsditch.
Mr Edwd King of ye King's Stables, now at Zell.
xx Christopher Talbot Esqr,* Lincoln's Inn.
Deere, Esqr. Temple.
White, Esqr. Ch. Ch. Oxon.
Gratton, Esqr. New Coll. Oxon.
John Day, Esqr. Bearhill Books.
Revd Mr Salter, Charterhouse.
Billy Woodfall, No. 6 Silver Street, Whitefriars.
Flexney, Bookseller.
Williams, Chancery Lane, Barber.
< Johnson Gildart, Cecil Street.
Humphry, Mins. Painter [Ozias].
Carwardine, do.

Persons I made acquaintance yth at Hamburg.

Mr Jno Parish – Lady & family.
< Mr Geo. do do do.
Dr Ross do do.
Revd Mr Vaughan & Miss his daughter.
Captn Wolffe.
Captn James (fat).

* Morris borrowed his coach and livery servant to elope.

Captn Painter.
Captn Mingie.
Captn Hill (water-drinker)
Captn Plowman.
       Hannan.
Mr Toderhost do do.
Mr & Mrs Evatt.
Mr & Mrs Sadlier – Germans.
Mr & Mrs Schaland.
Mr & Mrs Stephen.
Mr & Mrs Toder Horst – Germans.
[erased]

At Brunswick

Captn. Langdale (a Rom: Cath: Engl. Officer).
Mrs Luttelow (once Mrs Metsner).

At Zell

Mr Elderhost – stall-meister.
Mr Cook – equerry or rider.
Mr Komp – a stall meister.
Mons. Professeur royal Rocque & Mlle sa fille, & Fil.
Captn Deering.
Captn Schwellenbergen.
Mr Secretary Struhve.
Herr von Insanrotz (Schauroth?) some other officers.
Mr M'Douall.

Other acquaintances contracted abroad

Brunswick
Lieut Speke.
Captn Sir Jas Murray.
Mr Byron ⎫
Mr Dalton ⎭ a little.

Gottingen
Mr Vaughan (acquaintance yth him in England).
Mr Boyé, his tutor.

On ye road
Baron Klopman, of Mittau.

Cassel
    Mr Boulanger, Captn Dutch Cavalry.
    Mr —— a Swiss, his Friend & travelling conductor.

Frankfort
    Mr Morse of Norwich, Manufacturer.
    Lieut. Williams, of ye Welsh Fusiliers.
    Mr Alexander (Scotch) English Language master.
    Mr Baron Groetheuse, Ld Chesterfield's companion.

At Geneva
    Mr Mussita, where I lodged, Italian master.
    Mr Lullen, Banker.

At Genoa
    Mr Wm Munro.
    Grace.
    Mr Guillaume – a Scotch gentn.
    Captn Gray ⎫ ship
    do Eales ⎭

At Marseilles
    Mr Bierbeck (& his Lady) (English Agent).

At Paris
    Mr Rosenhagen, & his Lady.
    Mr Boosy, Wine Merch (English).
    Sir Jno Lambert, Rue des Beaux Enfants.
    Lady Lambert, his mother; by ye mint.
    Mr Mann, King's Messenger.
    Mr Pasquié, Sr Jno Lambert's Clerk.

At Rouen
    Mr & Mrs Louis Durand, Rue St Elois.

NOTE:
Robert Morris also kept a detailed list of all letters sent, received and unanswered during his time abroad.

The Diaries

20 February – 5 July 1774

1774

Having delivered my last journal book (which was kept regularly from the time of my coming abroad May 16, 1772 until Feb. 19, 1774) into the hands of Mr Durand at Rouen for safer custody, I begin this on Sunday Feb. 20, 1774.

ROUEN. On which day my sister Jane dined with us at our Inn. I settled my Sister's board & Lodging with Durand for one quarter, from Sat: Feb: 12th last, being the day she went to his house at 600 Livres or 25 guineas (An infamous imposing demand; but in the distress I then was I could not refuse it) the sum his Lady set it at, for every article of expence: and this I paid him in advance. Went on yth packing the Trunk, preparing for our departure from Rouen. Supt at Durand's. All these French have a notion of the English drinking nothing but strong Liquors: & therefore poison us with Goblets full of *Liqueurs*.

21 February Rainy. Trunk packt. Mr Billinghurst (an English merchant established in the Birmingham way at Rouen) & Captain Osborn dined with us. La Fosse was to have come, but sent excuse. The same Company supt with us. I begun to be apprehensive for my sword lent to La Fosse. I had received several shuffling answers from him about it. His own, which he had forced upon me, by way of a present, I had return'd him. I intended to go off the next morning with the Coach for Havre de Grace; but was resolved not to go without my sword. The last return to my message this Evening to La Fosse, was that he had given it to the Jew (his usual messenger) to bring me. At 2 after midnight I walkt out to call upon La Fosse. I was forced to make a great noise at the outer Door. The landlord looking out of the Window; said to me, 'I suppose you are come for your sword.' I said, 'Yes & to speak to Mr La Fosse too.' He offered to put the sword down to me out of ye window, but I refused to take it so, telling him he must give it me at the Door. He kept me parleying for a quarter of an hour; telling me at one time he cou'd not find a Light; at another time, he c^d not find the key. So I thought it best to take my sword, as I cou'd get it, out of ye Window. Having told him, I wanted to ask Mr La Fosse, whether he w^d accompany me that morning in ye coach, as he promised, since he said he wou'd set out with me, whenever I went to any quarter of the world I pleased He replied to me, 'I might spare myself the trouble of speaking to Mr La Fosse upon that subject: because supposing Mr La Fosse w^d go, he himself shd not let him; for he owed him money, & he w^d not let him go till he paid it.'

This evening Captn Osborn pretended to tell any card that was thought of. I gave him a pack of Cards, & before hand I in my mind pitched upon the seven of Diamonds. He went out of the Room; came in again afterwards, pretended to make some calculations yth ye Cards, & then told me, I had thought of ye King of Diamonds. 'You have hit upon it' says I; and he & all the rest of the company really thought he had done the Trick: In which manner I suppose it is generally done.

22 February At 4 this morning set out in the stage for Havre. A little room the Coach is, capable of holding 10 persons. A young Lad in ye Coach sick all the way, & oblig'd to walk; a woman too, vomiting & as sick as ever I saw any one at Sea. Women in this Country were [wear] an odd cap, with long full Lappets: sometimes these Lappets pinned up. Lay upon ye Road; and arrived at Havre the next day at noon.

23 February Havre de Grace.

Came to ye Golden Eagle Inn in the Great Street, Havre de Grace. Dear & imposing: Ask 50 sous a night for ye Lodging of a two-bedded Room up three pair of Stairs: Got it down to 30 sous: & afterwards made them change it me for ye first floor. In the Evening about 6 saw a boat preparing for Honfleur: Called King & we both went into it; where we arrived (3 Leagues higher up the mouth of the Seine, on ye opposite shore) in an hour & a half. Went to ye Post house: a good Inn: Askt for Potatoes, & they drest us some Jerusalem Artichokes: They have in this Country what they call *poire de terre* as well as the *Pomme de terre*: perhaps it was ye former they gave us. All sorts of Potatoes rare in these parts: None to be had at Havre; & Only of one Person at Rouen; for which when there gave 5 pence English to a pound: He took some unbroke ground in hand at a low rent, set it with Potatoes, & though as yet he can get none, but the Poor to eat them, he is already said to have got a fortune by it.

24 February Wind high, & no passing back, all this day to Havre. At 2 in the afternoon mounted Biddies for Caen: which place we got to in 5 hours & a half: Some part of the road just like the Sands & Boroughs from

Swansea to Britonferry; but worse; the part nearest Caen, not upon ye Sands, most execrable, & I believe as bad, or near as bad as ever I rid: for some very bad roads before now, both in Wales & Herefordshire. Put up at the sign of the Place royale de la Ville at Caen; the Inn fronts the Place, & is a very good one. Inquired after La Fosse's family, found his mother kept a Lace & Mercery shop: He perhaps might have been concern'd in it; but too idle to continue: He had been not long since married; & has a Child not 5 months old: & yet he goes on getting the Clap, & giving it to every girl he can lie with: Of the *Mal au Cul* he makes as light as one w^d of blowing one's nose: Has two Sisters, the completest whores in Caen: Upon one of these some verses were lately stuck up in the Town by a young fellow, who had apparently suffered by her favors:

> Jeuns Gens, Qui aimez le vice
> Ne Foutez pas La Fosse, car Elle a
> Chaud – du-Pisse.

He suffered again for his wit; for he was put in prison several days for posting up those verses. In short, by the best accounts, this La Fosse has but slight pretensions to any other character but that of a shopkeeper, except being abandoned to idleness, vice & Drunkenness.

25 February Went to the Academy. Received very politely at the Riding-house, which is under the inspection of an old Fellow about 60, Chevalier of the order of St Lazar. He has been in England: a great admirer of Sr Sidney Meadowes: He askt Mr King; who mounted 2 of his Horses: At first he found fault to me yth King's riding, as to his heels sticking out from the Horse, & his Elbows being constrained: but he soon became a Convert in his favor: greatly admired his riding; praised the nice touch of his hand; enter'd much into Conversation with him, & invited us to dinner: There were about 20 horses for riding in ye Stables; some good, & showy: Several English come here for Education: at present about half a dozen: What names I c^d learn were these: Poyntz a nephew of Mr Castleton with ye wooden leg: Ramsden, nephew of Colonel Ramsden, Equerry to the King: Meynard, was of Eaton school; some relation of Sr Sidney Meadowes: Brenan, an Irish Officer. Mr Smelt was also at Caen; but not one of ye Academy, except to ride: He was sent over from his regiment in North America by his Uncle, who is Praeceptor to the Prince of Wales; & is at Caen for ye purpose of learning French; being intended in all probability to travel yth ye Prince abroad. He is brother to Mr Smelt the Russia Merchant, at Mr Symond's Salters Court. We dined at the general table for all ye young men, who boarded in the Academy: being to appearance of near 30. The Chevalier & his Lady sat towards ye

Head of the Table: His Lady handsome; about 24: This as usual gives the husband ye reputation of being a Cuckold: & so ye world says the Child is not his own: After dinner drank a bottle of wine, with the Chevalier & his Lady in y^r upper apartment. The Chevalier, an ingenious Mechanic, Mathematician, & Musician: His Lady plays too, well, as was said on ye Violin & Harpsichord: The Chevalier quite a Valetudinarian. Seems not difficult, for one of ye English to succeed with Madam: & one of them has the reputation of it. The Chevalier show'd, a very curious, well set skeleton of a man upon a horse: both of very small size. Went & saw a very fine Convent of Monks in ye skirt of ye Town: where is William ye Conqueror's Tombstone: A fine Church to this abbey, very fine long Gallery in ye Habitation of ye Monks: The Church beautifying; never saw a finer Abbey unless I shou'd reckon that at Genoa to be so. Took Posthorses & at 6 set out upon our return: Went no farther this night than to Dive, a little poor village, where the Count Lauraguais has a Chateau close by. The English made some shew of landing here last war. The whole country long then in alarm: a Chain of troops upon all the Hills. Ten thousand men within a few Leagues of Cherbourg, when as they told us about 40 of our people came in & took; they not minding the descent of 40 people, who they esteem'd w^d never throw themselves in ye way of being cut to pieces: I heard this Cherbourg was a very paltry little place of no Strength or consequence.

26 February Having lain at Dive to wait for Low Water, that we might pass along ye Sands, the road at high water being impassable, at 3 this morning we set out on Chevaux quitté. (Messenger's horses quitted Chevaux de Messagerie quitté) This is ye only part of France I have met with that term or usage; they are cheaper than the Post, or at least you need not with them have another horse with a Postilion, for you are trusted alone: We kept company with others going ye same road; & got in good time to Honfleur. Here I met with the Longest Posts I ever found: From Honfleur to Dive 3½ Posts; from Dive again to Havre 3 Posts; & each Post is well known to be 2 Leagues: The Leagues in this Country too, not being of the shortest. Crost over in ye Passage Boat to Havre: Some in ye Boat, who had serv'd as sailors during the last war in the French navy, were giving us an account of what part they had had in it. They agreed together in abusing their officers. One engagement was mentioned, where the Captain, 1st 2d, & 3d Lieutenant staid down in the Hold: The 4th Lieutenant commanded upon deck; but a shot happening to come very near him, which besprinkled him with the blood of another, he took that occasion to pretend, or really thought he was wounded, & so he went down too to his superior Officers. Conflaus was greatly abused, for Cowardice. After the defeat of his squadron, one ship was chaced up into some river, where the Officers (I suppose here was meant the Land officers) wou'd have gone out into a Chaloupe from the Cabbin Windows: The men threatened to fire upon their officers, if they left the ship, saying, when they had left it, they were no longer their Commanders: The French Sailor was telling this story to a Chevalier of St Louis, who was next me in the boat, saying to him, among these Officers, there was a hatfull of Croix St Louis, taking his hat, & shaking it, as if he had them all in there together.

When our fleet was off Brest, Boats were suffered to go ashore for refreshments for ye Officers; & Market Boats permitted to go to them with Fresh meat & Greens. I question whether we w^d have been so civil to them; or whether it w^d not have been deemed adhered [adhering] to the K.'s enemies.

Havre

Came over in 2½ hours. Was not sick, going or coming as most are, even many sailors, when rough as sometimes this passage is extremely so. Called at Mr Le Monayer's to whom I had a letter from Mr Durand: Should have thought him a principal merchant: Lives in a most shabby house. Several Old Families are protestant, about this neighbourhood of Caen. De la Fosse, Moisson's family is so.

27 February A fine Bason for the ships here. Full of West India & Guinea-men. Was in ye Public Walks of the Town: but the Gentry do not walk out much in this part of ye Year. Heard at the Coffee-house that no French Officer of ye Garrison here is rec^ed in any Gentleman's house of ye Town, upon general agreement; owing to some of ye officers of the regiment now here, having forced their way into a Gentleman's house, who gave a Ball, & had not invited them. Drank some punch at an English public house kept by a Yorkshire woman married to one Parrie a French Sailor. She told me of an English Lord lodging about 4 or 5 years ago at ye same Hotel as mine here; who by her description I guest to be Lord Balti-more; & so it was. The time was, when he retir'd upon that Bitch Sarah Woodcock's affair. She represented him, as most extremely lavish of money; that she alone for washing for him got to ye amount of 300 Livres of him: that he appear'd mad; that he w^d talk to a person, & not seem to know what he was saying; & that he w^d acknowledge of himself; was made a Free-mason here, which cost him 20 Guineas: used to send his man Dick every fortnight to England for money, as she said; Came here at first, with one Gentleman & a Lady: that gentleman I suppose was Perrini

& the Lady, Mrs Hales: Some time after came a Servant with an^{or} Lady; they I believe were Broughton & Mrs Griffenburgh: Lord B. was sweet upon this Mrs Parry; always presenting her with Ribbons; then pulling them off her head & giving them to others: w^d have his shirts washed by her, if she charged a Guinea a Shirt: one of the Ladies no doubt Mrs Griff: wanted her to leave her husband & go off with them – offered a hatfull of Louis, as she says: This Mrs Parry has been pretty; but battered: Lord B. after went into a private house at Havre, & then saw less company: from hence to Rouen, as she says; & thence to Paris: Ld B. lay in ye very same room as I did up 3 pr of Stairs: used to be in bed, when this Mrs Parry came of a morning; told her, she need not be afraid, for he had vow'd he never w^d touch another woman, as long as he lived: In ye mind he then was, I suppose, he spoke as be believ'd: Ld B. w^d have Mrs Parry also to roast his meat for him. None must walk in ye streets here, as they told us (at this time of ye year I suppose) after half after nine in ye Evg without a Candle; like as in Hamburgh in ye winter after 10. No fire or Candle allow'd in any of the ships in this Harbour either day or night. At Hamburgh none allow'd after 8 at night.

28 February Wrote some letters in the morning. Very stormy. Dined at a Writing Master's who keeps *pension*, or board. Our dinner at 30 sous a head; Gras; very good; only us two: Might dine if we pleased, with some of the young merchants of ye Town; and they assured us too, that there was one Gentleman even among them; yet all of them were brought up to Commerce, & substantial people's sons: these they called *Bourgeois*, to distinguish them from Gentlemen; a distinction wch they keep up very religiously: An officer, for example, w^d not be seen in this Company for ye world. He also kept a table apart for ye Jeunes Eleves de la Marine; for whom there is an Academy here; & these young people are of good families, appointed to this education by the Court. We askt if we c^d not dine with them; but were afterwards informed that we c^d not even, if we had ye *Croix de Louis*. I supt in the Evening at this house with these Burghers; and Blackguards indeed I found them; so that I shall trouble them I believe no more with my company. An honest day-Labourer is a good companion but something above the Degree of a Day Labourer & under the Degree of a Gentleman (those that may be called in England your 2 shilling swearers, being what they are assessed at for a prophane oath) such are intolerable. I have lately taken Juvenal in hand, & find a great deal of pleasure in the reading; but I am often obliged to cast my eye upon the French translation.

1 March This month begun here with a very fine day. Begun Fencing:

The master a common Grenadier, as often in France: Is engaged from hence to ye Academy at Angé & is to have his Congé in May: His terms only 9 Livres for 24 Lessons, ye first month; & 6 Livres the other: Promised him a Livre a day for us two. Mr Carmichael & Mr Stewart, the only Merchants, or Factors here. Had some conversation yth ye Former. I was addrest by Durand to Mr Le Monayer: I saw in his *Comptoir*, that several vessels in the tobacco trade were addrest to him from Glasgow: He was of correspondence with ye House of Cunninghame there: also yth Harries in London. I find we live at this Hotel at the rate of about ½ a guinea a Day to ye House: It is reckon'd here a dear one, & so it is.

2 March Past a very uneasy night, owing I believe to the eating of some muscles for supper last night: Itching all over me, & some pain in my Bowels: Drank a glass of Brandy in the morning, & was well. Eau de vie D'Andaye is excellent Brandy; but is sweet: Price 50 sous a Bottle. A large Ship arrived in the Harbour from Baltimore in Maryland with Flower. Several small Craft from England with Flower. Was askt by a Captain of a French vessel bound to Brest, 100 Crowns i.e. 300 Livres, for our Passage yth Jack there, & to be maintained by him: I suppose the price is not above one third, or one half at the most of what he askt. Begun to learn the Soldier's manual exercise of our Fencing master. There is also an exercise of the Firelock for officers: all the French officers practice it. A Raw recruit is fitted to mount guard in 14 days; yet some take longer, even as far as 2 months. A French Soldier, who is observ'd to be after the rest in putting his hand to his haunch after shouldering his musquet; is sometimes sent to prison for 3 days for it. A Captain of a Dutch Vessel here, with whom I intend to go to Amsterdam, came in ye afternoon to drink some Punch & smoke a Pipe: He found his quarters so good that he staid with us to supper. Took our usual round of Backgammon at ye Coffee-house; & went early to bed. Loup Loup (ne merds pas Loup Loup) not well.

3 March I believe I may say of a truth, that I never fail to dream every night, & during the whole of the night, of that dear young creature, whom I do not know whether to speak of only as my wife or my misfortune. Spent the Day in Fencing & doing ye Soldier's Exercise. Was aboard the Galloway, a very fine Vessel from Philadephia: Of live Oak; ye upper works of Cedar. Mahogany Cabbin; came here yth Flower. (French make little use of Mahogany; yet they have it in St Domingo. They call it Bois de Cajou.) The Captain assured me, it was bo^t at a higher price there, than sold here; and supposed bo^t up by ye French ministry at a loss, to prevent scarcity. Smoak pretty often in ye Evening; & can almost master a pipe; which I chuse to be able to do, to be sociable, yth some that cannot be sociable without it. A Fine day. At ye play for a quarter of an hour, & c^d suffer it no longer.

4 *March* Very rainy. Usual Exercises of Fencing & the Fire-lock in ye Morning. Wrote some letters. Le Jeune Cadet de Province, who fenced in ye Winter Vauxhall at Paris, was in the Regiment now here, which is ye Regiment de *Province*, and in that regiment he has killed 20 men upon slight quarrels, at single Combat, either with a small sword or Sabre. Brags to have killed 50 men in his time; & he is now young. The more he killed, the men [more] caressed by the Officers. Common soldiers here often fight Duels, upon ye slightest affront: a look across ye street may effect it: If a Grenadier was to refuse another's Challenge, all ye rest of ye Troop w^d cut him in pieces. Yet Challenges (pour donner un rendezvous) & Duels, are agst Law here & punishable. A Grenadier has one Sou pr day more than a Hat-man. When a soldier has serv'd 8 years, He has a blue Bar on his arm ⬧ Called un Chevreuil. Then receives 2 Sous a day more pay; after 16 years he has the distinction of 2 Bars ⬧ and has 4 sous per Day increase pay; after 24 years he has upon the breast of his Coat 2 swords in Blue Cloth sowed in a cross, un croix d'Epees ⚔ and receives then 8 sous a day more than a common man first enter'd. None enter in France for life: The engagement is always for 8 years; & never denied the Congé at ye end of ye Term: This Congé they call their Cartouche. Mr Carmichael (an Irish Merchant here) supt yth me; as well as did 2 Captains of the Pennsilvania & ye Maryland ships, & an^or Captain – Names I don't know.

5 *March* The French Coffeehouse joke upon ye Weather is, that it has got the ague. No Fire nor Candle allowed in any of ye Ships either day or night: 500 Livres penalty; reason is, that ye Ships are left dry, & some burning ye rest c^d not be removed. There is no river at Havre; all a factitious Port: as it seems to me. No Fires or Candles allow'd at Amsterdam; when ye ships are froze up: None at Hamburgh at any time after 8 in ye evening. Took a very long walk into ye Country; seems to have pretty capabilities of pleasantness in Summertime. Though this is ye principal port of entrance for Sugar in France, yet Sugar here, is one Shilling Eng: pr Pound; the best indeed; but then that is very far from being refined; & w^d not fetch 9 pence a pound in London. They dont refine Sugar well in France. None do it so well as the Hamburghers. Most of the Sugar Refiners in London, I am told, are Germans.

6 *March* This morning Prêt-a-boire (my Fencing master's) Partner or

friend partaking in ye same Salle, wch is between them, though the Scholars not, came to inform that Prêtaboire, drinking last night with another Grenadier, who also taught fencing, & disputing about Arms, had fought upon ye spot, & rec^d un Coup du Sabre, wch had laid open the side of his head: His antagonist had also receiv'd a stroke on ye top of his head & on his arm; Prêtaboire the worst; & now both in ye Hospital: He said, it w^d be an affair of 8 days: I askt if ye Regiment w^d not take notice, & he said, most likely Officers w^d & both of them receive punishment. I took my Lesson of this man instead of Prêtaboire, & I think he is a better Fencing Master. Le Monoyer called here in ye Evening – to keep up conversation is ye most disagreable thing in ye world to me. 2 ships sail'd for Chichester: I wish I had gone yth them. Fair wind for Holland; but no ship ready. This harbour once at Harfleur; 2 Leagues higher up ye country: This Port all made: The Town now, where Sea was.

7 March Got up at 5 to go afishing in one of ye common Fishing Boats; & though we desired no more, than to sit in the Boat, & let them do their own affairs, & go where they pleased, as they intended of themselves, yet one fellow had the impudence to stick to half a Guinea to be given him for that; another w^d not take less than 6 Livres (saying very ridiculously he cou'd not afford it under, as it cost him 5 Livres 10 Sous), though I show'd them we had good provisions in Beef & Brandy, where they shou'd partake, & promised 3 Livres & even 4, when we return'd with them in ye afternoon. Went to see Prêtaboire in ye Hospital; but did not see his wound; the fellow look't hearty. He & his antagonist will for punishment both be forbidden to practise teaching Fencing, & be put for about 15 days, in prison. I now understand, that the Officers are far from encouraging these single conflicts among the Soldiers; though some among them may applaud those, who in that manner revenge real affronts & injuries. But for drunken quarrels, it is quite otherwise. Every soldier upon his ent'ring take upon them a military name, as they chuse themselves or as the Major gives them. Thus one is called Lajoye, another Monte-au-Ciel, another La Tulipe & so on. It is only permitted *aux gens de Condition* to retain a Family name.

8 March Spent the day in the usual manner – Fencing & Learning ye Soldier's exercise. King employ'd in writing Letters. (Spent the Evening in Company with ye 3 American Captains here, another of Biddeford, who had often been at Swansea; & the Scotchman, Mr Carmichael: Jolly, & drank an exceeding deal of their wine; committed some follies, & have been since very much ashamed of my debauch in such company.) This Evg is misdated: it shd be Mo. 7.

This morning we made another attempt to go afishing; but before we got out of ye harbour, ye wind drove us agst ye Jettee (or Pier) & we broke our Rudder. (Le Gouvernail, which we thought at first, they called, *their Gouverneur*) So we were obliged to return.

9 *March* This morning at 7, we actually did put in Execution our long planned Fishing Scheme, going out in one of ye Common Boats, wch are open, but very large. We only dredged for Oysters, of which in 2 Hawls, there being 2 dredges each time, we took 800; There were also a few Maid-fish, & a vast number of marine productions. About 2 Hours after I had been in ye boat, I perceiv'd a Sea Sickness, which forced me to bring up my stomach, as I did once again in about ¾ of an hour afterwards: I then took to lying down & found myself during ye rest of our sailing pretty hearty & well, but I did not chuse to trust myself to move about. About 6 in ye Afternoon I began to have a little appetite, & eat some Cold Beef: Before that during ye whole time I had only eat one oyster, & drank a little drop of Brandy. King had also a Seasickness. Jack, to whom it was his first time, was very bad; for ye first half-hour he found himself so well, that he thought it was not possible he shd get sick; He grew however pretty well again towards ye latter end of ye Day. I gave ye fellows as by agreement 6 Livres. We were upon ye Seas 12 Hours. All under sail, except when we were drawing up ye Dredges. They said, we made 20 Leagues of way; In ye same time we shd have been, had we gone on direct pretty near in sight of ye Isle of Wight; which is from Havre 28 Leagues. There was during most part of ye time a good deal of wind & swell. We return'd to Havre, a little before 7 in ye Evening.

10 *March* Went as usual to the Salle d'Armes twice. Havre a famous place for wet wet weather; They say they have not thirteen dry days in ye year. By our experience we found ye assertion very likely to be true. All ye poor in France depend upon charity of individuals, or charitable institutions. No Rate; or necessary provision for them. One Institution here, & I believe in many other places is, what is called Les Pauvres de la misericorde; of which certain Ladies are named the directors, & they take it by turns to visit the poor, make soup for them, distribute it, & collect charity in churches upon their own solicitations. I was so accosted, as I acted the momentary Catholic in one of their Churches, pour les pauvres de la Misericorde by a very genteel Lady; in such a graceful manner she presented the little purse to me, in wch she collected the money as if she was going to present her hand in a minuet: so that yth ye least spice of Gallantry I could not help being charitable also. In ye Evg supt at le

Moneyer's upon Meagre; crost themselves both before they began their supper. They never suffer a bit of meat to enter their doors in Lent time: A couple of the most rigid Catholics I have met with. The Price of Coals here I learnt to be from –50 Livres to 300 for a quantity equal to 14 Tons, & have a ready market here.

11 March   This day West Indiamen sail'd out of ye harbour, as did the Galloway for Philadelphia, the Pilot of which going to leave the Vessel, as soon as he had brought him to ye Jettee head, I saw the Captain force him back (for ye Pilot had got ye outside of the Vessel to fall into his own Boat) & then slipping the rope of ye Pilot's Boat, he carried him off along with him; to get safe & clear from all Land: Whether he afterwards re-turn'd him to any of the Fishing boats lying out in ye Bay I know not. I learnt, that the coming directly here from America was contraband: that ye clear'd for Portugal, & took with them back clearances in Portuguese, as if they had actually discharged in Portugal.

12 March   A fine day; & the first we have had here. A ship launched, directly into the Sea. Invited at night to drink a glass of Champaign by a strong Paddywhack Irishman, lodged the next Room to us.

13 March   In the Ev^g Mr King happen'd to cast his eyes out of ye Window upon an old acquaintance of us both, Dan Hales. We had heard of him (in passing) in Germany, with Captn Stuart, 3d Son of Lord Bute: He had been upon some business of his from Ratisbon (German Regensberg) to London, & was now returning to Ratisbon, with a sulky Maitre D'Hotel of Captn Stuart's. The History of this young Hales is already extra-ordinary, nor is he yet more than 20: His Father is a Navy-agent in good circumstances; but upon acc^ot of his manifold past extravagances (mostly in ye Company of Clopperogge, another acquaintance of King's & mine) he leaves him at present to shift for himself in the wide world. Paddy-whack & others supt with me; & we induced Hales to stay with us till ye morning. The Commandant refused him ye favor of having ye Gates open'd in ye Night-time, though he had already granted it for midnight to some others: But I believe he refused it because ye Post-master accom-panied us to him; & he does not like ye Postmaster.

14 March   Our Passport for Holland was granted only for 3 weeks, & had now for about a week expired. However that caused no difficulty, for it was registered & accepted, without hardly looking at it.

15 March   Spent the day in ye old stile; i.e. Letter writing; reading Juvenal, Horace & Caesar; fencing, walking & Backgammon playing at the Coffeehouse. (Su. 13 Our Holland Schiffer, Jelle Jacobs, supt yth us) N.B. I had 2 of the Musicians of the Regiment to play upon the Clarinet here at Supper Sunday night: Required 6 Livres apiece; Was obliged to ask the Lieutenant Colonel's Leave: One of 'em said he had 600 Livres a year, & Clothes; but was to find himself; He was also a dancing, Music & singing master; not enter'd in ye Regiment. Free to quit at 3 month's notice: Was willing to go away: Had some inclination to take him: Had a conversation yth him ye next day upon it: Said he wou'd not wear a Livery, nor serve as a servant: but to go to accompany a travelling gentleman; or to be engaged as a Musician in a great Family; I then saw it was time to amuse him, & no farther; so I talk'd to him about his being my Maitre D'Hotel: He w^d have even run off, without giving his warning: I appointed another time; & then took care to see no more of him: But had my affairs gone on well, it w^d have been a most agreable thing to me to have hired one yth his Talents.

16 March The Irishman (Mr Brenan) dined yth us: A good natured fellow: is of Wexford: Gave me very readily one of his hoard; value 1½ G^a. I gave him my Pocket Book, silver Pencil Case, Silver Knife (wch alone cost me 25 shillings) Paid off the Fencing Master, & gave him a Guinea for teaching me & Mr King, 16 Days, 2 Lessons each a day – the Soldier's exercise some few times – & Jack to fence about 8 or 9 Days: He was well content; gave them afterwards about a Crown to drink.

17 March Settled Mr Monoyer: Spent £30 at Havre &c in 3 weeks living moderate: the House Bill in that time was only 11 Guineas: Bought some Sailor's Clothes, Hats &c. About noon sailed in the Wakende Hoop (the Wakeful Hope) Capt. Jelle Jacobs, for Amsterdam; the first Ship ready since we return'd from Caen. Passage 12 Ducats for us 3 & Baggage: to find our own eating. Fine Day. In the Ev^g Thunder; but were out of the Storm; which seem'd to be very great at Havre. At first sailing very calm; after the Thunder sprung a gale, not great. S.S.W.; the rightest wind for Amsterdam: Quite well: Eat Heartily: to bed at 10.

18 March Fine weather, still a wind but now S.S.E. About 7 in ye Morn^g Got up. Then had proceeded about 10 or 12 Leagues: about opp^e Dieppe not quite so far. At 11 Beachy Head in Sight; bearing North. A Wren quite tired out came aboard; frighten'd & flew away; & soon through fatigue fell into ye Sea: then 5 Leagues in Land: Several Dieppe Fishing Boats in Sight; nearer ye Coast of England. Wrote this Journal about 1. Continued quite well & hearty as did King & Jack. Fine Weather; Wind S.E. Eat a hearty dinner. Went to sleep about 7; waked at ½ after 10. Then made some Punch; & eat some Bread Cheese. Staid up till 1 in ye morning. Sea very white; where cut by ye Ship: The rest a very dark

Green approaching to a Black. A Ship's light just before us. The 2 Lights at Dover in sight at 2.

19 March Still fine weather. Past within about half a League of Calais Cliff at 7 in ye morning. Wind S. Got up at 9. Breakfast on Tea, & Biscuit & Butter. Went atop of the Mast; beyond ye Shroud. Eat ye rest of our Oysters. Read some of Horace, 2d Vol; as yesterday; also Holland's Grammar & Juvenal. The Captain, as all of 'em do, touches up our Brandy when he can get at it. No Land in Sight about noon; opposite to Ostend: Another Land Bird (a sparrow) came aboard, & rested himself several times. Can write very easily with the motion of our Smack or Gallootte. Wind S.S.E. Bed hard last night; but slept uninterruptedly; which I did not the night before. Dined at 2 upon our Cold Beef. The provisions we brought were 2 Fowls; a piece Roast Beef; a leg of Fresh Mutton; Cheese, Salary, Potatoes, 24 long Rolls of Bread; 7 Bottles Brandy; a Ham: 3 Bottles of Soup: Tea; Sugar: Salt: Lemons. I was drest, in Check shirt, Blue Jacket, & Trowsers. Wind came to N.N.E. quite the Contrary point, to where we were going; or we shd have been in the Texel by tomorrow evening. Went to sleep about 8 intending only to sleep an hour or two; & did not wake till 3 in the morning; when I got up, as I had resolved to do, whenever I waked: made some punch, & eat some Bread & Cheese.

20 March In the morning 'till about 4 very rainy; Wind still N.E. Sea luminous. A light upon ye mast head; but did not see it myself. Lay down again about 6, for a few hours. Then fine weather: Sun powerful; & wind to ye S. but very little stirring. A Whiting caught, by a hook, baited yth a bit of an oyster: Cut off ye tail of the Whiting; & about a third of his body yth it; then baited that upon a large hook, but caught nothing more. A small Bird came aboard; though no land for 5 Dutch miles off: Each Dutch mile is 4⅘ English: because 15 Dutch miles make a Degree; & 69½ Eng: do so: Jack caught this little Bird after chacing him for half an hour or more; when he sometimes fled a long way from the Ship & returned: Put him into a Cage in ye Cabbin. The two Dogs, Cartouche & Loup always afighting: We fastened Muzzles about yr mouths, & then set them together to do y^r worst, thinking they c^d not hurt each other; but they continued to open their mouths a little; when Cartouche bit a piece of Loup's Ear off: & afterwards Loup got so fast hold of Cartouche's mouth that I was obliged to knock him on ye nose yth a stick to make him loose: Both of them had wounds about their eyes; so they must have no more fighting if we can help it. No wind stirring till Ev^g & then it turn'd to N.N.E. The Captain despairs of getting in to the Texel, even by morrow. Such are the little transactions of our voyage. The Theatre being small in wch we act, we are not to expect mighty feats to be done. 21 March Begun to be in fear, that the provisions wch we laid in for ourselves will not hold us out. The little Bird dead in ye cage; we intended after giving him a night's rest to have let him flown. Sowed Loup's ear up. Wind verges still to the N. from that to N.N.E. all the morning. Within 18 Dutch miles as they pretend to tell us of Amsterdam & we have been within 20 of it these 2 days. A small English Sloop past close by us: He seemed to me to bear upon us, as if he intended to board us: I said immediately, 'Out with our swords; here is a Pirate acoming.' We hailed him in English: He past close by our Stern, & said he was going from Helvoet to Harwich; & had Turbot & Tongue aboard. A fine day. Hazy night. See only 2 Ships length.

22 March Loup tore off most of the sewing of his ear. A Bad Day: still 15 D. miles from ye Texel. A good deal of Wind, & that E. Lay abed in order to lose the time, till 1 o'clock. A Prussian Vessel from ye Baltic past by; & hailed us, asking if we had seen ye English Pirate; which we took to be ye little sloop that past by us yesterday. A Swede 3 mast ship past by; Made towards a Fisherman & hoisted a flag, for him to come to him, by way of piloting him into some harbour close by, as Rotterdam or Helvoet: But the Fisherman took no notice of his signal: And the Captain told me, they never did, not chusing to get y^r money in ye way of pilotage, & being in too great a hurry to bring their fish to market. A Chaffinch caught aboard & shut in ye cage; & begun to eat.

23 March A Hazy, raw Day. Wind E. by S. That better than any point between ye E. & the N. 3 or 4 points nearer the S. & we shd have a wind to bring us into ye Texel. Now 10 D. miles off. The Bird caught yesterday eats & does well. Qu. Finch? (Fink) in Dutch is to chirrup, hence our name for several small Birds. Finch. A Starling came aboard. Another Chaffinch caught. Cold weather & the wind likely to hold to ye E. so but little prospect of coming into ye Texel, & our provisions have a poor appearance. Our Bread & Potatoes all out. The Captain but 1 Loaf more: after which must come to his Biscuits, wch are all mouldy. Still keep free from sea-sickness; though in this unpleasant weather am now & then mawkish, & a little giddy. Ship tosses very much. A good deal of wind. Came at night into 10 fathom water. When you come into 8 fathom, you must not go nearer the Land upon the Holland's Coast. The Captain thought himself too near for the night time; & made a tack. In the morning found themselves a vast way off at Sea; & now, as they say, 20 D. miles from the Texel.

24 March This completes our first week aboard; upon a voyage that is often made in 2 days. Find myself better if I take exercise & run about the Ship. I am then quite well, & in good spirits. At all times since I have been aboard, good appetite. Obliged to doctor Loup's Ear again; & to cut off the Bit wch was tore. The ear seemed putrefying, & had begun to stink monstrously. A Raven came aboard: The Captain held him in his hand, escaped, & soon fell into the Sea, & was drown'd. One of the Chaffinches lives & does well, the other dead. A Sailor working his passage home aboard, that had been in ye East Indies: to ye Whale Fishery, & the Coast of Guinea: Was a Cooper & only 23 years of age. Said he shd make 2 more voyages to Guinea, & for which he shd get 1100 Guilders – 100 Gs & then marry, & take to his own home. Some of ye stories he told us were of this nature: All wch I cannot say I believe. He was shipwreckt on ye Coast of Bengal. Came home in a French ship to L'Orient. From thence walk'd to Havre. Passing through Brittany, travelling with 2 others; he was told at a Village, that there were Robbers upon ye way, & if they ventured to go on, as they were, the Landlord desired them to leave their names wch he wrote down in a book, in case any of their Relations shd come to inquire after them, as he was sure they w^d be murdered: However they went on, & coming to a wood, there they were attack'd & robbed of their money, & Clothes; but their persons were not hurt. At the Whale Fishery he was one of 2 ships, wch together caught 17 whales in 19 hours. He was cutting up a Female Whale & fell into the Vagina, up to his middle, being obliged to have a man to help him out. Saw upon the shore, 3 or 400 Bears. Whales run sometimes under the Ice, but they pull them from under again. Sea smooth there. The Ice always floating agst the Wind. Each sailor has treble Clothing on him. Upon the Coast of Guinea, men have all some private trade for Gold-Dust. None of the Blacks on Board ye Slaving ships suffer'd to lie yth the women; But the Sailors may lie with as many of them as they please; taking them into their Hammock for ye night. He has lain with one only 8 years old. I am sorry I did not see ye *Combat des Animaux* when I past through Lions. Jack was giving me an account of it: that one Dog alone attacked & overthrew a Bear; that afterwards the Bear got him in his Paws, & whilst he was squeezing him, the Dog was always trying to bite his Lips: & that the Bear did not kill him by this squeezing. A Wild Horse, was turned loose, & hungry Dogs set upon him, some of whom got under his Belly & begun to bite & eat him, keeping always their hold, clinging to his Belly, though he kicked & caper'd at full Gallop. I remember the name of their famous Dog; it was called La Montagne.

A Bear at loose upon an Ass; squeezed him till he broke his Back Bone: then whilst he was eating him, & the Ass braying in a most monstrous manner, 3 Dogs let loose upon ye Bear; who was obliged to quite the Ass, & fight with the Dogs, for ye Prey he had left. Then came a Bull; & so on. A Heart was brought in Broil'd; which they called the Heart of a Wolf: This heart was fasten'd to a string, wch went over a Pully: A Little affamish'd Dog was brought in who seizes upon the broil'd meat, which is hoisted up by ye Pully: the Dog never quits his hold of the meat, but is drawn up with it; then they begin to let off Crackers & Serpents underneath him, making a monstrous fire & smoke but the Dog still keeps fixt to his morsel in ye air, which he endeavours to eat, as fast as he can. Nobody allowed to bring Bears into Holland, May any other animals.

I hope some time or other in my life, to make all ye following voyages.
1. To the Whale Fishery
2. to the Coast of Guinea
3. The West Indies & America
4. The East Indies. Then
5. Home by Land: After which have only to visit the Baltic & the Mediterranean. Yet still I shall hardly be contented without a visit to
6. the Ota-h   shall not be without longing for a view of
7. China, & even with a Dutch Ship to
8. Japan.

Whenever I shall have made these voyages, then shall I be able to say, that even, that disunion so much lamented by me from a tie once to me the most dear, since it will have made me more free, will have turned out my greatest happiness.

In giving a Traveller's history to ye Public, when it is only designed to entertain the reader by some comical adventure or curious exhibition, as long as ye adventure is probable & the sight what has really in some place or another been exhibited, it matters not whether ye real adventurer or has been the actual spectator. There is hardly a book of travels, where some adventure or sight has not been related from imagination or hearsay.

Begun towards night to be warmer. I foretold a change of wind: That is more to ye South. Tomorrow I said w^d be calm; the next day we shd have a southerly wind.

In ye Ev^g we were upon ye *Brie Vierteen*, that is a bank where there is 14 Fathom water. This Bank is ye richest for fishing, hereabouts. Fish enough upon ye English side; but more upon ye Dutch.

If ye Wind had been Westerly instead of Easterly, where we are now w^d be full of Pilot (Lote's) Boats, looking out for ships from ye Channel: Now they are all looking out for those from ye Elbe.

Obliged to take a Pilot, going into the Texel; but the Hollanders, who knew the Entrance, sometimes cheat the Pilots, by making sign that they have got one aboard already.

Play'd a trick upon ye little Cook with regard to his bird, substituting a dead one in the Cage, & pretending his was dead: Which he took in good earnest, fell into a great passion, & charged us yth killing him: It was agreable enough afterwards to see his pleasure & surprise in finding him alive again.

Came upon a Bremener, who sail'd from Havre a day before us.

25 March King & I having agreed last night upon my proposal to up to ye top of ye mast, this morning we set about. King went boldly up first. I next. I thought I shd not be such a fool as to let go, therefore there c^d be no danger: However my Legs rather misgave me, for I cou'd not help this trembling a little when I was upon the Shrouds. I had good hold by my hand, & that is what I trusted to. I went up to the top of all, & turned the Vane with my hand.

I afterwards tried my art in climbing up (or what is called swarming up) a single rope a good way, which I did. Jack attempted to go up to the top of the Mast. He went a little way above ye Shrouds; but his heart fail'd him to go higher. I cover'd Loup's Ear with Tar.

Drest ye last remant of our provisions. The Bremener all day in Sight. No land to be seen. A very fine day. Wind S.E. but not much stirring, yet too much to fish. Quite brisk when I take exercise; a little lifeless otherwise.

Keep on with my Horace, Juvenal & the Dutch Grammar. Spoke with a Vessel, wch turned out to be one, wch sailed from Havre 2 days before us for Bremen: This is what the Captain declared yesterday, at a considerable distance to be ye Bremener. He told us, that the Texel bore S.S.W. We directly after spoke with another vessel from Groningen: Who told us, that the Texel (the Hollander call it Tessel) bore S.S.E. Our Captain said neither of them was right, for it bore S.E. The quarter, from wch exactly the Wind came. Drank out our last bowl of Punch: & now for meat & drink must come upon the Captain. King saw land first this afternoon.

26 March Captain says he saw Land in ye morning: it grew thick in the Horison, & could see it no more; all the morning looking for it: At 12 begun to think they had past the Texel: Water, 15 Fathom. Took ye Tar off Wolf's Ear, & found it much ye better of it: Took it off his Hair: by putting Butter on last night, & now washing ye butter off with very hot water. I caught a Raven alive with my hand: Clipt his wings, intending to keep him aboard ship; but the moment I let him loose, he hop'd overboard. When Bird's Wings are cut to prevent their flying, they must be cut unevenly; or one cut, & the other left untouched.

Caught in all 5 live Birds, & 5 or 6 we killed. I am sorry I brought no Gun with us. Very easy to catch a bird aboardship; are mostly very tame & tired.

Wind S.S.E. Expected all day Pilot's boats but none came. Saw the Land about noon; & kept it in sight the rest of the day.

Jack took heart to go up to the Top of the Mast, & turn the Vane, as well as we had done. Made a good fare upon ye Captain's Salt Beef. Spoke with a vessel, from ye Texel, bound for Looxtoo, or some such place, in the Prussian territories in the East Sea (the Baltic) as the Hollanders always call it.

27 March Still we have fine weather: Wind S. About 8 took a Pilot aboard: At 10 came to an anchor, just by one of the mouths of the Texel, to wait for the tide.

Clean'd & shaved myself; a little. Wrote some letters to be ready to send by the first boat ashore: But afterwards I found no opportunity of sending them sooner, than I shd arrive myself. We came into the Amsterdam River (or rather Sea) by the Brie, & not by ye Texel Island. At 3 weigh'd anchor, with the Tide. At 5 came to an anchor again, that the Ship might have its' clearance to go up to Amsterdam: After Sunset the Clear-master, as he is called, comes out to no vessel; and this being Sunday we expected he w^d not come to us: However he did; & so drunk, that he c^d not write & Mr King was obliged to write for him, what he dictated, as well as he cou'd in Holland's. Bought 24 large Plaice for a Guelder.

28 March Weigh'd anchor with the day. Wind got to ye E. of the S., by which we are to hope to get to Amsterdam by tomorrow evening; otherwise we c^d not have expected it with the Wind S. in less than 3 days; now it will be 2.

At noon drop anchor opp. Warkomin in Frieseland: another little town above it called Stenderlopen: above that again (as I think) Stavorn: from this latter town they say the first ship sail'd that ever found the passage through the Sound into the Baltic. The Captain sent his boat ashore with the little Cook, who was afterwards to walk all night, to go & acquaint the Captain's wife at some village in Frieseland of his arrival that she might come & meet him at Amsterdam; the little Cook had 12 Dutch miles to go; a walk he set out for with pleasure: We went to the shore along with him, but not near enough to go into the Town; & staying at land about half an hour, we returned to the Ship, which before we reached it had weigh'd anchor again & shortened the way to us by meeting us. The Wind being now exact S.E. & N.W. being the course we had to steer, we had the wind directly fair for us; a fine breeze: the Pilot resolving to go all night, with this fair wind & clear moon, we have to expect to get early to Amsterdam tomorrow morning.

29 March Wind continues fair. Captain being sick I let him lay all night in ye Cabbin bed; & I lay upon a sail in a little hole in the Steerage where Jack used to lie.

Past by Warkham about 9. Another story of the East Indian's: that he has seen people all red hair & skin, of a blood red; & that there are such people at Surinang. If I do not misremember, the ancient inhabitants of the West India Islands (the Caribbees) are said to have been of that colour. I believe Voltaire also takes notice of such a race of men.

All the passage up to Amsterdam from where we took in the Pilot, which they call a river, seems to me a Sea. Crowded with vast numbers of Fishing Boots; & yet they talked, of there being sometimes many more. This is the first voyage of any consideration I ever made without being sick; as I have not been at all this voyage of 13 days. Arrived at Amsterdam about noon. 8 stivers is the price of a Boot from the ship to the shore. Qu: if not 4. Made 2 trips – brought out Baggage; askd 3 Guelders & paid 2. Was obliged to pay the Captain about 2 guineas for our victualling aboard his Ship for these 5 or 6 days last. Put up at one Mr James Norman's; who had been a master of a Vessel; he kept (now) the Dog & Duck: Price 6 Stivers a night each bed. (4 Stiv: for that of the servant) 6 Stivers for Breakfast; 12 for Dinner; & 6 for Supper: Porter 8 Stivers a Bottle, or Pot from the Cask: Company, Captains of Ships; & all of them great Blackguards; But that does not matter much: Breakfast & sup generally alone. Went this first night yth some of ye Captains to visit those extraordinary asylums of men & women called Spiel-houses. They begin to have their company about 10. A large room. Benches all round. Music consisting of a fiddle & a Lute; or 2 fiddles. Girls sitting in the Benches, of all fashions & ages; some even old women of 40 or 50 down to 16: Some drest à la française, some quite like the Baur-magdkins of Holland: these girls dance sometimes 2 girls only together, a Holland dance, where one often stands still, the other dancing, sometimes quick sometimes slow; this each does alternately; sometimes both together dance: And sometimes a man & woman dance this dance: Then again at other times parties of 3 or 4 Couple of Minuets; some of ye men smoking their pipes at the time:

The men dance in the most awkward, clumsy manner; in some of their dances, they use as much labour & as many contortions in the most graceless way, that half the pains they take might under a french dancing master perfect them in the most graceful manner: More girls by far than men: The men don't in their appearance give you the least idea of young rakes; many of them old fellows of 40 or 50; all in the dress of Journeymen Shoemakers or Taylors: The waiters in the same stile; Dusty Porters in the day time; some now more hired to knock you down than to wait upon you; their business is to ply you with a bottle of wine, as soon as you come in; the price of this wine, at most of these houses is a Golden or 20 Stivers; at some you may get wine for 16 stivers a bottle. The white is a small french wine, wch is drinkable; the red, is a most abominable composition, I shou'd think it was a mixture of the Juice of Elder Berries & Sloes, & is really not drinkable: The Girls here very forward & impudent; they make nothing of talking to you in ye grossest manner, which conversation they will begin, by naming everything in plain terms: Some of these girls live at these houses, & you may lay with them there all night; others you may pick to go to their own homes; a Ducat for a night's sleeping will well content them; a Florin is enough for what we call a Flyer: The Girls have most of them the disfiguring fashion of wearing a very large patch upon some part of ye face: I think they have most of them a better appearance than most of the Covent Garden Street-walkers; Many of these girls are Germans, some French: These Houses are Licensed; we beat the round of them, 'till about 2 in the morning; having visited about 7 or 8 of them: for which expense 5 of us put in a couple of Florins apiece, & that sufficed. Never any riots, as I cou'd hear of in these houses; at least we saw no disposition towards it when we were there. Sent some letters off.

30 March Put my things in order, which took up most of the morning: In ye afternoon called upon Messrs Larwood & Van Hasselt; rec^{ed} some letters there; & was very politely & kindly rec^{ed} by them, from Mr Parish's recommendation. Walk'd about the Town; vastly pleas'd with it. Visited the Stadthouse; one of the finest buildings in the inside I ever saw (grand also without) Spacious Hall & arcades; all white & Blue vein'd marble; a fine Celestial Hemisphere laid down on ye floor; the Stars represented in Brass; the lower apartments free for every one to walk; had now workmen with scaffolding in ye large Hall repairing or beautifying: Went up to ye Top; Fine view of ye whole Town; about the 6th part of London, & ye 3d or 4th of Paris: Much fewer ships here than at London: Saw also ye Justice & Council rooms in ye Stadthouse, upstairs & below; very fine Dutch pictures.

31 March Visited the great riding-house; very spacious & excellent; Riding master a very awkward little fellow. Terms 30 Florins for the first 20 Lessons, afterwards a Florin a Lesson: Price in London is 2 or even 3 guineas for 16 Lessons, a month; here it is only 1½ guinea for ye same time & number of Lessons. A very fine new playhouse building; at present act in a tiny wooden Booth temporarily erected, where the old Playhouse was burnt down; & that is close by where the new one is built. An English horse, merely for ye saddle sold here lately for 2,200 Florins – 200 guineas: No English horses in ye Ridinghouse; but there were 3 or 4 Spanish horses. Several Ladies learn here, & gentlemen may see them ride: 3 or 4 other riding houses in Amsterdam, though smaller. I hear there are 7 in all at the Hague, where the terms of riding are rather higher. Also Ladies learn there; some in the English stile, sideways; some in the French across. The King's at Buckingham gate, the largest riding house in Europe; that at Hannover with the Copad Ceiling a very large & fine one. Spent a great deal of the rest of the day in reading English newspapers, to as far back as the Beginning of this year. 5 Coffeehouses at Amsterdam take in the English Newspapers: New English Coffeehouse, Lond. Ev. P. & Lloyd's. Paradise Bird C.H. – Whitehall & St James's. The French Coffy H. – ye Gazetteer . . . all in the Colbert Street, close out of the large square before the Stadt house.

1 April This Day being Good Friday I found pass here just like any other day: All full of Business: Change (which is a very good & large one) all full of People: Piazza's all round the inside of ye Change, Pillars number'd; so that such & such persons acquaint you they are to be found between such & such numbers. Vast numbers of singing Birds for sale in little cages: Canals through most of ye Streets: Town clean; & people too: A Shopkeeper will hardly let you come into a shop, if you are followed by a Dog: No English Booksellers here; though several at Rotterdam.

2 April Saw an imposter for ye first Beggar in ye Street; yesterday he was acting fits, which I *almost* thought real, though I even then had my doubts; However I contributed some little money to him: Now he was acting his part again in another quarter of ye Town, with ye same young fellow about him administering relief to him as if ye old man was just a dying: Amsterdam I shd have thought the last place for attempting such an imposture: I dare say his Carrier [career] won't be long. Furnish'd myself yth a Book of travels into Arabia by order of ye K. of Denmark. In the Coffeehouses observe, taken in Periodical papers, like our Adventurer or Rambler: One was called The Thinker: They have also very clever monthly productions; Registers of all that pass like our Magazines.

Wind very cold from ye South East; Clear Sun: but rather too cold to walk for pleasure. Saw a small collection of Birds & Beasts; mostly Parrots & monkeys; kept at a Wine-house; where calling for a Bottle of wine, you see these things gratis; the Collection was once larger: Saw there a small figure of a Woman (like a small doll) which mechanically play'd upon a small Lute. Expected to see or hear of a pack of Runaway Thieves & Rogues, at such a place as Amsterdam. There is one Lightholder comes to our house, chaced from Preston in Lancashire for coining: Many ingenious English Workmen settled abroad, from offences wch they committed at home. I found this Lightholder talking of an Allum work set up some 30 years ago at Trwyddfa near Swansea: He said his father was concerned in it, in company with Mr Thos. Pryce of Penllyrgare, & others; in all to the number of 12; that if they had stuck to the making of allium alone, & not copperas, they had an inexhaustible rock of it over ye coal, but that having lost some money (to the amount of about £500) at first setting out, the undertaking was dropt; 7 of the Partners being for dissolving it, against 5 for upholding it. He also spoke of my father's works (i.e. the Battery mills) as set up in that neighbourhood; I then acquainted him who I was; & he said, he had known my father & uncle very well. I talked to him a good deal about Swansea & its neighbourhood, all wch he was well acquainted with as well as the people thereabouts. He mentioned a circumstance of one Joe: Morgan employed by my father in his mills, who had gone away from him with a plan of them into the employ of Patten & Co. & that he was suspected of giving him ye plan, wch he denied, but if there was any such plan taken, I thought by his own story, it was probably given to Morgan by himself: He confessed, that he had [been] upon his trial in Lancashire for High Treason in coining guineas & shillings, that his trial last'd 13 hours, that 8 witnesses swore positively to seing him in the fact, but that he proved, he was at that time in Holland: However he admitted to, that he made some advantage from the copy of ye Indictment not being given to him in due according to ye Statute before ye Trial. There is one circumstance I shall not forget; & that he told us, Sir Fletcher Norton being counsel agst him, Sr Fl. told the Jury they had before them one of ye most notorious offenders in ye kingdom, that he was guilty beyond all doubt, & so certain was he of that, that he himself cd swear he was guilty; upon which Lightholder interrupts him & the Court, charging Sr Fletcher with being an accessory; because if he was so positive, he must have been present & concerned yth him: This put Sr Fletcher to such a Raid [rage] that he was obliged to tuck his gown up under his arm, & march out of the Court.

This same Lightholder pretends to all manner of arts & sciences, says he was concerned in establishing a Copper Rolling mills in Hungary, a Plate Glass manufactory & other works; He is now employ'd here in setting up some works for the Glazing of Cottons: he says, he has seen the Copper mines in Barbary, that he c^d have put them there in ye way, of bringing their ore in ye first melting to Regulus (or Regular, as he called it) & in ye second to fine Copper: that there are means enough for any european who understands the art of refining metals to make his fortune there. He pretends that he cannot now go to England on account of the works he was engaged under the Court of Vienna; but he allows also, that Mr Chamberlayne of ye Mint must also first be consulted previous to his return to England. He abuses L'Anglois, who was Secretary to Ld Stormont, when he was served with process at Vienna to return home; & says, he is an Alien born, at Naples I think or Venice, his father too being an Alien, though he is himself in ye British Parliament & has an office in ye Tower.

There is another strange talkative pretending Character comes here, a horse-doctor, called Langford, came from Bedford, was a Dragoon (though a little fellow) or Light horseman in ye last war, & had been in employ under the Prince of Monaco at Versailles.

I must not forget too of this Lightholder, that he declares he has travelled all over, Arabia, & also in China; that he has been in ye inner City of Canton (through favor of his Uncle, who was a Missionary there) & also in Pekin: N.B. He himself is a Catholic. He says London w^d stand in a corner of Pekin, that he was 3 days riding round that city; yet he questions whether there is not more building in London; no house being at Pekin more than one story high.

3 April Beggars enough & impostors too, in this Town of Amsterdam. Walked round about one half of the walls this morning: The Town is very little bigger than Hamburgh.

4 April Now walked round the other half of ye Town, between ye River & the Amstel, which is the pleasantest side: A fine Canal to Harlaem: A great number of 2 wheel Phaetons; with 2 horses, driving upon ye road to Harlaem; close by ye side of ye Canal; drive very fast; fine Black cattle; mostly all mares, from Frieseland do not esteem Geldings. Drivers of these Phaetons, all sit on the left side; which in England we shd esteem very awkward for holding the whip.

5 April Went down with our Landlord Norman in his Boat, as far as the Pampus, which may be called the Bar of the Harbour: Was aboard an American Brig; where ye Captain had his wife aboard, who begun crying & roaring because he w^d not bring her up in our Boat. Was also aboard an American Sloop, who had bro' Rice here from New York, without calling at any port in England. Saw a Dutch India-man upon Camels, as  they are called; being 2 large covered Barges, as long as ye Ship, one of one side the other of the other; these fit the sides of the Ship, the Camels being concave on one side; they are lash'd under & fastened together yth ropes: but first when put to the sides of the ship, they are filled instantly with water, by opening a part; then being fixt toye Ship; all this water is pumped out of ye Camels, which makes them rise & the Ship with it, which so sails drawing very little water, & so all ships as Indiamen & Men of War, though without their Stores, must do to sail in & out of the Port of Amsterdam.

When we returned up, we had rain & very squally wind, which brought us gunnel to, & made our mast bend so much that Norman was fearful it w^d break. King staid at home.

6 April They give a great price for walking canes here; even as far as from 20 to 50 guineas: Most brought from London.

A great many more pleasure boats kept here than in London; These pleasure boats they make at great expence, some as far as £200; there are places paled in on purpose for ye boats, called *Yacht-harbours*; where for a small pitch to put their Boat in, they give 50 or £100 for ye inheritance of it. Dined at Mr Van Yasselts; a Dutch Dinner is a stupid affair; 5 minutes at silent prayer before they begun to eat.

My inclination for ye Greenland Fishery is more turned towards a voyage to the Coast of Guinea.

7 April Fenced a good deal; & was in the Evening at the Play; seated in what is called the Bach; Same as our pit, with Seats; but genteeler company; price 24 Stivers: Many pretty women there; dress'd in English fashion; some abominable ugly Jewesses: Zemiri & Azer was the play; a piece with pretty music & decorations.

8 April Consumed the Morning at home; preparing to pack off some of my things for London. In the Evening was present at the most agreable concert I ever attended. The two Mlles Pocorny from Prague played most delightfully on ye *French-horn*; and sung many airs; After wch they danced some allemandes; with all wch I was so taken & with ye beautiful person of ye Youngest that I fell most desperately in Love.

9 April In ye afternoon was at an entertainment in ye Great Riding house, wch they call (very preposterously) a Carousal: There were 16 Cavaliers: 2 at a time ride different ways or sides round the Riding-house, & at different Corners 1st they take a ring off a hook a little higher than

their head with a pike; 2d they throw a dart. 3d fire a pistol at a paste-board head set up; 4th strike at this head with a sword; or 5th pick up from ye ground at ye fullest gallop a past-board face or mask, which the pistol has blown off ye head: During all this music accompanies; & to conclude they perform ye Exercise of ye Cavalry: These are ye Gentle-men Scholars of ye Riding house; Ladies are introduced by Tickets into ye Gallery; & there are many spectators seated atop by ye windows of ye house.

10 April In ye Ev^g 8 o-clock set off in ye Track-Sckyt with King, for Utrecht: Hired ye Cabbin, or as it is called, the Roof: 4 St. 4 D. & 2 D. besides, for our passages.

11 April Arrived at Utrecht ½ after 4 in ye morning: Had ye pleasure of a very fine day: The Spring very forward: Horse Chestnut trees & several others out: The Town very pretty; clean; Houses excellent: Streets wide: Vast quantity of fine garden-ground about ye Town; putting one in mind of little Chelsea: A fine mall just out of ye Town, inclosed with low boards, about 2 feet high, for some sport, as the mall was in St James's park.

Beau Russel with his wife lodg'd at the New Antwerp Castle Inn here. (Le Nouveau Chateau d'Anvers)

Visited in a Chaise a little place about a couple of Leagues off, towards Guelderland, called Size; where there is a society of people called, *Les Frères, et les Soeurs, Evangeliques.* The men live in one large pile of Building, the women in another: Each employ'd in different suitable employs & manufactures: Among ye men there are Silver-Smiths, Toymen, Sadlers, Tinmen &c &c. Women; Ribbon & weavers milleners &c: All their goods displayed in a very neat manner in different apartments according to each assortment; equally civil whether you lay out money or not; but hardly possible to avoid doing so: They have also several articles, which they do not make themselves, as Whips from England, Hardware from Do. &c; Gentlemen & Ladies can both visit the Brothers but only Ladies ye Sister's apartments: The Sisters may marry any they please but are ex-pected mostly to marry yth ye Brothers: They are of all nations, but mostly Dutch: Their religion I believe is what we call Moravian in England.

12 April In walking round ye walls, was follow'd by a fine pointer; whom I brought to Amsterdam: Perhaps this might in England be called stealing him. At 1 in ye Afternoon set out again in ye Track Skuyt on my return: but it was in ye Daytime; did not hire ye Roof; for both our passages, we paid this time 31 Stivers: or 2St. 7D. I suppose I paid some-thing more for our having cushions put for us, as also some others had, on ye common seats of ye Skuyt. Got to Amsterdam by 8 in ye Evening. The Borders of ye Amstel down wch we came & all the passage from Utrecht very rich, & finely set off by Gardens & Buildings.

13 April Was again at the French-horn Concert. Still in Love, but not desperately as before. It w^d have completed my story to have married this girl, & brought her to England as my only wife.

14 April Few people w^d be pleased with this house, except Captains of Ships. Too full of company. Grubb's genteeler. All the English settled in these sort of Houses abroad are those, who have fled their own country for Crimes. Grubb was a Pawnbroker who run away with all ye goods in his possession: And I suppose, did we know his history our Norman, who told us this story of Grubb, w^d not turn out much better.

15 April Astonishing the ignorance of Sea Captains: One of them, an old opinionated fellow called Langton from Whitby w^d persist to me that the Frozen Zone was a river, which he had often passed: Neither did he nor any others here know ye difference between an Island and a Continent. Any large County [Country] as England for example they w^d call a Continent. Preparing to set out for Harlaem: Which we did at 5 o'clock; Track-Skuyt going every hour, as from most Towns in Holland either every hour or every 2 hours. Arrived in Harlaem at 8. At the Golden Lion: a good house, civil & reasonable. Supt at a Round Table, with some other gentlemen, but most of the company consisted of a set of high German Players, then in the Town, who gave some very good, German & French songs; there were 2 Actresses also; who were tolerable.

16 April Went to see the Flower Gardens, for wch this Town is most famous, vast shew of them; particularly of Hyacinths. Learnt than [that] in England they succeeded most in Carnations and Auriculas; in Holland, Tulips & Hyacinths: The Beds consist of a compost of Sand, Cowdung, & Tanners Bark (or much rotted Leaves) equal parts; Let this bed rest every 6 years; Change ye flowers therein every year. Among the seeds of ye Single Hyacinths, 1 in a thousand may be double, so that they esteem their trade a Lottery, & when they throw a pod of seed away, they say perhaps there goes 3,000 Florins, for a Hyacinth root has been known to sell for as much; they never bear a constant value, but decrease very fast as they become common. Colours in these flowers are esteem'd more for their oddity & rarity, than beauty: You give at some Gardens a trifle to ye servant who shows 'em to you.

LEYDEN. At noon went to Leyden: which we reached in 4 hours; University much decreased there; there have been 200 English Students: as they tell you, there at a time: Ld Baltimore studied at this University;

now not above 4 or 5 English. A pretty neat Town: At $\frac{1}{2}$ after 6 we set out again for the Hague; but I falling in Love with a fine mastiff Dog, who took to us in the Street, I Christen'd him More, stole him, & to be more sure of my prize, walk'd or rather run all the way to the Hague wch I reach'd a full half hour before ye Skuyt. Put my dog up at a Stable, at a Guelder per week: Then went & took up my Lodging at one Mrs Heywood, called the London Punch-house, next door to the Inn, where puts up the Amsterdam Post-Waggon: And was soon afterwards joined by King & Jack, who came with the Skuyt.

17 April Saw the Parade: Some Swiss here; the Prince in Person was upon ye parade as he almost always is: Wears the Prussian Hat; an ill-looking little Dutch figure; yet has likeness of our King; seems good-humor'd. Soldiers look well. Hague a fine town; the only one I have seen in Holland, with several open places in it: & here there are fewer Canals through ye streets, than in most others.

Palace nothing extraordinary. Walk't in ye Hague-wood, which is very fine, & the Prince has there a Seat. Dined at the Marechal Turenne; good ordinary, but little company. No Plays in Holland for a Sunday. Saw no Street-walkers here, yet the Hague full of Girls of pleasure, as I have heard.

18 April Saw Mr Maddeson, Sir Joseph Yorke's Private Secretary, an acquaintance of Mr King's; affable & polite. Dined today at the Parlement d'Angleterre, this with the Marechal Turenne, the Best houses in Town; much frequented by ye English, seem good ones, but dear: The one we are at Dear enough, 3 days costing us, 2 guineas & a half.

Was at ye Play; pretty compact Theatre; a fine illuminated Box in ye Center for ye Statholder. Saw here again ye young Baron Schimmelman; whom I before saw at Amsterdam: very affable & good-natured; now here from Gottingen; Mr King saw him there with my Sister.

19 April Pester'd with the Company of a fellow calling himself Ld Lenox, the most empty vulgar & open impostor I ever met with: Remember to have seen ye fellow before in London. Mrs Heywood, a widow left with 9 children; her eldest being wild, she got him trepan'd into a Prussian Garrison, & there detain'd as a Soldier.

In ye afternoon set out for Rotterdam which we reach'd in 3 hours; ye company of some very noisy fellows, partly English, partly Italian; we joined our noises to theirs, & a most glorious uproar we made all ye way; sometimes playing too at l'Amore: (Cinque, due with our fingers) My mastiff, bringing up his Stomach & the Ld knows what, enough to poison a regiment; yet no Dutchman dared to say a word. (James Moore ye name of one of ye Englishified Italians)

ROTTERDAM. *20 April* Put up at one Moses Maultby's in ye Wijn Straat; an English House, which Captains frequent; seems a civil fellow; His waiter is from Norfolk, having till last Mich-mas [Michaelmas] had a farm there of £100 a year; before a groom in some Baronet's service for 12 years; now a fugitive here with a wife & Child, for ye Debts he contracted in Farming, from keeping too many horses: Hardly an Englishman abroad, but some private history wch show you a reason yr [they] w^d not wish to own: 2 Coiners lately arrived here: A general Amnesty every 20 or 30 years necessary to restore many English with y^r families to their own Country; and after ye pennance they had done some of them might turn out very useful subjects: They all to a man behave very well abroad: Those who have committed Felonies are not so secret as to ye cause of their being abroad, as those who are only in Debt. I suspect our boat-acquaintance, Jas Moore, because he had been to ye Hague to get a Passport from the Venetian Ambassador to Venice which he might as well have brot with him from London. That fellow assured me that 6 months ago, he knew a young fellow of 17 a Housebreaker hanged at Tyburn, & recover'd as soon as brought home to his father's house: After wch he went abroad. One of ye Coiners came over here, now gone to North America. Consumed a good deal of ye Morning in arranging my baggage, now seperating Mr King's things from mine. N.B. The Day we arrived here, there was an exec^on [execution] of a woman for the murder of her husband. The circumstances were these. A man was taken in Prussia for a Thief: He confesses, & adds to his crimes that he was concerned with a certain woman in Holland in the Murder of her Husband: The Thief is executed; the Confession sent over here: That is esteemed sufficient to put the woman to ye Torture, which she suffer'd & then confess'd that she murdered her husband, & *boiled* her Child: Her execution was made by tying her to a post & then strangling her: After which her body was left to hang upon a Gallows to rot: These Gallows were [where] the bodyes hang are enclosed by a wall not easily scaled but have a door in them.

King as usual went to visit a Riding house; in which every town in Holland abounds. In the afternoon paid our old score to ye English Newspapers at the Coffeehouses, of which there are two, that take them in here. *21 April* Walkt about the Town. Inquired after vessels to Dieppe & Havre. Read some of Virgil. In the afternoon saw a game of Billiards play'd in which a Captain of an English Vessel took a Ball in his mouth & blew it out for his stroke, chusing his stand, & giving Mr King 8, but he lost: Nor did he seem to do it well.

N.B. There is a woman in ye Stadthouse Prison at Amsterdam; who suffer'd the torture & survived it: It was done by dislocating every joint in her Limbs, drawing her lip, with a weight at her feet: Tho' ye evidence was strong agst her for murder, yet by y^r foolish Laws, they put her to ye Torture, worse than Death, but c^d not execute her: The torture was over in 5 minutes; & so was then the custom; but now they extend it to 15: Few endure it: This woman is now living, but confined for Life: she has so much the use of her arms as to sew, but seems a good deal pent to her body; as I was told, but I did not see her myself; for wch I am to blame.

Went in ye Eve^g to some Spiel-houses; but they are poor affairs here to what they are at Amsterdam. Saw General Stewart at the Coffeehouse whom I before saw at the Hague: Has a redgment [regiment] in ye Dutch Service: Have heard he was deprived of a Com^{mon} [Commission] in our service, for a speech in Parl^t during the late King's reign; but my authority is not the best; being from that knave & fool the pretended Lord Lenox. (Left off 'till May 5)

22 April Everything prepared for setting off for Helvoet. Went down first to the Brill. Cost for us (exclusively of what others paid) a Ducat. 5 hours this down the Maese.

HELVOETSLUYS. Hired an Extra-open Waggon; & arrived at Helvoet-Sluys, by 9 o'clock in the Ev^g. Put up at Mr Wood's.

23 April This & Wensday the regular days for ye Packets to sail; Usually sail about 3 in the afternoon; the Mail arriving from Rotterdam about 2. This day the wind coming from the West, which is quite contrary & blowing very hard, the Captain determined not to sail: though he had order'd an hour my things aboard. Lownged about the rest of the day.

A Swiss *Half-Gentleman* arriving about dinner-time, we permitted him at our table; & he very coolly took poss^n [possession] of our Room, as his own: As an antidote to the insipidity of his company, I always had our Landlord to dine & sup with us.

This Wood is famous for being the father of the Young man concerned in ye Forgery for £4,500 upon the Bank in Vamneck's name; & afterwards another more extra [extraordinary] forgery in a public Coffeehouse upon Walpole & Co. He has never been turn'd [tried] because he turned insane; & as such has been ever since in the Compter in London.

24 April Helvoet seems entirely a factitious harbour; yet so advanced into the Sea, as never to be left dry: Water deep enough in ye Road close to ye Harbour for any Man-of-war. 2 Frigates & an Indiaman now lying off the mouth. Saw some company set off in the Captain's Barge: Rowers all in an uniform; of white Course shirts, tied yth Green Ribbons.

25 April This day King departed for Rotterdam in ye ordinary; Passage Boat. Fare thee well! Pleasant Companion & good Errand. From Rotterdam he sails for Havre, to conduct my sister afterwards for Rouen.

26 April Wind & tide presenting a moment a little more favourable; About 3 o'clock in ye afternoon, we set out yth ye Packet; Captⁿ Cockerill; an old Fellow; said to be worth £40,000.

Most of our Passengers comprised of Jews. You pay 14 shill^{gs} apiece for a permit to go over; which money goes to our Post-office; & nothing more need be paid: But you pay for a bed on Board the Packet a Guinea. A servant, when he is joined in his master's pass, pays 7 shillings. The Captain will ask a guinea too for his bed; but will take half a guinea. I had taken a Hair-dressing German over yth me; because he was very clever; & had thoughts of keeping him for his [my] servant. His name is Joseph Francis born near Vienna; has travelled all over Europe & talks most languages: Behaved very well a Ship-board; had been much used to ye Sea; cooks well; was very assiduous & serviceable. I stood the first 4 hours, without being sick; & then begun the usual course upwards & downwards; But cannot say, that I was very sick: I could even amuse myself with reading all the time.

27 April In the morning, again a little sick: But stirred & moved about; above Deck & below: Was soon the only Passenger that could do as myself: Forced myself to eat at dinner: In the afternoon quite Brisk & well; & eat a very hearty supper. Wind all this time very high; but had got tolerably favorable. Now quite well from ye Sea.

28 April At 6 in the Morning arrived at Harwich: Our persons searched by the Custom-house officers aboard.

HARWICH. Put up at ye 3 Cups. There found a Letter from my Brother. Had my Baggage easily delivered from the Custom-house; nothing hardly that c^d under any pretence be seized; but for civility tipt him half a-guinea: The Jewfellows gave him 6 lb of Tobacco: another Silk Handkerchiefs & so on as a present. I had been generous to my Servant-fellows; giving them a Guineas apiece; on account of their beds if they had chose to have taken any; which Jack did (being very sick) but the German not. However there seemed some falshood & Chicanery on ye German's side, in dividing this money, I absolutely turned him off: The poor Devil made all the precations in the World; & afterwards, run after the Coach, or holding behind it, for the first 10 miles. I then took pity upon him; recollected his poverty; considered some circumstances that still appeared in this matter in his favor; (though upon my first inquiries he told me a plain lie, that he had given the Captain a Guinea, when upon my asking the

Captain, he assured me he had given him but half a one) and so I took him again. Three of these Jew Merchants, the Swiss & I took a Coach & 4 horses between us: We set out at 8: changed 3 times horses; cost us a guinea a-piece: I paying also another for my servants on ye outside: and arrived in Town at the King's Arms Inn Leadenhall Street at 10 at night: Where I took up my abode. I think I was past by on ye Road by W. Eden in a Phaeton with Poll Jones, his whore.

I was used to forget these fellows with us were Jews, & was plaguing them every stage, to partake of some of the meet I ordered; But they excused themselves, under not being hungry, not having time; eating only an Egg, & so forth.

29 April This Day my Eyes were once more blest yth ye sight of my most dear & affectionate Brother John Morris; & of my sister Margaret,* with those sweet Motherless Infants, my excellent Sister† Lockwood's Children! My Brother had his abode in Conduit Street, ye corner of George Street. My Brother here speedily informed me of his happy prospect in his speedily going to be married to a daughter of Sir Philip Musgrave's of ye County of Cumberland; a most amiable young Lady;‡ fortune sufficient; & family most respectable & opulent. How happy for him! How happy wᵈ such a match have been for me! But how sincerely did I partake in his Joy! I had the pleasure too of seeing Miss Molly Lloyd (of Mabus) who had come up to Town on purpose to see my sister, & taken her abode within a couple of doors. There I found when I first came into the room Mrs Vaughan, of Golden Grove & another Lady, I askt Miss Lloyd, audibly enough for the others to hear me, whether those Ladies were of my acquaintance: She made no reply; for they were just upon the move & it was too dark to distinguish them; However I heard it was Mrs Vaughan; my long acquaintance, even from our cradles: But she chuses to be huft upon account of that long remembered disappointment from me & my little Heroine, when we left England, instead of observing, as accurately as she expected, her invitation to Ranelagh: Let her be offended: I have tried to remove the offence: And let her be ever so much my enemy, I shall take no revenge.

Nullum memorabile nomen
Faemineâ in poenâ est: nec habet Victoria laudem.

30 April This day I spent mostly in my Brother's pleasant society in

---

* Margaret Morris married Noël Joseph Desenfans, born 1745, who became an Art Dealer with the aid of her £5,000 dowry. His pictures were left to Dulwich College.
† Bridget Morris.
‡ Henrietta Musgrave.

Conduit Street; & there I dined. The rest of the day with my Sister & my little Nephew & Nieces; whom I all found to have been taught to bear an extreme affection for me. I called upon Mr Cox, the attorney, Castle Yard, Holborn, upon Mr King's affairs; but found he was unable to do anything.

1 May I dined with Mr Thos. Lockwood, by whom I was received very kindly & politely. The rest of the day dedicated to the company of my dear relations. This & the former Evenings I spent at the New-York Coffee house by the Exchange in the company of my good & obliging friend Mr Wm Tolson, whom I first knew at Wansbeck.

2 May I wrote a Letter this day to Prevost, that I shou'd be ready to be forthcoming in the Court of Chancery before the conclusion of this term, if he would agree yth me to appoint a Day: the only answer I had was information from Mr Geo. Jones, that a messenger of the Court of Chancery was already in pursuit with a warrant out against me.

The inveteracy of their persecution & their ungenerosity of proceedings will ever go together. This Evening I called upon Mr Richard Jones, in Castle Yard; my solicitor in all these matters. I supt with Mr Tolson at the Exchange Coffee House; a fine new room near the Bank Buildings. At night I lay for the first time at a Lodging I had taken in ye house of some Jewesses N 118 Fenchurch Street: I had drunk a full Bottle of Port to my share this Evening; a stronger wine than I had been for some time used to; & therefore when I came into ye Air, more than I w^d well bear: Overpowerd in this manner I made some advances to ye Jew Maid, & thank God I did not succeed: Had I, I sh^d have been miserable: And I can assert upon my honor, that since with Fanny I went abroad, this is the only woman I ever made the least attempt upon, contenting myself with ye posson [possession] of one I esteemed my lawful wife, & whom from taste of pleasure I prefered to all women: yet from her have I been debarred ever since now September last.

3 May This morning I was plagued before I set out with a pack of fellows, who called themselves City Drummers, to congratulate me upon my marriage, & to give them a guinea: A pretty Burlesque truly: Another fellow calling himself the Beadle of St. George's Parish had been to make the same modest application to me at my Brother's.

I sallied forth with a determined resolution to resist with my sword, any person who under colour from the court of Chancery shou'd attack me. I walked to Anderson's Coffee-house, Fleet Street, where I had ye pleasure of being met to Breakfast by Mr Howarth.* I appointed to dine with him

* Of Mitre Court, Inner Temple.

at the Horn Tavern. From here I walked to Mr Richd Jones's; & with him I staid all the rest of the morning. Finding myself not quite well from the Wine of yesterday; I took a vomit to clear my head; which I workt off in his office, amidst all his Clerks. Mr Bearcroft being told by Mr Howarth, that I was come to Town, resolved to dine with me: In wch he did me great honor; & I esteem it a mark of his friendship & partiality. He was too open & candid to tell me, that he could approve or justify my conduct in going off with the young Fanny: But he said, it was a matter that admitted of palliation; We have all faults; & a man is not for a fault to be given up: He said of all those, who spoke slightingly of me there was not one, who, if I had happened by my marriage to possess my wife's fortune, would not have come to my table, upon invitation so far to partake in it. He readily accepted to be my Council; He advised me by all means, for ye present to keep a little up; & in order to be prepared in my measures; & especially upon ye account of my Brother's expected marriage which ought first to be concluded. He said, he would not insult my understanding by advising me not to resist by force of Arms the officer of the Court of Chancery. There dined with us besides, the two Jones's my good friends. After Dinner I retired by Mr Howarth's kind Leave to his Chambers, Mitre Buildings Temple. There I intend to keep up, till all my affairs are ready to be brought upon ye Carpet. My Brother called here at 11 at night: & staid with me till one. His prospects of happiness become every day nearer & more certain: Everything now concluded upon but the day.

4 May Employ all my time in preparing my defence. I saw my Brother for a little while this morning. In the Evening Mr Tolson supt with me.

5 May All this day I had not the pleasure of seing my Brother, who was too much engaged in his matrimonial affairs. Mr Tolson dined with me: For supper, I had none. Mr Howarth's Clerk & Servant, Mr Williams, as he calls himself, is ye greatest Puppy, Rake & Coxcomb I ever knew: I fancy however he is faithful to his Master's Interest.

6 May I had a little more composed rest: For some time my mind had been so much disturb'd I cou'd not sleep beyond 5 o'clock. Today I did not get up 'till 10. Howarth's Clerk is for ever filling the Chambers yth Whores. My good friend Edmondes of Cowbridge called upon me, who I was happy to see. He, with Franklen, Mr Geo. Jones, & Mr Tolson, supt with me.

7 May Begun the Brief to my Counsel; which I am resolv'd for greater perspicuity, to give them in Print. I did not see my Brother all today. Tolson I had again to sup with me.

8 May My Brother I saw in the morning. His affair goes on swimmingly. The Bridal Present of a Watch is bought; the Coach is preparing. The 25th everything will be ready. The whole Town rings with the news, that he is going to be married to the prettiest woman in it. Mr Humphrey Howarth (Brother of my friend ye Councillor) dined with me. Howarth not quite well. Conversation came about – talk'd that I had better have ye windows open to enjoy ye air: I resolved to sally forth immediately: I took my sword under my arm; Slippers on; & great Coat; an odd figure I cut: Unfortunately I met a fellow who seemed to smile; I return'd back; threaten'd him a Slap of ye face; & was for drawing my sword; which however I gave into ye hands of Howarth's Clerk, who came out with me, & then wanted to call him aside to account: He was too prudent: And I by my hastiness only disgraced myself in the adventure. I must begin to call myself a Tomahawk: a Set who make themselves particular, & when any stare at them, draw their swords & demand satisfaction: A proper term for us would be Anti-Basilisks; we do not kill, by looking ourselves at others, but we kill upon their looking at us.

9–12 May These days I passed, employed in Mr Howarth's chambers entirely in the consideration of my affairs; & have now pretty nearly finished my Law researches, & my instructions for Counsel. The only person I have seen besides those before mentioned is Mr Wm Woodfall; Printer of the Morning-Chronicle; my constant & very good friend: Wensday, I found myself in very good spirits; & why I could not conceive, unless it was that the report of the King of France's death, by this time came pretty nearly confirmed: I do love Bustle variety & disturbance, to my very Soul. Mr Franklen informed me of his Brother Will having left our Employ in the Copper Works and his being now in Town: His plan is to make something more of a gentleman in case he sh^d succeed to his fortune. Franklen is the prudentest fellow I know. Edmondes* I fear is in a bad way, as to his finances.

My Servant Francis I sent for to me on Wensday: He seems an assiduous useful fellow; & I shall now keep him by me. Jack as less useful I must part with: I hear he has already cause to lament the stinging embraces of a London whore. (In this I mistake as to Locality; for I must substitute Marseilles instead: the effect of what was there obtained is lasting, as ye distance is great.) I believe he is honest. I sh^d not like to have any distress come upon him; Neither must I upon his account too much distress Myself.

13–14 May Still in snug quarters at Mr Howarth's. I had proposed

* Of Cowbridge, Glamorganshire.

bringing my matter on in ye Court of Chancery, as soon as my Brother's marriage was over: but every proposal I made upon my part for voluntarily appearing being disrespected I became less inclined to appear at all. Edmondes comes to inform me that the Chr̄s Mēssr̄ [Chancellor's Messenger] says he is to have £100 if he can find me. This alone, I esteem provocation enough to be off; it arguing a doubt, whether I will appear & being a sort of Challenge who shall have more management in ye matter. Besides whatever reason they have for pressing my appearance, the same I must have, though I do not know it, to keep it back: and I have no doubt, but the ambiguity they will now be thrown in will a good deal distress them: already not knowing what to do with the person, whom by their absurd management & pretended care they have already so much distrest. I am also more prest to be off, because Howarth informs me, that he must absolutely have the Chambers to himself the next week on account of his Sessions Clients.

15 May   This morning I resolved to take some decisive steps: Accordingly I got up a little after 6. I left the Chambers a few minutes after 7, walking with Will to Fleet Ditch through the Courts where I took a coach, & came to the Exchange Coffee house; having before appointed to meet Mr Tolson to breakfast at the New York: I sent to him there; & he soon joined me. From hence Mr Tolson & I walkt towards Moorfields where we hired a saddlehorse: I staid a little while at Moorgate Coffee house; & then Mr Tolson hired a one Horse-Chaise besides: In the mean while Will having gone home to prepare his dress, he came to see us again, & we set out upon this Party for an airing. At first I went in the One h. [horse] Chaise; & we took our route to Highgate returning through Hamstead; thence by Tyburn Turnpike.

In the new buildings the outside of the Turnpike we had the pleasure to see my Brother looking out of a window; for this was at Mr Greville's Country-air Lodgings. I stopt & he came down to speak. I there explained to him, that I was resolved to go off for Hamburgh; because I was certain that my presence there wᵈ both facilitate & expedite every question I wanted to have determined. He suffered himself to submit to my discretion; & therefore approved of my intentions. I pluckt up my best chearfulness: He was himself a little low; complaining of a head-ache: I tried to leave him both with giving & receiving as little pain as possible. We now therefore went on our way, which was laid out for me to pay a visit to Mrs Hales at Castle-Bear near Ealing. At present I was got a horse-back; a circumstance I had like to have had some reason to repent; for my horse being of ye true hackney Breed, & beginning to be foundered, he made a most dangerous trip with me, which brought his nose to ye ground, & me over his head. However I had ye good luck not to be in ye least hurt: I mounted him again, but soon thought it best to let Will ride him; which he did, not without similar danger.

We stopt at a house at Acton, & there ordered a Dinner: And then went on for this Castle-Bear.

I had the pleasure of seing Mrs Hales, & her 2 little Children, who seemed very promising: Sophy even gets handsomer in the face than Betsey: Mrs Hales has a very pretty little house & garden for £16 a year; & reced [received] me with great pleasure. She told me, that Fanny directly after she came to her mother had said, that all her happiness in Life was then at an end. Fickle creature; under weak & wicked advisers.

We returned & took our dinners: & got to Moorfields again about 8. Will rode ye horse, but not without 2 falls: He then met us at the Swan in Lad Lane, with some things of mine; as I had purposed to set off that very night for Leeds, intending thence for Newcastle, Leith & Hamburgh: But we were too late for the Leeds Coach; or ye Leeds Coach was full.

We did not take up our Lodging here, but went to another Northern Road Inn, close by; the Cross-keys in Wood Street: There I was very near going off in a Lincolnshire Coach; but at last I chose to lie there that night.

I must not omit, that coming home on Sunday Evening, I chose to pass through Rathbone Place, for the first time since I came to Town. The Dining room parlour windows were shut: But I think I saw that nasty bitch Miss Hogson [Hodgson] looking out of the 2 pr [pair] of Stair Windows in her usual nasty Bed-gown.

I stood up in the Chaise on purpose to make myself conspicuous. I past into Percy Street: then desired Mr Tolson to step out, & go to demand the young woman as my wife, in order to ground an action, if necessary to try one. He readily did so. He found some difficulty to be admitted; but finding himself at last obliged to declare to ye Maid his business, Mrs Harford, putting on her best termagent voice hails him from ye top of ye Stairs, first of all ordering the Street door to be Shut upon him, perhaps thinking it was me.

When he said, he came from me commissioned to claim my wife: 'He claim a wife: he claims a gallows: Why does he not claim her of his [her] guardian, the Lord Chancellor?' Then she said 'Let the fellar out.' He soon came & reported this to me; & it served us at least for a little present fun; as well as it must have served them for surprise.

16 May I thought it was now time to alter my counsels; & Mr Tolson coming to the Inn about 10 in ye morning, I drest & went out yth him: taking a Coach at Guildhall; for a few Streets; then going out of it, & seing that nobody had observed; I walked into Moorfields; & took another Coach to Islington Church. I then went to a house called the Gun, where in an hour or two's time I was joined by Mr Tolson: In the meanwhile I had been occupied in preparing directions for what was to be done in my absence.

We afterwards walked a little about Islington fields; & then dined at the Jerusalem Tavern, Clerkenwell.

From thence we walked to Hick's Hall; past through Charterhouse Square, Cripplegate & to Moorfields: then I parted with Mr Tolson, who went to prepare the necessaries for my new intended departure; which was now designed for Liverpool, thence to Glasgow, Edinburgh & Hamburgh: Had I gone ye other way I proposed revisiting a little my old School acquaintance at Heath, & when passing through Cumberland to have taken a peep at my Brother's new-intended Lady's paternal seat. I sauntered about Moorfields, & all the Jews' residences about Houndsditch: At last I took it into my head to go to Hoffman's Bishopsgate Street; where I staid a full half-hour, & eat some ices.

Returning to Moorgate Coffeehouse I was met by Mr Tolson; who had prepared everything for my departure; & was ready kindly to accommodate me with £20 in cash.

I gave him ample written directions for what more was to be done; & also a letter for My Br. [Brother]. Then I went with him into Houndsditch & from Mr Mundeford Allen's old Situation where my dogs were in keeping, took up my dog Loup; & now being joined by my little Baggage, we sauntered away a little remnant of time at a Porterhouse: At 8 o-clock I took Leave of my good friend Mr Tolson; & set off in the Liverpool Coach, having taken a place as far as Warrington.

17 May Having set out last night in ye Liverpool Coach, I was first accosted at a little Alehouse at Highgate; by one who was riding upon ye outside as far as St. Albans, by his saying, that he remembered my face, & thought he had been a School with me. He askt first if I had not been at School at Newington; then he askt about ye Charterhouse, which I chose to acknowledge; then he purposely recollected me in every other respect than my name; in which I to the last deceived him; for I told him it was Chapman, & so He thought it was: His was Green; the same wild Haram-Scaram fellow as ever: He is one of those animals that lie mid-way between a Jockey & a farmer; the latter his occupation & the former his choice: He said he was very intimate with Johnson Gildart:* I afterwards went a little way on ye outside, & held a good deal of old School chit-chat yth him.

I shd not omit to mention, that stopping at a little Alehouse at Highgate, where that ceremony of swearing upon ye Horns is used to pass, I was there taken for ye Oath, wch is well enough conceived & deserves ye Shilling wch at the same time gets you the quantity of Punch. When it talks of being constant to your wife – I had like to have shown a little weakness.

The company of ye inside of ye Coach, consisting of 2 men & a woman, the wife of one of them, were most stupid & abominable to be conceived: To make it worse I could not look upon ye woman without being strongly put in mind of that execrable creature Miss Hogson.

Bedfordshire & Northampton I found very fertile low countries: growing too west quantities of Wheat. Coventry is an ugly town; but the grounds all about it are most beautiful & fertile. There is a very pretty situation of an Inn about 6 or 8 miles this side of Coventry.

We came to Litchfield about 8 o-clock; & there we are to lie.

The most disagreable part of stupid low company is their affectation of civility. This sort of affectation they had not at least to complain of agst me. Before 2 this morning we set out again.

The part of Staffordshire we past through was most extremely beautiful; particularly of each side of Newcastle. The more we came among the Coal, the less fertile the ground seemed to me to be.

At 5 in the afternoon we came to Warrington: there was I very glad to get quit of my vehicle; owing to the stupidity & impertinence of my vile blackguard company: the worst of whom was a cheesemongering Scotchman of Liverpool, called McKnighty to whom to be sure I was as rude in my turn as possible; but he w^d take no rebuffs.

The Coach went on this night to Liverpool; where it was to get about 10. About a mile & a half off from this Town, we crost over the Duke of Bridgewater's Canal. I took a walk again to it. Nothing to be compar'd to a Dutch Canal. A poor miserable Trackskuyt sets off to-morrow for Manchester; & I purpose going with it: Afterwards again to return here. However ye Canal is not to be despised. It is ye more beautiful for not being straight. It is so much sunk in some few places, as to lose the prospect. The environs of Warrington extremely picturesque. The river Meyser [Mersey] adds greatly to ye view. It is within half a mile of the Canal.

* Later of 7 Surrey Street, Strand, and Ranston, near Blandford, Dorsetshire. A correspondent of Wilkes.

I put up at Mrs Dale's the Red Lion: Has ye reputation of a very good house, & I believe not without cause.

19 May I begin to question how far I shall keep up my spirits, whilst I travel alone, under that real load of anxiety by which from the particularity of my present situation I cannot help ever carrying with me. N.B. What next follows, to my arrival at Liverpool, to save time I copy from a letter to King.

'I left Warrington at 8 this morning, setting out in the Duke of Bridgewater's Trackskuyt on his new canal for Manchester: This canal does not come nearer than within one mile of Warrington. The Boat performs the distance to Manchester, which is 20 miles in 5 hours: 1 horse, & that not changed: Stops twice for a 10 minutes rest, & refreshment for ye Passengers.'

NOTES
There does not seem much navigation on ye Canal: I suppose it will increase when completed through Sr Richd Brooke's Ground. The Duke's navigation, of some detriment to Warrington, as not passing through the Town. Yet the old Navigation of ye River keeps up pretty well: Some improvements have been made by ye Proprietors of that navigation. Liverpool is also something hurt by ye Duke's Canal.

We were between 30 & 40 in the Boat: Price 1 shilling, Passage. The Trackskuyt not so large or well shaped as those in Holland. Here too short for its Breadth. The surprise & wonder everyone is continually expressing about the Trackskuyt & the Canal &c becomes tiresome from its sameness & repetition. The Canal is more beautiful than any in Holland; except as to Width. The Banks & prospects are much more beautifully variegated: The Curvity of the Canal adds greatly to the pleasure of going upon it.

There is no great ingenuity in making a canal through a flat country: there is however great merit shown in the Contrivances in Holland to restrain the influx of Tides, the excess & defect of Water. The Duke's canal is made over very irregular ground; though a Level is sought as much as is practicable in making it, which occasions the Canal to be a little curved. When the ground falls only a little, then a bank is thrown up for ye Canal to go upon ye Top of it. If it falls very much then arches are made for ye canal to go over them. As roads must be preserved, those that are very low go under the Canal by means of an arch: Where roads are about the Level of ye Canal then they are led over it by Bridges. Sometimes we sail upon a Level with the tops of the neighbouring trees: again in other places we are sunk down considerably below ye adjacent ground. This necessarily happens, if the water is to be preserved without Locks, as no Level can otherwise be gained, over ground unevenly high & low. These parts where the Canal is lower than the intersected ground had nothing stupendous in ye cut, for it was nowhere of great depth.

When we came within 3 miles of Manchester I parted from ye Boat; & to lose no time as well as to save expence, I took a quick walk for 5 miles along another cross canal to Worsley. In this path I saw the most considerable work, where the Canal is led over a bridge of 3 very large arches above the River Mersey; which river is here very considerable, & navigable itself yth Locks. Yet even this part of the Canal has nothing in it, that ought to surprise a thinking beholder. However both the thought & the attempt were meritorious: the thought, not the less so, because it was natural & easy: the attempt, because it was grand & new. As to a Bridge being the Basis of a Canal running upon the Top of it, what were all the Roman aqueducts, though not used for navigation, but in effect so many canals of this nature? An arch is very well understood to be easily made impenitrable to water. Yet, in one road under the Canal, I saw water oozing through the sides of the Arch; which, if not redressed, must I think in time bring it down.

At Worsley is ye entrance into the hill from wch ye chief quantity of Coal is got: this I entered along ye continuation of ye canal in a long narrow boat; & here ye work appears to be a most noble useful undertaking. There is a large quarry here which makes ye chief grandeur of ye prospect. One is however rather hurt to see the entrances into ye hill made only through 2 very small apertures; through which a man cannot I believe stand upright in passing. For utility, to be sure, nothing higher is necessary. The reason of ye 2 apertures is that ye first was made too narrow for ye double passage of Boats: yet the archway stands better & is thought safer than through the new passage, which is considerable wider.

I saw at Worsley 2 more Trackskuyt, just ready to launch; one merely for ye Duke's pleasure; ye other, a very considerable one for a Passage Boat. I think it superior to any I have even seen in Holland. It contains 3 rooms with Fireplaces.

Upon ye Hill at Worsley the Duke's Steward (Mr Gilbert) has a handsome house, where also ye Duke resides when in this part of ye Country. There is a grand prospect from this house: Below you see a very large Moss, much improved by the Duke. There were then grazing up it 80 head of Cattle, where no cattle ever formerly c^d tread a foot. I learnt, it was principally improved (besides cutting of Drains) by carting up it great quantities of Bricks burnt on purpose for that use, & brought there by a cut from ye Canal, which goes through it.

NOTES AT MANCHESTER
Many new buildings going forward; Mostly small houses. Byron Street Buildings the handsomest of ye Town.

In the Trackskuyt from Warrington (which I must here observe is only in this Country called, the Passage Boat, & sometimes the Pleasure Boat) there came with me 2 young students piping hot from the College of Dublin. They afterwards took horses from Manchester for Worsley & came there just as I was going away. As for myself I took my solitary walk on to Manchester now 7 miles more. At Manchester I associated afterwards with these Irish Gentlemen. There is a vast uniformity in the understanding as well as in ye manners of the Irish. Their ideas I think in ye general run exceedingly puerile. They are all affectedly civil & obliging, & yet amidst all this show of politeness, they invariably mix a particular native sort of impertinence; which however (and I believe it is from indulgence to their ignorance) one cannot help being greatly inclinable to excuse.

20 May   All this day I had nothing to do, but to look about Manchester, of which, though some skirts of the Town & all the environs are pretty, I grew heartily tired in ye progress of 12 hours. I put up at the Bull's head: Old house, which I perfectly remember ye situation of, when formerly returning from Heath School in Yorkshire. Happy times those! Not happy in being at school, but happy in returning from it. There is a very good house the other side ye river called the King's head; the Landlord is a civil jovial fellow; his wife is an authoress; a proper authoress for an Inn; having published a considerable treatise upon Cookery. I found late at night a returned Chaise to Warrington, to which I committed my carcase; not returning there, 'till between 4 & 5 the next morning. In our way stopping at a hedge alehouse, I met with a curious old fellow, who called himself an estated man; he pretended to discover I was a Lawyer, & put a serious case to me about some dispute with his neighbour relating to a small incroachment of 2 or 3 feet; in short I was to tell whose ground it was, upon only being informed that it was claimed on both sides. This estated man turned out only pŏssed [possessed] of a small cottage an encroachment itself upon ye walk, but he said he had pŏssed it these 19 years, & now feard no man. As to his cottage it was all in ruins, & he had had no bed to lie in for these 7 weeks: Soon after he pulled out a little Book, which he called his Brief; & there it was set forth, that the under-written persons taking into their consideration the miserable condition of

John Swallow's house had subscribed as follows towards repairing it. Then one subscribed 100 of Bricks, another a hod of mortar; one a Shilling, another 6 pence: He gave me the Book, & I subscribed this. 'The famous John Wilkes subscribes towards rebuilding this house by way of giving strength to ye builder one Pint of Beer.' Without his reading what I had subscribed, I put my hand in my pocket, & taking out a flat white-metalled Button, which I happened to have there, & which had much ye appearance of a Shilling, I made a display of it, & put it into his hand. Then was the Contrast glorious in his countenance, when he came to perceive, what he had got, & what he had expected: I intended to have made good at last by Subscription of a Pint of Beer by it's value in 2 penny-worth of halfpence: but I really was so struck with the grandeur of his indignant silence upon what had passed, that in going out of ye room, besides the twopence, I made amends by slipping a silver Tester over into his hand.

NOTE

There is a Mr Lever about 5 miles from Manchester has a good collection of natural curiosities, which he calls a Museum, & wch he is proud of showing. He is a great Connoisseur in Horses: & has a fine Stallion, that he has taught to play several tricks, particularly to go into a Room & fetch a person's hat &c.

21 May After a little refreshment of Sleep & some writing occupation after I was up, I set out a horseback to visit the rest of the Duke's canal towards Runcorn. There is nothing more particular here, except it's communication at Runcorn with ye Mersey, & consequently with Liverpool. The communication is made by means of 15 locks (3 Locks make what is called a pair of Double Locks; so there are here 5 pr of Locks.) which gain a fall of 21 yards, and give a most grand & powerful idea of human industry & ingenuity. There is besides a very curious contrivance to deepen ye channel of ye river close before ye entrance of ye Canal. That is done by impounding the water when it is high tide; & when it is low water letting it out again, that by it's rapidity it may carry away before it all the Collection of mud that that has been making; this water is impounded in a channel cut along ye side of ye River into ye Rock, upon which 400 men were at work at once: The Rock was sawn on each side, then blown up. The Channel of ye River used to take on ye opposite side; but [by] means of this cutting it is now greatly brought round to the Cheshire side on wch ye Canal is. I took care to visit the part where ye canal is stopt at Sr Richd Brooke's estate: the Circumstances of that dispute have long been the general talk of the Country.

I saw at Runcorn a pack of Aberystwith Sailors; I enquired after my Aunt Lloyd; Several of them had also been at Swansea & knew all my family connexions there; of wch they put me too strongly in mind not to leave them something to remember me in ye drink, when I was absent. I daresay if £1,000 had been offered upon one's head, a fellow-Country-man might have trusted his person with these fellows.

Returning to Warrington I was prest to drink Tea at Mr Turner's (a sail-Cloth manufacturer) to whom I had brought a letter from Mr Tolson; but I dread [above] everything a family appearance; It puts me too much in mind of what I had lost.

'Indeed my present feelings are so truly distressful, that I find myself very little capable of taking pleasure in anything that offers. My time hangs heavy on my hands, & I become a prey to my own reflexions. From what I feel, from what I suffer; & from what I think, I fear that my temper my constitution & my reason will be materially affected through Life. I must take some decisive steps to remove the uneasiness, that is at present such an unbearable Load upon me. Nothing to this end seems to me so effec-tual, as what will bring ye question of my marriage to a nearer crisis. Could I see any end to it I might be happy, could I but hate her, who by her fickleness & treachery is the cause of all my misery. Could I take even temporary notice of another female I might find momentary relief. But the misfortune is, all the rest of Womankind have lost their charms for me; they are even become odious; and her only can I figure as an object of my passions, her alone do I love, whom I ought above all others to detest.'

In the Evening I set out with the London machine as it past for Liverpool. Coming out of Warrington I found there was a Copper-work there belonging to Patten & Co. which I was sorry I did not know of, that I might have visited it. Patten has a grand house at a little distance before it.

I came to the Talbot Inn at Liverpool, which seems a pretty good one. My Servant Francis I found had arrived the night before, with Cartouche, & those of my things, which I wanted.

22 May   Visited the Docks, which I think are as grand & spacious as any I have ever seen. Ships not in such numbers as at Hamburgh. This is now reckoned the 2d place of Trade in England. By a return made from ye Corporation here to Queen Elizabeth, upon a general inspection into ye number of Seamen, it appears there was only returned from hence to be 35, whom they called Fishermen.

I took a walk up ye Hill, where the Corporation Quarry is, which I suppose is as grand as any Quarry in Europe: There is a Road into it under Ground, with large Tunnels for Light: In ye Quarry is a Spa spring, though but weak in quality, with persons to serve you to it: There is a grand view of ye river & Town & Country from ye top of ye hill; upon which there is also an exceedingly elegant public-house with walks prettily & usefully laid out. Consumed some more of ye Day in writing; & at ye Coffee house.

A good ordinary here at a Shilling a head: the usual price in this Country.

Took a long wandering walk about the Town towards ye Evening, Supt alone.

23 May Begun to have my Letters reach me here; the answering of which sufficient employ; or I intended to have gone to see ye Copper works at Warrington: No other copper works in this County, as I can hear of. They are entirely under the management of Mr Patten, son of ye late Proprietor; he is also a Colonel in ye Militia. He is said however to have others concerned with him. A late Partener with his father was one Mr Watkins; & he took it into his fancy one Sunday to hang himself; upon which others took into their fancy to saw [see], that he saw a bad state of affairs. He came into ye works with the same rope in his hands that he directly afterwards went into the Warehouse to hang himself with. I cannot find there are any Mills here, but horse-mills, in which I hear they roll some Copper: These Works make Manillas for ye African trade.

There is one James here, who has risen himself for [from] nothing to be poss[ess]ed in his own name of 32 African ships; He never makes insurances: Last year he had losses to ye amount of £40,000. Different Ideas are entertained of his wealth; Some thinking him very rich; others, far from it. He said to have 2 others privately concerned with him. Many Adventurers in trade in Liverpool: yet not 10 of them to be worth £10,000. Are bad paymasters: make no scruple of refusing to pay a Bill; saying, the ships are not arrived: This does them no Discredit; & it passes for the Custom of ye Place.

I met yth a young Clergyman in ye Machine from Warrington here: We discoursed upon general matter: I find he took notice of my discourse; has been pleased to compliment me to others; for I learnt from a Gentleman at ye Ordinary today that he had before described me to him.

Having found a ship going for Air [Ayr] in Scotland, to touch ye Isle of Man, I am likely I think to go with it.

24 May Today I set on foot a Porter to inquire after shipping for Scotland, who found me a little vessel ready to sail yth ye first wind for Greenough (within 10 miles of Glasgow): & I think myself likely now to sail with that; In short I shall go with ye first, that sets out for anywhere thereabouts; for I begin to find myself uneasy here.

Bought some stuff for a couple of straw mattresses aship-board: & Francis has undertaken to make them: He seems an useful ready fellow. I saw at the Coffee house called Pontack's one of ye young Haywoods I saw & knew at Hamburgh: I did not chuse to acknowledge & soon marchd off: I shall take now to another Coffee house called George's: The Coffee Rooms here are large rooms; but they do not seem much frequented. The sight of any acquaintance I have known abroad in happier days is now too afflictive to me.

I have just learnt that Rowe & Co. have a Copper work in ye skirts of this Town: I thought indeed to have heard so before.

25 May The Copper work I went to see today: It is about a mile from the Town upon the River Side; once it was in the Skirts of ye Town, but being convicted of being a nuisance was compelled to be removed. The Works are single, & seem very cool & well contrived: As far as I recollect the construction, there was something particular in the Roof; for where one w^d have expected cross Beams, *(this* ⋀) there was instead a small arch of Brick carried up *(this* ⌒) but perhaps these were only the casings with Brick of ye Beams: Here they call the Regulus Metal, saying, 'Now This is not Copper, but it will be Copper next smelting.' They roast or calcine all their ore. Most of ye ore they have from Cornwall. A good deal from Anglesea, & from Flintshire: Most from these 2 places comes in a burnt state to them; & then it is of a red Color: I also saw some Ore from Cornwall, which was red, that they said had not been burnt before it came. They have their Coal from ye works up ye River near Warrington. They said, they made more Copper, than at Patten's Works: But they seemed not to know: The Foreman was ill: And they have but one Foreman, who has 20 Shillings, for ye 7 days of ye week: One of ye workmen, more informed I suppose than the rest supplied his place. The men when they come here to work first have immediately 15 pence per Day for ye 12 hours; for ye first year; after which they have 16 pence a day; & can expect to rise no more. A Labourer in a Stone Quarry told me his wages were 18 pence a day. Close to the Copper-works, there is neat Row of small houses, to the number, as far as I can now guess, of about 12 or 14 for ye workmen. There did not seem to be above 20 workmen employ'd at a Time in the whole works. I forgot to reckon ye number of Furnaces: But the works are not even so large as those at Middlebank at Swansea.

I went to visit these works along with a couple of young Irishmen just piping hot arrived. They are certainly entertaining companions these Irishmen merely from their simplicity.

The wind is too much to ye North for us to get out of ye harbour & sail for Scotland. Cold & dirty weather. I took today an inventory of the things which I have here with me.

26 May Finished today a long letter to the Chancellor; & sent it off; with several others to Tolson. My two young Irishmen gone. Today I saw Mr Kenyon, returned from Manchester Races: Seems a polite obliging young man. Still less prospect of getting off; and the Scotch Captain is going now to bring his vessel into Dock again.

I went to see the China-manufacture here: It is but a Course sort; but however pretty good: They only do in Blue & White: the Colour before glazed & burnt is a Grey, like some Indian Ink; then turns by Baking a strong Blue: There is a person that pencils for them the China in the Copperplate way of any colour when bespoke.

N.B. This was the Day of my Brother's* happy Marriage.

27 May Was employd most of this Day in writing a long letter upon my case to Bearcroft.

Weather a little finer, but wind not changed; & very cold: Sit by a large fire all Day.

One Mackintosh, Optician in London, came down here by ye Coach last night: tells a long story about one Capt. Angell of ye Stag Frigate; who he says is now somewhere in Hanover Country, being dismissed his majesty's imploy for a disgraceful crime, which he caused to be found out. Qu: if not related to that Angell at Altona.

28 May I got up late to-day, & have not marked this day by doing much: neither had I much to do: Yet I sent off another large Packet of Letters: The Wind N.N.W. No removing. I was plagued at Dinner with ye society of an ignorant fellow who because he had been upon some comm̄on [commission] to Cadiz took upon him the travelled Gentleman; & to be instilled to plague every company with his nonsense, deliverd in a tone of voice, that was shocking: Such a tone as nonsense is generally convey'd in, when accompanied by affectation.

29 May The players begin to flock down: One of them, called Bradshaw supt with us tonight. This Even^g the wind begun to show a disposition to change. Today I had the happiness to hear news of my Brother's marriage yth Miss Henrietta Musgrave daughter of Sr Philip Musgrave Bart. of Cumberland.

---

* John, knighted in 1806, and his wife are buried at St John's Church, Swansea (now St Matthew's).

30 May Happily we are now destined to sail off from hence to-day for Greenock in ye Nell Sloop, Burthen 60 Tons, Lading Wood, James Simpson Master. Time begun to hang heavy: I should have had little to fill up my Journal wth if I had staid here any Longer. It is a good time to decamp, when the Journal becomes happy: At least for those who calculate happiness for ye variety of Events. Variety of Events are however no pleasure to me, while they pass; only in recollection afterwards; & not all then, neither.

At 2 in the afternoon we sail'd: Wind S.E. quite the reverse to what it had been, blowing a pretty gale. Vast numbers of Vessels left the harbour at ye same time as we did; among the rest many Guineaman: who all gave 3 cheers, as soon as they got under Sail.

A long Course down the River from Liverpool. We went without a pilot: The entrance very contiguous to that up to Park Gate: Fine view of ye Welsh Hills: Among the rest Penmaenmawr. Weather very pleasant. Eat a hearty dinner. Francis cooks excellently. Towards night going pretty brisk, had very near turned sick. Went to bed, & soon got the better of it. Woke well. In the night past by the Isle of Man. Hazy & c^d have seen nothing of it to signify.

31 May Saw the Isle of Man at a Distance. In the afternoon of to-day the wind begun to slacken. Two Dogs fell a fighting, & Francis had his hand sadly bit. I never saw a poor fellow frightened more. My fellow passenger, a most stupid fellow; as most of the Irish are. Saw a most glorious fine round rock (I forget it's name) entering the Straight up to Glasgow; said to be 2 mile round, & 2 mile high: the latter it cannot be; perhaps it may be 2 mile to walk up it: Has rabbits upon it; & they say some Goats: Vast numbers of Birds. Sailing up this Firth most beautifully fine.

1 June I find my Captain, if he had not been prest for time intended to have gone over to Ireland to bring home smuggled Brandy.

Passage up continues delightful: Past by Bute Island. Lord Bute's house seems indifferent at ye distance I saw it. The Island large, containing high & low grounds: but seems mostly poor lands. Scotch hills of all sides now; & seem very barren. On the left, they talk nothing but Highlands: The [they] name it Gallic. All the Sailors in our Vessel talked it. Mostly calm to-day: But arrived at Greenock about 2 in the afternoon: A dirty Stinking town, owing to native uncleanliness; because situated on a slant might be clean enough: Common People seem very poor: Children & many others without shoes & stockings. Our little Captain's son without hat: The Girls (to 15, or 16) without Caps: See but one pretty child in ye Town.

Paid the Captain 10/6 for my passage with Dogs & Baggage, & 5/- for my servant's. Very well contented: People very thankful for a Shilling: did not even think of asking for the remainder of my provisions.

Took a most pleasant walk to ye environs of ye Town; fine prospect; of the Land-lockt Sea here, which looks like a lake: Not a deal of Shipping here: There is another place for Glasgow shipping, about 2 miles higher up than Glasgow, called Port Glasgow; about as considerable as Greenock. Sir Michael Stuart, most property about the Town: Saw some Ladies, as I walk'd in ye adjacent Wood: But where can I walk for pleasure: My mind is a perpetual prey upon me. Boys about 6 year old go about in a sort of Jacket & a petticoat or Trowsers that go round both legs, without Breeches.

2 June Very rainy morning. At 8 a Coach set off for Glasgow, 6 persons, each to pay 6 shillings: At 12 a Boat goes, each to pay 6 pence: I shall surely go by the latter.

Something must be done to remove the present Load from my mind. I neither pass the night nor ye Day without the image, that torments me. It must be destructive I am sure both to my understanding & to my health. Let us bring it as hasty as possible to some conclusion: Any end is better than suspence.

A little after 2 I set out in a common passage Boat for Glasgow: By land it is 25 English miles from Greenock to Glasgow; they call it 16, Scotch, or computed: By water I do not conceive it much more. We pay only 6 pence a piece for our Passage; but they required me to pay 3/- for my Luggage, reckoning 6 pence for each parcel: By right I suppose they could not exact near so much. Goods pay a Duty for improving the River at Glasgow of 1/- per Ton. My Baggage paid 2 pence. Considerable works are carrying on for improving this navigation; which is at present extremely shallow, as small Boats drawing 2½ feet water cannot pass, but with the Tide. The improvement is making by casting out Causeways in several parts into ye River: In other places Sand dug up from the Bed of ye River & formed into Banks upon ye Side of it, contracting the Passage. I saw full 200 men at work together: Seemed all Highlanders; without Breeches: strong fellows, who work hard; but I am told, there are also some Irish employ'd among them. The works done stand well. The Ice hurts them a little, but they are not washed away by ye ordinary course of the River.

Where sand is taken out of the River, this is done by fixing up a great number of Windlasses (perhaps 20) very close to each other, along the shore, opposite is moored in the River a Raft as long as this line of Wind-lasses, upon this Raft are other Windlasses just opposite; between the Raft

& the Shore are then drawn Dredges under Water, which scoops up the Sand, & brings it to the Shore; the middle between the Raft, & the Windlasses on Shore is the Channel Deepen'd. I conceive there wd be no occasion for ye Raft, but that it saves the fixing & refixing of Windlasses, at least on one side of the Shore: On ye other it is necessary, where the Bank directly before the Windlasses is to be raised.

There are 30 of these Windlasses at Work together. Upon ye side the Sand as [is] drawn up, 5, 6, or 7 men are used to each Windlass: On the other side men only to draw the Dredges down to the Bottom, 2 men to ye Windlass (moved by Poles) are enough.

A A the Dredges fixt at each end by a Rope to ye Windlasses.
B B The Ropes, sunk down that Boats may go over them: N.B. They are not ropes, only the Ends near ye Windlass, the rest Chains.

The Undertaker employ'd about this work, is an Englishman. The Scotch are hardly such fools as to be National where their particular interests are concerned.

The Passage up the Water is most extremely beautiful: Wanted nothing, but a Companion to enjoy it with me. We were 6 hours going up, sometimes rowing, but mostly sailing. There is a remarkable Rock projecting in the River, though joined to the Land, just before the Town of Dumbarton, upon which is a Fort: The Water is here too shallow for any ships to pass: it serves therefore only for a Land Fort, particularly covering the Town of Dumbarton.

Several beautiful Situations of houses along ye Water side: Some they called Lord's Houses: I forget their titles: Land fertile; but mountains at a Distance barren; & no Woods: Some few groves & young Plantations about all the Gentlemen's houses. Approach to Glasgow very fine. Two Bridges very near each other. The new one quite superb. The Town not so handsomely built as I expected it: Yet a fine Town:

A. The Highlands. B. Dumbarton. D. Dumbarton Castle-Rock. C. The Governers House. E. The River.

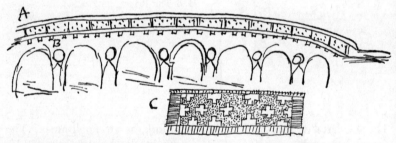

A. Rough sketch of the New Bridge.
B. Each Pier lightend by a Circular Hole, on the principles of the Great One-Arch'd Taff Bridge
C. The Parapet at Top in stone – Hollow where light.

The Streets well paved; but Dirty: Vast numbers of idle Boys & others assembled in the Evening about ye Cross, as ye call the Place, though no Cross there: It is where the Exchange is, & where is set up an Equestral Statue in Stone of King William: The Horse seems very Badly executed; the figure of the Man better: He is crown'd yth Laurels: The People here seem very loyal, yet they speak with very great respect of ye Pretender; calling him by no other title than ye Prince: Great fuss made here & in all the Scotch Towns on ye King's Birthday. Put up at the Bull; kept now by one Herron; seems a very good house.

3 June Breakfasted at the Exchange Coffee house: They had no English

Papers. See several Highlanders, in their Highland Dresses. The Petticoat I spoke of, as ye little Boys wearing, is a species of the Highland Dress.

Went to see the College: a despicable building. Saw the little Printer, one of the Brothers, Foulis: I desired to see his collection of Pictures: He first of all introduced me to his Book shop: as is his custom: there I saw the Grand Glasgow Homer, & Virgil: There is very nearly a complete edition of the Classics: And a very cheap common Edition of the English Poets, consisting of 40 Vols. in 12 mo. at 1/3 per Vol. half Bound: in Calf neat at 1/6 per Vol: the whole therefore in the first was £2.10.0. In ye 2d £3.

His Collection of pictures, but paltry & ill-disposed. Some good copies made at Rome by young Scotch Artists sent out by these very Foulis at their Expence; particularly a large one from ye Vatican, though not as large, as that in the Vatican, of the School of Athens: One of these Foulis, went abroad himself on purpose for ye collection of these pictures: Everyone who sees them puts a shilling into a Box. They have rather impoverished themselves by their schemes; and their collection of Pictures, they intend next year to sell by auction in London.

Some of the Gentⁿ Students at the University here live in the College; but most lodge out: At present it is vacation time.

I went next to see an old Cathedral: a fine grove upon a [an] eminence just above it: Remains of an old Castle just by.

Went again to examine the deepening of the Bed of the River. I find ropes were first used with the Dredges, but they wore out & broke.

They were mostly Irish Labourers, first employed about this work:

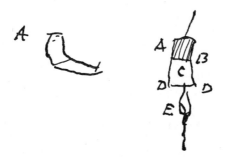

A.   Dredges
B.   Only a small end of the Dredge that has any bottom to it.
C.   Open part: yet when drawn up all full of sand
D.D. Iron to draw by, but does not cut the sand.
E.   The Chain

189

afterwards Highlanders & Irish quarrelling, most of the Irish are gone off:
They got for each drag 1½d by which they could get 11 sh a week: About
7 are requisite for the Drag; sometime 8 are used: 11 sh. a week at 1½d
each Drag among 7 allow them to make each Day 103 Drags. Among 8
it makes 118 Drags. It seems hard work; but then there is frequent relief
by Pauses; while the opposite 2 men are drawing back the Dredge:

As the Dredge must work in furrows, & so make ridges, the ridges are
afterwards workt away by a little shifting of the raft, which brings the
Dredges then to work upon these ridges.

The greatest effect is expected from narrowing the channel, which in
many places is done considerably.

The [they] pretend to tell me, that the hollow Cylinders of the Bridge
were made because the Piers were too low; & these Cylinders are [to] let
the water have a passage through on high Floods: And that they have
seen the Water so pass through the 2 end ones.

I saw a Thread mill at work; one man moves it by pushing round with
his hand: He told me, he works when light from 4 in the morning, 'till 8
at night, & can get at it but 1/- per Day; It requires a careful eye to attend
the breaking of the Threads. There is a Green Glass bottle house in Town,
but no White Glass. I can hear of no other manufacture. I see none, or
very few, great Warehouses; & there seems but little appearance of Trade;
& very few boats up. There are however many considerable merchants,
who live here: However their Goods must principally be at Greenock or
Port Glasgow.

I have seen now pretty near the whole of the Town: It certainly may be
called a pretty place: Yet there is not one perfect Street; & many of them
mean & nasty.

As a Preparatory to the celebration of the King's Birthday, Boys go
about, with a miserable Black figure held up, which they call Wilkes;
And they accost everyone, 'Won't ye give a Baubee to burn Wilkes?' I
gave it to them willingly; for the fun of saying I had done it. I wrote
Letters: Read some of Virgil; wrote some of this Book; & instead of
going to the Play stay'd at home in the Evening.

4 June The people here, mad for celebrating the King's Birthday: Proof
of the Disloyalty in the neighbourhood. At least the disloyalty that was.
No such particular notice w^d be taken here, diff^t from other parts of
England, if the Country equally affected.

The Foulis's hang out in the College-Quadrangle all their Copies of the
Italian & Flemish pictures: But few of which have merit: Now viewed by
mobs of People.

Laid out about half a guinea in Books with ye Foulis: for which I had
1   of Tibullus & Propertius.
2d. 4 Vols. Milton's Poet. Works.
3.   Tucker on Trade.
4.   Seldon's Table Talk.
5.   Sr W. Petty's Polit. Arith.
In all 8 Books in Duo.

In ye cheapest manner I c^d not buy these Books under Double the Price
English Edition.

The numbers of dissolute Boys & others in the Street under pretence of
celebrating the King's Birthday, quite a nuisance.

Perpetually plagued about the burning of Wilkes. The Magistrates out
all in their formalities yth the Burgher's watch: Windows ornamented
with Garlands; Houses & heads with green Leaves & Branches. And at
the Theatre pompous entertainments given.

To ye Play I went; & most of ye Characters very well performed, being
the Merry wives of Windsor: At the conclusion of the Farce, was sung,
what they called ye Loyal Chorus of God save the King, in which many
Gentlemen in ye Boxes joined: House pretty full; Women very ugly:
Young Girls, 8 & 9 year old, Gentlewomen's Daughters, in ye disfiguring
dress, of hair cut short round, like Boys at School: Many of ye Ladies
disadvantageously set off: awkward & graceless: Men all broad scotch in
y^r tongue, except ye Actors, who spoke very pure English.

Upon ye famous Loyal Chorus, it is easy to observe, that it was originally calculated for another occasion.

God *save* Great George our King
Send him *victorious*
Long to reign over us.

Send is not so very applicable to one at present reigning; though it might
be justifiable, as a poetical word; a plainer word for such an unpoetical
song, is *Grant*. Then ye *Victorious* plainly shows there was a contest to his
reigning & that he must conquer, before he c^d attain ye Throne. *Long* was
soon to reign over us. Some more of ye Words are very absurd.

Oh Lord our God arise.
Scatter our Enemies.
Confound their *politics*
Frustrate their *knavish tricks*.

The solemn address to ye Divinity is finely let down to ye Level afterwards of confounding Politics, & ye frustrating of knavish tricks.

I entered for a few moments into a Highland Church, which was very full & some tolerably well-drest people; the Parson was very vehement in delivering his Gâlic. Afterwards I went to ye Cathedral; where I staid near an hour, & being included in a pew. Here ye Minister was preaching too, in a most drawling wretched manner: But his prayers were afterwards delivered in a worse tone, as if God w^d the better hear them.

The method laid out for Preaching in Scotland, is much better calculated for ye Delivery of a sensible discourse than in England: To take a single verse, or perhaps 3 words of a single verse: 'Abraham begat Isaac' – What argument c^d be drawn from these words: Yet it is well known, that a sermon upon the propriety of *Residence* was preached under that Text. 'To beget Isaac, it was necessary that Abraham shd be *resident*; and therefore, my Brethren, I am fairly led into an occasion of treating of ye Grand consequence of Residence.' People will preach what they like; there is therefore no use of tying them down to any text, for allusions forced or natural will always be made: the division of Sermons into 3 heads, is still worse: Few admit of necessity the ternal patition [partition]: But of Parsons I shd not wonder, if some were to take upon them to give their Sermons a *triune* head.

The mode in Scotland is to take a Chapter in ye Bible; And comment upon it Verse by Verse. It happened in ye Progress of ye Sermon, that the Parson had to fall upon ye Stumbling block of *Faith & Good Works*; and here he made no scruple roundly to declare, that by Works, was understood Works of all kinds & denominations* before belief & after belief not the mere Works of Ceremonial Law, and that Works of no sort whatsoever c^d avail anything to salvation, wch alone was to be obtained by ye Righteousness of Jesus Christ; and that even without faith good *Works* were a sin. Yet he insisted that this doctrine was no encouragement to Vice, because though good works avail'd nothing to Salvation, it was equally incumbent upon Christians to perform them, because they were not released from ye obligation to ye moral Law of God, though that of itself was only sufficient to condemn them & not to save them.

I think there is something in this: I have given his argument the best of it: I much doubt whether it is not the true doctrine of those called Apostles: But I conceive it too evidently contrary to good sense, to need a confutation.

After preaching a considerable time, he said, he had intended to have gone on farther, but he shd now leave it to ye next discourse; He then took a little pray; and afterwards they all fell to singing of Psalms: Upon which I thought the ceremony concluded: Far from it: For now this *next*

---

* A description large enough to take in ye Works of Carpenters, Masons &c.

discourse was to begin; & so he calmly open'd his Bible again, & begun to preach, as if a considerable distance of time had past since his last discourse, & all his hearers had sufficiently recruited their attention by their Psalm-singing: He gave us a half-hour's discourse, & then with all the composure in ye world, taking out his Watch, he said, that there was not time sufficient for accomplishing at present, what he had undertaken, & so shd conclude: But still there was to be praying & Psalm-singing; His Prayer was introduced by the Clerk, reading over about 20 names, some of whom, were sick of ye Small Pox, One was under ye Surgeon's care for a broken leg, another was afflicted yth ye Gout; Of the women, one was nervously inclined, or, as they termed it, afflicted with low spirits, another to lie in, & a third to undergo an operation for a Bubo; of the young men, one had weighty affairs upon his hands for which he desired assistance, & another was merely going abroad.

The Parson then begun his prayer in the Progress of which, he prayed, that God w^d be pleased to bring all nations in one mind, that he w^d bring us again his Auncient people ye Jews; but that he w^d particularly take care of Scotland, and of this large & populous City of Glasgow, blessing all the people in y^r Merchandize & other concerns. The illustrious house of Brunswick was to be sure not forgot; & it was not amiss, when he prayed to God, that as he made them great, he w^d make them good.

The Cathedral is now divided into 2 Churches partitioned from each other, though under the same Roof: & sometimes service is performed in both, ye one not interrupting the other. The Scotch are not so absurd, as to pay adoration to bare walls; so that when divine service is not actually in ye spot performing, you may walk about their Churches cover'd.

As to Alter-pieces, or religious ornaments, to be sure there is no appearance of them. I c^d not even for certain discover where the Lord's Supper was celebrated, but I observed about the middle 2 pews, in each of which was a table & benches round.

There is only one more part of ye Parson's prayer I shd take notice of, & that is, as God was pleased to be yth them this morning, he hoped he w^d not fail to be yth them again in ye afternoon.

Tonight I go part of my way to Edinburgh, because ye Coach is full for to-morrow. To Falkirk is 27 Engl. miles: The driver requires 6 hours to do it in: I said I w^d try if I c^d not get a chaise from another house to do it quicker: The Landlady of ye house comes to speak with me upon ye matter: I was writing; she comes close up to my ear, & speaks so very loud, I c^d not help bursting out alaughing; she too begins to smile thinking to have found me in a much better humour than she expected: Upon wch

I c^d not help telling her, that 'I only laughed, because she spoke so loud, close at my Ear, when I c^d hear very well if she was at a distance.' This shockt my Landlady so much, that she retired abruptly out of the Room.

At 4 I left Glasgow. The Country open. No woods & few inclosures: Hilly at a distance; but none very great.

Past along side of the Clyde Canal Navigation. Superior Canal to ye Duke of Bridgewater, being much broader: But I question whether so well constructed: Said to leak: several of ye Bridges upon this Canal are Draw Bridges: none so upon ye Duke's as I saw. Most part of ye Canal, higher than ye Level of ye Country; none sunk much under ye Level, as I saw: At the Entrance by the Carron Works, it has 15 Locks; ye same as ye Duke's Canal has in Number to enter into ye Mersey.

I was near 5 hours coming to Falkirk, 24 Engl. miles. There I lay.

6 June This morning I visited with vast pleasure the works at Carron: You apply at an office at the works there for a ticket of admission, by writing your name & abode, & you easily obtain it: A man for ye purpose accompanying you; this man was extremely well contented with a shilling. You are not askt for anything by any of the people; but if they show you anything particular they may expect something. I saw 24 pounder Cannon Cast: It is amazing what heat ye People stand in ye operation: I c^d not help giving a principal man here 1/- to drink, at that time as he was all running down with sweat: The mould of the Cannon, is deposited in a hole, now well closed up with sand, so that the mouth of the cannon is a

F. the Hole of ye Furnace, where the metal is let out, by driving in a Bar: moderated or increased in it's flow as ye man pleases, who stands there.

F. to D. the Channel in the sand goes in a strait Line; through a furrow made so $\bigvee$ perhaps about a foot Deep.

At D. it is stopt by ye sand; when ye Current begins then to turn by C. The reason of this is, that the first of ye Metal which flows out may not run into ye Cannon mould: When ye Metal has run, as far as D. a man throws sand upon it: which makes a stronger Dam to turn it by C.

B. Here a man stands with something like a shovel, which he puts across the flow of Metal; keeping off the Dross which swims at top; & letting out only the best metal at bottom under his shovel.

A. The Cannon mould.
This Cannon Mould consists of several parts; according as we may see marks in a Cannon.

Thus. A. one division
B. & C. so many others.

little below, the bottom of ye furnace; then the metal is let out, which is conducted in a channel through sand to ye cannon mould.

The moulds are made with moist sand. Each of ye Partitions first seperately: Then these moulds are put into an intolerable hot suffocating room, where there is a large fire in a grate, no chimney or passage for air, but from ye folding Door, which is opposite to it; though Shut, except when ye men go in, to deposite or examine the moulds, which are here set to roast, as ye call it; & fairly it is roasting before ye large fire. The room has a low circular roof, which is all Cast Iron; the floor is also of cast Iron: I c^d not bear hardly to step a foot into, yet ye men, would go up to ye fire, which is at least 12 feet from ye Door: The Coal is charred which avoids ye Smoak.

The sand is here I believe baked quite hard: at least I saw, after a Cannon had been cast; the sand was quite cemented together, & more like brick than sand.

The hole in ye Cannon is preserved in casting, by a fluted piece of Iron or Steel I suppose, which is inserted upright, & so fixt in ye mould, upon ye casting; this fluted Bar, is afterwards, as I observed easily taken out, by some men turning Levers inserted into Holes at ye End of ye Bar, when the Cannon with the mould is afterwards laid down horizontally. I shd at first have thought, that a smooth piece of Steel w^d sooner have been got out, but I suppose the Bits of ye Casts Metal that enters the flutes of ye Bar are easily broke off in ye turning round of ye Bar by the Levers; & so a larger Passage made to get ye Bar out.

A.D. Fluted Bar.
B.C. Holes for ye Levers, to get ye Bar out again, by turning it round, as a screw is drawn out.

The Bore of ye Cannon is afterwards made more perfect & smooth, by boring mills, in wch the Bore is fixt to the Axis of a large Wheel; the Cannon laid up a frame, which from time to time screwed up against the Bore, as the Boring advances. The Head of ye Cannon is cut off, by the Cannon, being put to turn round upon this Boring Pin afterwards, and a piece of Steel, applied to the end of ye Cannon, whilst turning with ye axis ye Wheel.

A most remarkable forced ore furnace is here: There are 3 Cylinders, with Suckers, Workt by one very large water wheel (the Diameter of which water wheel is I think 30, or 40 feet) yet there is very little water used to turn it: The Flaps or whatever they are called of the Water wheel, are very close set, & are like so many troughs. The Water falls close upon it, at ye top of the wheel. As from A. There being a small properly fed Cistern at A. for ye holding it. They use mostly Coked Coal.

Much of ye Ore is brought 20 miles off: None nearer than 6 or 8.

A large Hammer 7 Cwt – yet short in length. Used for making anvils. A large Grinding stone turnd by Water, for brightening Chimney Backs & other articles.

I saw here a very large Boiler of Cast Iron, for a Fire Engine to be erected at Peterburgh; for Drawing water out of or for filling some of yᵉ Docks: The Cilinder for which this Boiler of Cast Iron is made was 5 feet Diameter: The Boiler is cast I believe in 3 parts.

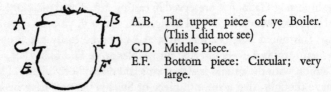

A.B. The upper piece of ye Boiler. (This I did not see)
C.D. Middle Piece.
E.F. Bottom piece: Circular; very large.

To cost about ye 3d Part of Copper.

They make vast quantities of Common Boiling Pots: They also make Bath Stoves, curiously cast in ornamental way; & also Warming Machines. such as Buzaglio; In short everything that can be cast, & some more things other usually [?not] thought to be capable of being cast. I saw here some cast Cinder Grates upon Hearths. The most is done in ye foundry of Cannon: They never made a larger Cannon than 42 pounder.

I arrived at Edinburgh, in a chaise about 3 in ye afternoon: Went first to the White Horse in Cannon Gate, kept by one Boyd: reckoned ye best, though an indifferent Inn: Here to my great Pleasure I found a Pack of Letters from Mr Tolson. I afterwards took a Lodging at Mrs Wight's, a genteel wdo [widow] Lady, Chapel Street, Nicholson's Park, the South side of ye Town: a very pretty front Room, 1st floor, concealed Bed: & Bed & room for Servt. 10/- a week – and adjoining room soon, if I chuse, & then ye whole Lodgings 18/- a week.

There were some people, who had the impudence to ask me for much worse accommodations in ye High Street, 2 Ga a week, though up 3 pr of Stairs & the lowest price they offered was 30/-

These Lodgings were taken for me by a Porter: There is an useful set of people here called Câddy's, like Lacquey's de Place, hire 2/- a day, very intelligent, though some Rogues; Do all y^r Business of all nature. But I did not want to employ one: I sauntered away most of my time at the Coffee houses; but I also wrote some Letters.

7 June No necessary belonging to ye House where I am or to any in the neighbourhood: I askt the maid; & she fairly told me so, if she & I understand each other rightly; the streets I do not find soil'd, as used to be reported.

I took my excursion this morning to see the Town: In the first place I mounted a vast hill, rocky Hill, where fine quarries, this South side of the Town; where I had a glorious prospect of ye Town; ye Country round, & the Sea. Edinburgh is not so large as Bristol; Leith is not at all capable of being said to be joined to Edinburgh; It is a full mile asunder, without contiguous buildings: Leith I conceive as big as Swansea:

The Sea has a fine Effect; a fine rocky island in view: Descended into ye Town: Holyrood Palace, a poor affair: Grass grows in ye Courts: A spacious Hospital.

College. Only ye Professors live in it: Now Vacance till October.

Royal Academy which is a building for riding & fencing.

Royal Exchange, a handsome Court. Streets well paved, Most Broad, & spacious foot way.

Edinburgh, built upon hilly ground, occasions upon steep nasty communications across.

New Bridge, ugly – but well constructed at top, for passage; having no rise: No water under it, yet a vast fall it goes over.

Elegant new Streets & Squares ye North side of ye Bridge, but not very extensive Buildings there: A fine House of Sr Lawrence Dundas's; not inhabited: A very fine House too of Mr Crosbie's, one of ye most eminent Scotch Lawyers.

Dined at one of their Taverns; called Wintner's. Had fresh Salmon: Lamb, salted Cheese, Beer; Reckoning 8 pence.

Coffee houses take a penny for reading ye Papers; some take 2 pence for a Dish of Coffee; but some others take 3 D.

I had a guinea & a half, both together wanted 10 grains of ye full weight; a Goldsmith weighed them, & had ye Conscience to tell me they came to 26/- I dare say many of ye lower sort, have been obliged to sell their Gold, much under value.

Francis lay abed all day ill. Complained of his Breast; says 'it is a return of an old Disorder from Riding Post in Germany, which he generally feels once a year.'

8 June   Weather before fine; now cold, & a little rainy; Find out a good Eating-place, called Ward's Chop-house in the High-street, in ye London Stile: This Ward an under Actor here in low Comedy; comes from Oxfordshire; relation of Ward the Upholsterer at Oxford.

Rec̃ d Letters from Tolson. Wrote & Read a good deal in ye Day. At home all the Evening. Fell in Love with a fine young Girl: Sent a Câdi to find her out; & learn her name to be Miss Brown: Perhaps I may know something more of her: I believe my Chastity will hardly keep much longer.

Got to reading now of Pennant 2d [Second] Scotch Taver [?Traveller]; which I have bought 24/- & intend to present to Mr Parish.

9 June   Six Haddocks now bought here for a penny. See Miss Brown as I walk along: pretty enough, & what is better, young, but I cannot venture to take any more notice of her. I Walked down to Leith: called at Mrs Parish's father Mr Todd: Saw his Wife, he was out: Left a Line, but not my name: Rather rejoiced I had paid the visit, without being known. It hurts me to see anybody, who know my happier connexions.

10 June   Busied this day 8 hours in writing. Francis comes out again; & seems as well as if nothing had been ye matter with him.

Took a close view of the Bridge: 3 arches all very large, & of equal size: The arches very fine, as well as some of the Upper works of ye Bridge: But the abutments or junctions to ye Ground at Both ends, are so monstrous heavy & ugly, that the look of ye whole is spoilt. I thought immediately there was a strange mixture of beauty & ugliness in this bridge. It is ye Work of Milne: However his original design was much alter'd by others; that perhaps is his excuse as well for ye bad appearance of the whole, as for ye accident wch happend 5 years ago, of one of ye End Abutments (nearest ye old City) falling down.

Sir Lawrence Dundas's new house, a very beautiful piece of architecture:

It stands insulated, commanding a fine view of ye forth, amid the new Buildings, which they call the new Town.

Mr Crosbie's the Lawyer's grand Cornerhouse is superb, but not so pleasing or so large as Sir Lawrence: Crosbie's Besides has too many large Pillars; & the Top heavy for so small a scale. Supt as well as dined at Wards.

11 June A very cold day & in the afternoon raining. Resolved soon to leave this place.

12 June Rainy till the afternoon. Heard in ye morning part of a sermon by Dr Blair (famous Preacher here) Preached rationally, & well: yet w^d be far from conspicuous in London.

In the afternoon heard a whole sermon, & attended the whole service at the Great Friers Church: Where the famous Dr Robertson Preached: His Sermon was preach'd upon a single text, of a few words, about seeking ye Lord & finding Salvation, wch had also servd him for anor [another] Sermon before. He preached well; but not remarkably; nor was his Sermon very long. In general the difference of Scotch religion from ours, is that they love short prayers & long sermons, we ye reverse. I do not know in wch there is most reason. It may be said, there is no occasion to be long in telling God what we desire of him, seeing he knows best what at all times to give us. The example of Prayer set us by Jesus, is short enough: & so is his Sermon from the Mount. It may also be said, there is no occasion to be repeededly telling men their duty; that is always known better than it is practised. A farmer having once told his men, when to plow, when to sow, & when to reap, is not for ever after telling them the same things over again. These arguments make for short prayers & short sermons both.

Dr Robertson in his prayer before his sermon, which here in Scotland is ye longest they have, was the first I ever knew, begin ye Lord's Prayer without going through it; He introduced it in his Prayer, & saying from 'Our Father' down to 'as it is in Heaven' He went off next to something else of his own head. Both Dr Blair & Dr Robertson had striking Twangs of the Scotch in their pronunciation.

The evening fine. Sunlight to read by, till 10 o'clock.

13 June Visited a Linnen manufactory: All weaving upon the same principles: Some fine Linnen in making. They call Flax, Lint.

Some fellows having things to sell in a Basket put a Bell hung to a shaking spring, which continually rings as they walk about.

In Glasgow, the Cryer went about with a Drum. The same I remember in Alsace. Here Fish in the Market is announced by a Man with a horn:

Who says thus e.g. 'There is a Corbelo (or what is that name which ye Dutch call Cod by?) & Salmon.' Everything that is cried begins with 'There is.'

14 June I went to Leith to visit Mr Todd, Mrs Parish's Father; & there I past most of the Day. He was a Ship-builder, but has now left off. Saw George Parish's little Son Georgy; to whom I brought some Cakes &c.

Saw a Captain who remembered me at Hamburgh: Forget his name. A ship going for Newcastle next week.

Past this one day without going to a Coffee house; wch is extraordinary: considering what a News-thirster I am. The Evening I spent as usual at Ward's. There a Mr Mason, whom I had just interchanged a few words with once before at dinner-time came & sat down with me: One Dr Gilson, a musical Professor, very drunk soon came & join'd us, with his bottle of Claret, which from being the worst in the world he insisted upon to be the best. Mason let me know, this Dr Gilson, was a Character taken off in Humphrey Clinker. His sense shone through his ebriety. Mason after supper said to me, we will go & have a little amusement, if you please; When he forthwith led me ad praesepe. This was no other than the Tib-Nairne's I had heard of at Liverpool. Here we were forced to have 3 bottles of wine: Claret I believe at 3 shills. a Bottle: We had the whole tribe in; all the Scotch names tost up together: but Douglas was ye finest in person as well as in sound: There was one very abandoned, though a fine Grenadier; she was called Killpatrick: But she insisted herself, that her name was Killpr - - k.

We took our leave about 2: in passing along he showed me into another place of amusement for the lower sort, where there were some a-dancing; but here we had no inducement to stay: & I came home: a good deal overpower'd by what I had been forced to drink.

15 June I slept uninterruptedly, 'till ½ after 11: now sad & sorry for my last night's debauch: but this is the price we pay for knowing life; & it is well we pay no dearer. However my head & stomach are not quite clear: & I am indisposed all day.

They ask you here, where a person stays, instead of where they live: that is the manner of the French; Demeurer.

At supper, I was plagued by the most shocking of all stupid drunken dogs.

16 June This morning Mr Todd from Leith called upon me; & of course we past the Day together.

Saw Holyrood house called here, the Abbey. A fine Gallery as to size; but the furniture of Scotch Kings pictures execrable. I judged them all by the same hand: & so I find Smollett declares them to be, in his Humphrey Clinker.

There is the burying place of the ancient Kings to be shewn here; but I did not see it. Lord Darnley's Bones may be still taken up & handled: He was a man of extraordinary stature & these bones are very large.

We were led through a suite of unfurnished apartments, but good-sized rooms. In one a scene was painting for the Playhouse. There are other apartments, inhabited, particularly one set by the Duchess of Hamilton, or by a sister of the late Duke's.

There is a Guard at the entrance into the Palace. What w^d a Scotch King have said, to have been told, that Grass should grow in the interior Court of their Palace

I question whether Scotland has gained by the union considering the loss they sustain by having no King to make his residence in their Capital.

At one of ye Windows of the Palace the young Chevalier used to show himself to the gape crowd, when enjoying his mock royalty at Edinburgh.

I next went to the Castle. This the Rebels never had pośśon [possession] of; as they had of the Town. It would have been easy to have driven them out of ye town by the Cannon of the Castle: but that was not to have been desired, since to effect it, the town must have been laid in ruins. Some few shot were fired now & then from the Castle: & particularly a Weigh house (where some of ye Highlanders were upon Guard) in the middle of ye High Street knocked down; there are only 2 Guns from the Castle, that point into the Line of the High Street: A Baker, looking out at his door, was the only inhabitant kill'd by any shot: A Post-Chaise coming to one of the City Gates, close under the Castle, & demanding to have them opened in King James's name, upon a signal hoisted up, a shot was fired, which took directly upon the Chaise, & did some execution: I suppose the Gate was only shut by a civil guard; but perhaps ye whole is apocryphal.

The Castle is very inaccessible: It was taken by Oliver Cromwell, & there are marks now of his shot: There is a broad ascent to it from High Street; but then there is a Ditch with a draw Bridge, & a Half-moon Bastion in Front from the Castle: This Half-moon was added by Oliver Cromwell: There is a company of invalids upon guard here: But there also some of a marching regiment, that do duty.

There are large subterranean caverns, Bombproof; now mostly applied to Stables; some contained French prisoners in the last war: There is an armoury here; kept as armouries usually are very neat; the musquets old:

I said I c^d tell the number there, once going round them: the armourer said I c^d not come anything near it: He w^d not allow me visibly to count them; nor to take a pencil cut: I walk'd round made a silent calculation, & told him there were 3,966. He seem'd struck: & declared it was very near the number, though he must not declare what the number is: He never knew any other person ever come anything near it: The armoury was disposed so.

The arms in 3 Lines: Each Line 6 muskets a Breast: 10 in highth: 10 in Length. that makes 660 each Line: & then 6 lines. So they appeared to me & it was upon these principles I made ye calculations I dare say 4 or 5,000 is ye number.

There are not many cannon in ye Fort; & none larger as I say than 18 pounders: All in good order; most are Brass: There are Bombs (under shelter) & a magazine of Powder. I was led into a very little room about 8 feet square, where Mary was deliver'd while a prisoner of James 6th (of Scotland) of England 1st.

There is also a curious grace recorded under the Scotch arms upon ye wall in Gold letters, which some Bishop said over him, as then customary, as soon as born: The Day & year of his Birth are also markt upon ye wall: there lives in it some old woman, having a menial employ in ye castle; much fitter habitation for her, than a Queen: Mary begun early to be accustomed to confinement.

There was a scotch crown kept here: but now no more: supposed to be taken to the Tower; as well as the immensely large cannon they had here; I saw the round stones destined instead of shot for its' use.

I visited Herriots' hospital; a fine seminary for youth, like Christ's hospital in London, but only admitting boys.

There is one large burying place generally for Edinburgh in the South west part of the Town. Colonel Chartres has a tomb stone there; but not with Arbuthnot's epitaph.

Having got pretty intimate with Mr Masson, I went to his apartment; there he show'd me some of his production, viz. an English spelling book, that has gone through 7 editions: He is a Teacher of English at private houses: once had a public school, for grown persons, to break them of the Scotch accent: wch however he has, some little of it himself. He has also composed & printed an Italian Grammar. He seems a sensible man. He has travelled a little, having been at Paris. I learnt of him, that Joe: Townsend (the alderman's Brother) famous methodist, also has been field-preaching here, where they are very strict about the Sabbath, even when not methodists, being at Paris went himself to the public diversions of a Sunday Evening, wch the Priests of that Country will not do.

I past the Evening among a set of drunken porter Blackguards: They drink here immoderately of Lemon Porter: quarrelsome in their liquor: Fond of the company of English: Could not get away till 2 or 3 in the morning.

17 June Got into the company of one Peter Williamson; who has had some surprizing adventure among the North American Savages during the last-war; of which he has published an account. A very lusty fellow; declares it was he that acted the Indian yth ye War-hoop in London, & throwing the hatchet; That once in Hyde Park he threw the hatchet at the face of a man chalked upon a tree, in presence of his present majesty then Prince of Wales; he had the dexterity to cleave by his hatchet the markt out nose directly in two; he was desired to perform again, but he feared there was too much a mixture of luck in this attempt, & pretended he had sprained his arm, to gain a greater reputation & save himself from ye possibility of a disgrace: Afterwards he entered into connexion with Foote, who learnt the war-hoop, & performed the Indian, but never could arrive well at throwing the hatchet. This man first set up a penny-Post here: which takes well, but he has other Rivals: He consulted the Lawyers, if the Post-office c^d oppose him, but they were of opinion not, as not the limits of a Post-station: nor does the Post-office oppose him.

The Evening past in the company of a shilling club of tradesmen; such as Smiths, Taylors &c: Decent people: & as good as any other clubs; meat supper, Porter, Beer, cheese, Punch; all as much as we c^d use; within the Shilling.

I heard some say, there were houses, where Clubs might have a hot supper of 2 dishes, for 4 pence apiece.

The article of Living cheap here; yet greatly increased. At the same Coffee house, where I am charged 10 pence for my Breakfast, they never think of charging me more than 8 pence for my dinner.

At night I went to visit another seminary of Girls, patronised by one Miss Adams: In this house there are 16. I only saw 6 of whom, one was very handsome; she & all the rest very abandoned, in manners & discourse: Which I suppose is the Ton for those sort of girls here, otherwise they do not take. Got off, Masson & I, for 2 Bottles of wine 7 shs between us.

The Girls here seem very independent of ye Lady Abbess: They all meal together; & pay 5 Sh/ a week for their Board: A male Lodger, if he pleases, may mix in the repast.

18 June Saw a Captn Schaw at the Coffee house, whom I remember at Cowbridge with his Lady: I am not certain whether he knew me or not; but I preferred taking no notice of him, not wishing to renew any former acquaintances made in happier times: He is with his regiment here, upon duty.

I dined with the members of an oratorical or disputing club: 14 or 15 most illiterate fellows; Lawyers' underlings, Tradesmen & mechanics.

Clubs I find most stupid assemblies; upon all occasions; especially, when the bottle toast & song go round.

In the Evening I was at the Edinburgh Vauxhall, hearing here the name of comely gardens: They are pretty gardens enough; were there about 60 people & tolerable genteel persons: A Band of Music from 6 till 8. Country dances in a very good room: Lasses danced well; men not.

Made an attempt to see the Cargo of another convenient house (Kate Walker's, or perhaps Mrs Forsythe's opposite ye Tool-Booth door) But c^d not get them to let us in: Suppose full of company.

We went to our old resort at Miss Nairne's, to visit once again the little Douglas – found her intoxicated; they lead terrible lives: obliged to drink for ye good of ye houses: Saw here a prettier girl than I had seen before any where: I forget her name; She pretended not to be quite sound, though the truth is, she was well; but she reserved her first favors after ye restoration for some old acquaintance.

I have seen enough now of all their humers; & shall go no more. The worst is, that it costs me a humid dream when I come home; but then it is a dream of another person, not yet eradicated from my mind.

19 June A rainy day. Dined at Prince's Street Coffee House, in the new City, a very genteel good house. Met by Masson there. Called with him upon a genteel girl of his acquaintance, ill with a pleuritic fever a-bed. This girl had been once his House-keeper: ill; went into ye Hospital: fell in Love yth by one of ye Students of Physic, as I suppose, oftens happens: kept by him: He gone to Barbadoes: Said to have settled something upon her: She seems melancholy. Called at a curious fellow's (Public) house: One who had served as Valet de Chambre abroad: talkt french: Had lost some money in Coalworks. In ye Evening at Wards. The same stupid Porter-drinking work. Came home late.

20 June This probably the last day at Edinboro. Every thing prepared for removing for Leith: Having rec̃d a remittance from Mr Tolson; Packt up, & wrote Letters. Went in the Evening to Leith, whither that fellow

Masson w^d accompany me, who begins to be very troublesome, because very officious. I was obliged to accept of his proferr'd society; & stay'd the night with me at Lawson's Coffee House Leith.

21 June A public Inn without a necessary. Saw again Mr Todd this morning. He very stupid, or insipid from his age & infirmities, so that I c^d not bear to keep company with him.

Found no certain prospect of the Newcastle Ship sailing; so set out again for Edinbr̃o.

Fooled away the rest of the Day in company with that Fellow Masson: He w^d have me dine with him. There he read me some of his magazine productions: He has some marks of genius, & some Learning: But everything is lost in idle dissipation that is not drowned in ebriety.

Finished my perlustration of the Edinborough houses of polite reception: Saw some more pretty girl[s] at a more private house: All abandoned. Had like to have been taken in at another with ye stale pretences of fresh virginity: the subject to be sure was young enough: Was relieved by Masson calling in, who had gone out on some business. Supt for ye last time at Ward's. Masson w^d go with me to the Inn, intending to see me off in the Newcastle Coach, where I had engaged a place. He exacted a promise from me to write to him: Apparently grew very fond of me: pretends an acquaintance, with Hume Robertson, & all the other Scotch men of Letters: The character I learn from others of Masson is that he has parts & had encouragement, as an English French & Italian Teacher, but his drunkenness has now lost him everything. He says of himself that one of his works, 'ye English Spelling book', has gone through 7 editions of 6,000 to each edition; & another, called 'English Collections' that is 'chosen pieces in English for Learners' 6 Editions, 6,000 to each: Which has brought him in a good deal of money; which makes him little solicitous about teaching, & now he is resolved to go abroad, for his pleasure, intending to winter at Rome.

He saw me to ye Inn, but there finished up his drunkenness to such a pitch, that he quarrelled with the people of ye Inn, under the pretence of taking my part, when I was not offended, when ye Landlord had like to have kicked him out. In short after all I was obliged to see him to his Lodging, instead of &c where I finally took my leave of him;

22 June & This morning half-after 3 set out for Newcastle in the Fly. Francis I sent same time by another Coach.

A blustering stupid Captain, bellowing at every stage out of ye Coach 'When they had had any troops pass by.' His name Jennings, Captain of or Lieutenant of the 36th? I think the worst of all the Military I have known.

He spoke wretched grammar: was amazingly stupid, swearing; blustering. The mail-pillion for a woman to ride upon he repeatedly called a Pinion. Distance to N'Castle 104 miles: Arrived at ½ after 12 at night; the Cock Inn, Wilson's.

23 June Race time here. Called at Winn's Publican Pilgrim Street & found letters there from my friends Tolson & King: Shd have taken up my Lodging there at Tolson's desire, but they had no room. By King's letter was to expect him this evening: Impatiently waited for ye arrival of the London Coach, but he did not arrive; which was to me a great damp & disappointment. Could not find any pleasure in ye thought of going to the Race; nor to the Play. Past a good deal of my time in sauntering to Coffee-houses. Took [as] a favor from Masson at Edinborō a 36 Shills Portugal piece, for which gave him Scotch notes: Found no portugal money wᵈ pass here at all: Was obliged to sell my piece of 36 for 32 Shs. But the Goldsmith said 9 grains it had been diminished: I ought then to have had 34/6: Coming twice to his shop about it, & taking his offer the 2d time, he said, 'as I seem'd poor the money he was going to give me he wᵈ take care to be good.'

24–27 June No variety. Races continued all the week. Only went one day. Cocking Plays & Assemblies was not at. Could take no pleasure in anything being alone. Dined always at the Race ordinary here. A pack of low-lived gambling Blackguards.

Watching ye arrival of every machine with impatience for King; & sending every Evᵍ to the Post-houses. Employed a good deal at home in reading & writing. Felt often some qualms of Listlessness.

All dogs to be muzzled here on accᵗ of madness; or to be killed. Qu. who a right to issue such an order? & yet such a right shd be placed somewhere.

28 June, Tuesday This day when I lest [least] of all expected KING HE ARRIVED: Because I hardly thought he wᵈ set out from London the day preceding Sunday. Delay'd his coming, at Tolson's desire, upon Cash matters: & I expected I shd have come here by Sea; & therefore not so soon.

I get a new life by the addition of his Company.

29 June Having delay'd seeing everything here & hereabouts, till King arrived; shall now set about my Progress. Drank a Bottle of wine at Thyzack's, a Surgeon's here. Strong Patriot; of great interest, on ye popular side here. The Thyzacks, the Henry's & the Fitzroy's came here originally from Switzerland, establishing the White Glass manufactory: Those of that name have still particular privileges in ye Glasshouses here.

Vide, Young's Tour. None now of the Thyzacks remaining in ye Glass-houses. Our Patriot Thyzack is a Surgeon; served in ye Navy last war: was in Belisle. He shews me great Civilities: I don't know why. Went with him & King to visit the Infirmary. A handsome Building; seemingly well contrived. The Chapel has the Alter to ye West; necessary from ye Aspect of the Building: created great Contests; & had near been ordered to be pulled down again. Went also to see a wine-Glasshouse.

Now clear that Francis either purloined or lost my pistols; for which I shall make him pay 5 G's: He defends himself by Lies: If I were certain he had purloined them, I certainly shd not keep him.

30 June From our intimacy with Tyzack, who is a leading man here, were taken for ye opposing Candidates. Rode out yth him to-day. Show'd us, a Vitriol work of his: Copperas is found among the Coal, laid in Sloping bed, 5 or 6 feet thick of Copperas, Rainwater soaks through it, & from the Copperas liquor oozes out into Cellars, from whence pumped into a Boiler[s], then drawn off by a large syphon into Vats or Pans of Wood 8 foot long, 4 wide & 5 deep, or thereabout, large pieces of Wood, like the Boughs of Trees in the form of Merrythoughts (人) hung from a Pole steeping in the Liquor, agst which the Vitriol shoots; all incrustating round, by a little smart blow the stick is afterwards drawn out from the incrustation, which with ye stick is taken up with ye stick from the rest of ye Liquor which does not shoot into chrystallisation; & this rest is boiled over again, with other liquor. A good deal of Vitriol also sticks to the sides of the Vats. There is old Iron thrown into the Cellars which first receive ye Copperas Liquor, which ye Liquor preys upon, but will not take more than is proper to saturate itself. I saw this process in Clausthall in Germany: The Vitriol was there of a brighter green, & harder Chrystal: The Chrystalisation was left to shoot upon very small Reeds, instead of stout sticks here an inch & more diameter; & this reed was left to remain in the Vitriol. Copperas is of a Brassy Colour; substance a heavy stony earth: something of the look of Mundick as to Colour but not so bright.

Observed the Position of some Collieries: Not so crowded about New-castle as I expected. They have a great range up & down the River: Near Newcastle a good deal workt out, particularly by Mr Ridley's grounds.

Saw a Staith by ye River-side for containing & shipping off the Coal into the Keels: Keels have marks to show the measure of the Coal; & it is not re-measured again.

Past Mr Ridley's Glass-houses; were not at work or shd have seen them.

Cookson's Glasshouses are in the Town. Shd have gone to see Shields, but it rain'd, King declined: It is 8 miles off Newcastle, a poor Town, fine harbour, much shipping.

Heard much of Seaton Delaval; sorry no good plan of going there: A Large Rock the Delavals have cut through for ships to come in at into their harbour; with the Stone from ye Rock they built a Glasshouse; but I heard, the Glasshouse c^d not be kept up, owing to the Newcastle People's opposition. Heard since of a Glasshouse set up near Whitehaven, & the Proprietors bot [bought] off by those of Newcastle. These combinations among Glasshouse Proprietors very universal.

Tried to trace the Picts wall near Newcastle; saw part of the Ditch. Observed Mr Ridley's seat., Mr Bigges', & another. Return'd to Dinner.

A Pack of noisy drunken Freemasons dining in ye Houses. Such a society with novelty on its' side might have past: Now it is astonishing it shd be continued or at all admired.

1 July This day departed from Newcastle, in ye afternoon going no farther than Durham.

2 July The Environs round Durham beautiful: Hill, dale Woods & water; pleasant walks; elegant new bridge of 3 arches building, near the Bishop's house: Went to ye Top of ye Cathedral. At night came to a little place called Brugh. Visited the Bishop of Durham's capital seat at Bishop-Auckland: The inside good & habitable; not overabounding in furniture or pictures: Beautiful view from the Paddock round ye house; a fine circling river: Gentleman's seat ye other side very conspicuous; fine Deerhouse yth Arcades: an excellent Sheephouse, besides a good Kitchen & Fruit-Garden: tempted the under-Gardener for 6d to steal me 3 Cucumbers; even at this time of ye year in this Country a scarcity: Offered him 2/6 for a Pineapple; wch he w^d have stole for me, but all green.

3 July Came to dinner at Penrith, called often in this Country Perith; dined yth 2 parsons: Excellent Dinner: 1/- a head: Very cheap all thro' ye Country.

Took a ride to see Sr Philip Musgrave's seat at Eden hall, 4 miles off: Situated in a wild part of ye Country; But its' own grounds very beautiful: a very good large house;. no form or fashion; & little furniture: Family dislike the Place: only Sr Philip comes down for about a fortnight or 3 weeks in ye Summer: Was shown the house by a genteel old woman, who refused money; we ask'd her if any of the young Ladies were lately married: 'Ay! says she, two in a week.' We askt her, if she knew to whom they were married: She said 'She did not know; but one (she answer'd almost laughing) I think they say, is a Welshman.' In our way back say

[saw] the remains of a fine old castle close to ye River: Counsellor Wallis marriage-acquired estate is close by Perith. Came at night to Keswick.

4 July Visited the Beautiful lake here; 2 or 3 prettily wooded small Islands in it: Belongs to Greenwich Hospital; forfeited from ye Derwentwater Family. What has an Hospital to do with a fine prospect? Saw this Lake from a beautiful new planted little hill.

The Black lead mines, 8 miles off to ye South, as I guess. (Lead 2 miles from Keswick to ye North; Ld Egremont,* property there) only open'd once in 7 or 8 years: A monopoly not to be suffered; was told at Amsterdam by Lightholder, that some great persons in ye management of affairs in Holland were in posson [possession] of ye Lease, & had the lead first sent over to them, from whence as there is demand re-shipped to England, to keep up an equality of Price: I remember when at Amsterdam Black Lead being shipped for England, which they said was English.

Pieces of this Blacklead sometimes washed down into ye Bottoms still, picked up by the Farmers: Some pieces in ye old rubbish of the Work constantly now still pick'd up by ye poor people. It was not enough for these monopolizing proprietors to increase in this shameful manner the price upon all the world, but they obtained a law that purloining or taking any pieces of this Black Lead from their mines shd be felony, which ye stealing of no other ore is.

Came to Cockermouth to dinner: not an inconsiderable Town. No Navigation: An old Castle in good repair; was a Prison for ye French taken in ye last war: Has a manufacturer of Shalloons & hats: No Coal, nearer than 6 miles off toward Whitehaven: After Dinner arrived at that our place of destination.

5 July Went & visited the principal Colliery here. 2 miles underground; all from a Level: Was 123 fathom, where they now work the Coal. drawn up 2 pits; 1st one of 28 Fathom, then another of near 100.

Veins of Coal dip much towards ye Sea: was half a mile under the Sea, where they now work. Horses there for drawing ye Coal to ye Pits: Horses come along ye Level: Are building a fire-Engine underground: At present only 2 sets of hands at work on ye Coal, each 9 hours: the other 6 in the 24 employ'd for drawing up ye Water: I never saw such dry workings: Will have 3 sets at 8 hours each, as soon as ye Underground Fire-engine finished; a Water Engine under Ground: A Man cutting Coal in Buff: A great number Girls & boys, 12 & 14, driving the horses with Coal on ye Little waggons to ye Pit: The workings under Ground very extensive: Coal all under a fine Rock, no faults: very warm, for want of

* In 1784 Fanny married his brother, Frederick William Wyndham.

free air; often fires: a vast number of Doors, to confine the circulation of air to the proper streets; great care to shut these doors after you; can't be hung to shut of themselves, because of ye horses coming through.

At Newcastle Coalworks still deeper: as much as 2 horses can well do to draw up coal 100 Fathom: the Baskets of Coal, way [weigh] here Basket & all about 400 Cwt. 9. Near Newcastle, Horses let down pits; have stabling & water for them under-ground; & never come up again, till past their work usually then soon fall blind: An old woman employ'd in hooking on these heavy Baskets of Coal: Boys after working 'till about 14, go much to Sea; Girls work till they are 17, & often after they are married.

Saw at a Collier's house a Steelmill, for giving light, where dare not employ a candle: mostly used for searching out old workings, not so much for cutting ye Coal: It is a small mill fasten'd by a strap from ye Neck; consists of one Brass tooth wheel diameter 6 inches, turning a steel tooth wheel diameter ½ an inch, to which axis joined a smooth steel wheel, surface ⅓ of an Inch across, Diameter 3 inches or so; Right hand turns, left holds a Flint, agst the Steel wheel. If used in working Coal one man turns, while the other works. A large fire at the Bottom of one of the Pits, to create a circulation of air, but saw nothing of any fire suspended in them; according to what Gabriel Powell* once told me.

Took a walk to see the Harbour: Left dry when sea goes out. Vast number of rail'd Waggonways upon ye hill above ye Southside of ye Town.

Ld Egremont lately purchased some ground on ye North side an estate of Mr Elliston for £17,000; & is said to be going to set up Collieries: Chief & almost sole trade to Dublin.

Some little North American trade. A Stone Pottery in ye Neighbourhood.

---

* Portreeve of Swansea. See B.M. Cartoon 7222.

NOTE. Robert Morris was in Swansea by September 1774, seeking distraction in writing his *History of the Copper Concern.*

Index